THE ECONOMICS OF SOCIALISM

STUDIES IN ECONOMICS

A series edited by Charles Carter, *Vice-Chancellor,*
University of Lancaster

Publications

Expectation, Enterprise and Profit: The Theory of the Firm, G. L. S.
Shackle [1970]

The Economics of Socialism: Principles Governing the Operation of
the Centrally Planned Economies in the USSR and Eastern
Europe under the New System, J. Wilczynski [1970]

The Economics of Socialism

Principles Governing the Operation of the Centrally Planned Economies in the USSR and Eastern Europe Under the New System

J. Wilczynski

Royal Military College of Australia

ALDINE PUBLISHING COMPANY · CHICAGO

First U.S. edition published 1970 by
Aldine Publishing Company
529 South Wabash Avenue
Chicago, Illinois 60605

Library of Congress Catalog Number 72-119643
ISBN 202-06036-5

Printed in Great Britain

EDITOR'S NOTE

Economics is a large and rapidly developing subject, and needs, as well as elementary works for the beginner, authoritative textbooks on special subjects. This book belongs to a series of such textbooks (more than forty titles are planned): the general level is that of the second or third year in a British university course, but the books are written so as to be intelligible to other readers with a particular interest in the subject concerned.

C.F.C.

CONTENTS

CONTENTS

Accumulation—investment, or capital formation or saving, i.e. that portion of national income which is produced but not consumed during the period in question. It consists of productive investments, non-productive investments (for direct individual and collective consumption), stocks (of producer and consumer goods) and the balance of trade.

Alienation—estrangement of workers against capitalist employers because, although selling their own labour, they have no control over its use and over the goods and services they produce. A. may also appear under Socialism in the case of highly centralized economic planning and administration and a weak or arbitrary system of material incentives. It leads to the indifference and even hostility of workers to enterprises and of the local management and administration to higher authorities.

Amortization—depreciation of fixed capital.

Autarky—the policy designed to promote self-sufficiency. This policy was pursued by Socialist countries up to about the mid-1950s, but since then it has been largely discarded in favour of the international division of labour.

Bilateral clearing—a system of payments between two countries whereby settlements are effected not by means of a convertible currency but through central institutions in the partner countries (usually central banks). Such an institution makes payments to domestic creditors in domestic currency out of earnings from the partner country. The condition of satisfactory operation is that the value of the partner countries' deliveries to each other are balanced over an agreed period (usually a year). Interest-free swing credits provide for temporary imbalances.

Bilateral trade agreement—an agreement between two countries, usually designed to balance the value of exports and imports between the signatory countries. In addition, quotas for some or all goods to be traded and details as to the method of payment, tariffs, transport, exchange of trade missions, etc., may also be specified. The period covered ranges normally from two to six years.

Bonus—incentive payment made to individual, or groups of, workers and management in money or kind to promote achievement and over-fulfilment of targets and efficiency. *B. funds* are usually based on enterprise profits.

Bourgeois—pertaining to capitalist societies dominated by the *bourgeoisie* (the social class which owns most of the means of production and hires and exploits the *proletariat*).

Buyer's market—a condition where the aggregate supply of goods and services tends to exceed, or grow faster than, aggregate effective demand at the existing prices. It is typical of developed market economies where consumer's sovereignty prevails.

CMEA, or *CEMA*, *CEA*, *Comecon*—the Council for Mutual Economic Assistance established in 1949 with its headquarters in Moscow. Its original members are Albania, Bulgaria, Czechoslovakia, the German Democratic Republic, Hungary, Poland, Rumania and the USSR; Albania has ceased its membership since 1961 whilst Mongolia has joined since 1962 and Yugoslavia has become an associate member since 1964. Its purpose is to promote economic co-operation amongst the member countries.

Comecon—see *CMEA*.

Consumerism—widespread pressure by consumers exerted on the authorities to increase the volume, variety and quality of production for direct consumption, even if it means curtailing investment and the rate of economic growth.

Consumer's free choice—when consumers have freedom of choice to purchase what is produced for the consumer market. It implies that the planning authority determines the size and basic structure of production for current consumption but there is no rationing. Market equilibrium is ensured by the authorities manipulating retail prices (i.e. in practice adjusting turnover taxes) so that consumption is adapted to production.

Consumer's sovereignty—the condition under which the consumers' preferences, expressing themselves through spending, ultimately determine the size and structure of production. *Absolute* c.s. can exist only in market economies. A Socialist economy can ensure only *rationalized* c.s., i.e. that which is in the interest of society—curtailment of anti-social consumption and a generous provision of social consumption.

Cybernetics—a branch of knowledge, based on advanced mathe-

14

matical methods, concerned with the organization and self-steering of processes through the feedback of information.

Democratic centralism—the principle (first put forward by Lenin) of participation and control by the masses in centralized planning and administration.

Department (or *Division*, or *Sub-division* or *Sector*) *I and II*—division of total production in the country into the means of production (I) and the means of consumption (II). The proportion between the two Departments is one of the most important factors influencing the rate of economic growth and it is determined on a planned basis.

Director—the chief executive officer or (general) manager of a Socialist enterprise (there is no relation to the 'company director' under capitalism).

Enterprise cost of production—see *Prime cost*.

Equimarginal principle—a condition of the maximization of economic welfare ('Pareto optimum'). On the one hand it presupposes a pattern of the allocation of resources in such a way that the marginal value productivity of each factor is the same in all industries. On the other, the pattern of consumption is such that the marginal utility for all households is the same. The principle implies perfect competition and consumer's sovereignty.

Extended reproduction—see *Reproduction*.

Extensive growth—economic growth achieved due to increases in the amount of the factors of production employed (elimination of unemployment, growth of the labour force and an increase in capital investment). It is typical of Socialist countries in the early stages of economic development (roughly up to the mid-1960s in Eastern Europe).

Fetishism of production—when production degenerates into an end in itself, merely to reach or exceed quantitative targets irrespective of the quality and suitability of the goods produced to satisfy society's wants. It is a consequence of a faulty system of management and incentives, typical of the European Socialist countries before the reforms of the 1960s.

Gosbank—a Russian term for the State Bank of the USSR.

Gosplan—a Russian term for the State Planning Commission.

Group A and B—division of *industrial* output into producer goods (A) and consumer goods (B). The classification can be based either on the immediate use of the goods or (more usual now) on the type of industrial enterprises according to the purpose of the major portion of their output.

Horizontal planning—the system of economic planning under which the central plan is based on contracts between enterprises enjoying substantial independence. Such contracts, once co-ordinated and approved by higher authorities, then become binding targets, the execution of which is protected by a system of differentiated penalties.

IBEC—International Bank for Economic Co-operation, established in 1964 with its head office in Moscow. Its function is to promote multilateral payment settlements amongst CMEA countries.

Intensive growth—economic growth attained mainly through increasing labour productivity consequent upon greater specialization, application of technology and more effective incentives.

Inter-branch balancing—input–output analysis. Although the method originated in the West (in 1931) its fullest application is possible only in a planned economy. The table of inter-branch balances (or *matrix*) expressed in monetary terms is constructed in the form of a chessboard and it usually has the same number of rows (representing outputs) as columns (representing inputs). Such a table enables the effective co-ordination of production and distribution plans at different stages.

Khozraschet—a Russian term meaning 'cost accounting' or 'economic accountability'. Enterprises under this system operate independently of the State budget for financial resources.

Kolkhoz—a Russian term for 'collective farm' where land is collectively owned and farmed by the members.

Materialized labour—also described as 'crystallized', 'congealed' or 'past', is labour embodied in the goods produced in the past. It contrasts with 'live' labour which is the current labour cost of production expressed in wages.

Matrix of inter-branch balances—a table consisting of horizontal rows and vertical columns of figures showing flows of inputs and outputs of recipient and producing branches of the economy in a systematized pattern. It is designed to ensure internal consistency of the national economic plan.

Means of production—material factors of production, i.e. land and capital (including raw materials) but excluding labour (and entrepreneurship).

Multilateral trade and payments—a system of international trade under which trade surpluses earned in one country (or a group of countries) can be used to offset deficits with another (or several countries). It is typical of the trade of the developed capitalist countries and it usually presupposes convertibility of the currency (or currencies) used in settling balances. Much of the Socialist countries' trade with the capitalist world is on a multilateral basis (using Western currencies) whilst in intra-CMEA trade a scheme was introduced in 1964 designed to gradually lead to multilateralism.

National income—or 'net material product' is the net (of depreciation) total amount of goods and productive services produced in a year expressed at realized prices (not at 'factor cost'). The national income figure calculated by the Socialist method is usually about one-fifth smaller than if calculated by the Western method.

Net material product—see *National income*.

Norm—a rule specifying the amount of working time indispensable under normal conditions to produce one unit of an article (alternatively it can be expressed as the number of units of output to be produced in a specified period of time).

Objectively determined valuations—a concept used by L. V. Kantorovich to describe rational prices arrived at computationally which are conducive to the fulfilment of the optimal economic plan. O.d.v. reflect the scarcity of resources (land and capital, in addition to labour) and thus they are indicative of opportunity costs on a macrosocial scale. Their proposed function is to guide the allocation of resources at the central planning level for programming purposes.

Optimal prices—see *Programming prices*.

Optimization—attainment of postulated effects (e.g. production, investment, consumption) with the smallest possible outlay of resources, or of maximum possible effects from a given outlay of resources.

Planometrics—a branch of economics concerned with the methodology of constructing economic plans, especially arriving at the optimal plan, with the aid of modern mathematical methods and electronic computers.

Prime cost—production cost borne by the enterprise. It includes wages, materials used, interest and depreciation of fixed capital. It does not include the cost of capital supplied to the enterprise by the State free of charge.

Procurement prices—prices paid by the State to collective and private farms on delivery of farm products to the State. They are usually differentiated according to a variety of considerations.

Producers' prices—prices paid to producing enterprises. They can be described as wholesale prices provided it is understood that they do not include turnover taxes and the wholesale mark-up.

Production price—cost of production comprising variable and fixed costs (wages and capital charges) plus an average rate of profit proportional to the total of the two cost components. It is usually higher than 'value' (q.v.).

Productive—contributing directly to material production. *P. capital*—working and fixed capital engaged in production. *P. services*—transport, trade and paid-for services rendered to enterprises engaged in production. *P. consumption*—utilization of raw materials and intermediate goods in the process of material production.

Programming prices—prices applied by the central planning authority in determining the allocation of resources according to macrosocial cost–benefit considerations. In the past prices were either disregarded (in physical planning) or producers' prices were used. In recent years attempts have been made to work out optimal prices by mathematical methods and computers corresponding to the optimal plan.

Reproduction—continuous process of production involving productive consumption (q.v.) and investment. *Extended* (or *expanded*) *r.* signifies economic growth or a rising scale of production involving positive net investment. *Simple r.* is typical of a stationary economy where used-up capital stock is merely replaced, whilst *contracting r.* involves negative net investment and a decreasing scale of production.

Seller's market—condition prevailing in the market when aggregate effective demand tends to exceed supply at the existing prices, so that producers and sellers are in a dominant position over buyers. It is usually associated with a Socialist economy, although it may also appear under capitalism, especially in wartime.

Shadow prices—prices not used in actual transactions but only applied by planners to determine the allocation of resources at the planning level. These prices embody corrections to actual (producers' and retail) prices to take into account scarcity of resources and other social cost–benefit considerations. Besides, resources which are not subject to trade such as socialized land, are assigned differential scarcity prices.

Social product—in Socialist national income accounting, the value of the total output of all productive enterprises (i.e. 'unproductive services' are excluded) in a year. As it includes final as well as intermediate goods and productive services its total is inflated by double-counting.

Socialization—expropriation of privately owned enterprises, farms, agencies, etc., as a rule without compensation.

Socialized sector—that which is owned and operated by society. It consists of State and collectively (or co-operatively) owned enterprises, farms, agencies, etc. The remaining sector is 'private' (or 'individual').

Socially necessary labour—the minimum amount of work performed by efficient labour under the normal technological conditions prevailing in the economy to produce a particular commodity or service. It is the determinant of 'value'.

Sovkhoz—a Russian term for 'State farm' owned and operated by the State. The workers employed are paid wages and are treated in most respects like factory workers.

Subbotnik—a Russian term for 'Saturday work'. Work done without pay on a voluntary basis on days off or after working hours, usually on Saturdays.

Surplus value—a portion of the value created by labour but appropriated by capitalists. It consists mainly of profit but it may also embody elements of rent and interest. In the Marxian formula, $c+v+m$, it is represented by 'm' (c = constant cost, v = variable cost). In a modified form surplus value also arises under Socialism but it is called 'surplus product' or 'product for society', and is partly absorbed by the State budget and other social institutions and partly retained by the enterprise in which it was created.

Technical coefficient of production—a fractional figure indicating the input–output relation applicable to a particular industry or product. It is calculated by dividing the outlay of input per unit of output expressed in physical terms and it can be derived from the *matrix of inter-branch balances* (q.v.).

Trade protocol—renewal for the following twelve (occasionally for less or more) months of a trade agreement between countries trading on a bilateral basis. It is more specific than a trade agreement. If the partner is a capitalist country, it merely means that the government undertakes to issue import and export licences to the entities trading with the Socialist country in question, to the amount agreed on, but it does not guarantee reaching the quotas or totals agreed upon in the protocol.

Transferable ruble—also called 'clearing' or 'conversion' ruble, a medium of settling balances amongst CMEA countries as an instrument of the gradual multilateralization of the member countries' trade. It is divorced from the Soviet financial system although its official gold content (0·987412 grammes of fine gold) is the same as for the ruble in internal circulation, but both are inconvertible into gold or hard currencies.

Turnover tax—sales (or purchase) tax levied usually on consumer goods and exceptionally on producer goods. Apart from profits it represents the main source of State budgetary revenue.

Value—the amount of socially necessary labour (q.v.) embodied in a particular product. The price of the product, or its actual value-in-exchange, may depart from its value according to the conditions of supply and demand in the market.

Vertical planning—a system of 'command' planning where there is little participation from below. Instead targets and even methods of their implementation are imposed by directives from above. It is associated with the highly centralized system of economic administration and management and was typical of Socialist countries up to about the early 1960s.

CHAPTER 1

Background of Modern Socialist Economics

The term 'Socialism' became well established in England in the 1830s, although its first use can be traced back to at least 1826. Since that time Socialism has had an extraordinary career, and less than a century later a British social scientist could compile over 260 definitions of Socialism.[1] Today, the regimes which pursue Socialist economic policies can be found in monarchist Sweden and in communist China, in developed France and in underdeveloped Tanzania, in Catholic Argentina, Moslem Algeria and in Buddhist Burma.

However, more specifically, the designation 'Socialist' is used to describe the fourteen countries controlled by Communist Parties—nine Eastern European: Albania, Bulgaria, Czechoslovakia, the German Democratic Republic (or East Germany), Hungary, Poland, Rumania, the USSR and Yugoslavia; four Asian: China (or People's Republic of China), the Democratic People's Republic of Korea (or North Korea), Mongolia and the Democratic Republic of Vietnam (or North Vietnam); and Cuba.

To avoid confusion, which on this score is pretty common in the West, it must be pointed out that in Marxian terminology two stages of communism are distinguished. The first stage (called by Marx the 'lower phase'), or 'Socialism', is a transitional stage during which some elements of capitalism are retained. All the fourteen countries listed above are in this stage. Contrary to Western usage, these countries describe themselves as 'Socialist' (not 'Communist'). The second stage (Marx's 'higher phase'), or 'Communism' is to be marked by an age of plenty, distribution according to needs (not work), the absence of money and the market mechanism, the disappearance of the last vestiges of capitalism and the ultimate 'withering away' of the State. The USSR, socially the most advanced Socialist country at present, is vaguely scheduled to start entering the second stage about 1980.[2]

[1] D. F. Griffith, *What is Socialism?* A Symposium, London, Richards, 1924.
[2] See V. I. Lenin, *The State and Revolution*, Ch. I; *The Road to Communism*, Documents of the 22nd Congress of the CPSU, Moscow, FLPH, 1961, p. 512.

21

The subject matter of this book is, as the sub-title conveys, the principles governing the working of the economies of the advanced European Socialist countries which have embarked on far-reaching economic reforms in the last decade or so. This group of countries (Bulgaria, Czechoslovakia, the German D.R., Hungary, Poland, Rumania, the USSR and Yugoslavia) represents one-tenth of world population and one-fifth of world area. It also contributes about 10 per cent of world trade, 20 per cent of world national income and 30 per cent of the world's industrial output (see Fig. 17, p. 207).

A. THE SOCIALIST ECONOMIC SYSTEM

All Socialist countries subscribe to Marxism–Leninism, which in addition to economic philosophy also embodies sociological, moral and political precepts. This system of ideas provides basic guidelines for institutional organization, and the driving force directed towards ensuring social justice. The general characteristics distinguishing the Socialist from the capitalist economic system can be reduced to four fundamental elements.

a. *Concentration of Power in the Communist Party Representing the Working Classes*. The system of government based on the monoparty rule has important economic implications. The Party provides the continuity of economic policy and it makes overall value judgments. As the national scene is so overwhelmingly dominated by the Party, economic and non-economic objectives are intimately integrated in the State's totality of actions.

b. *Social Ownership of the Means of Production*. Most natural resources and capital are socialized, including land, manufacturing industries, banking, finance and domestic and foreign trade. Taking the eight European Socialist countries under consideration as a whole, 92 per cent of farming land is in the socialized (State and co-operative) sector and 95 per cent of the national income is contributed by this sector (for further details, see Chs 4 A, p. 64 and 8 A, p. 114-15).

c. *Central Economic Planning*. The market mechanism is largely replaced by, or at least substantially supplemented with, economic planning which is normally the responsibility of the State Planning Commission in each Socialist country. Economic processes are subordinated to macrosocial objectives laid down by the Party.

d. *Socially-equitable Distribution of National Income*. Property incomes (rent, interest, profits) are virtually eliminated whilst earned incomes are based on the quantity and quality of work. Private consumption is supplemented with a very well-developed system of collective goods and services provided free by the State.

However, it must be borne in mind that the former sharp distinctions between capitalist and Socialist economies have been obliterated to some extent by the developments described by some Western thinkers as 'convergence' of the two systems. This process is marked by increasing equality, departures from free enterprise and increasing State intervention in the capitalist world, and with liberal economic revisionism incorporating several elements of capitalism in the more developed Socialist countries (for details, see Ch. 15 D).

B. MODELS OF THE SOCIALIST ECONOMY

Up to about the mid-1950s, all Socialist countries had highly centralized economies, all fashioned on the Soviet model developed under the autocratic Stalinist regime. It was generally assumed that this was the only model possible or desirable under Socialism, and those who did not agree could not easily articulate their views. However, the Yugoslav reforms (after 1951), the possibility of 'different paths to Socialism' officially acknowledged at the 20th Congress of the Communist Party of the Soviet Union (in 1956), and the remarkable revival of economic thought that followed have effectively undermined the former orthodox uniformity. Today, Socialist economists distinguish four basic models, according to the management of the economy and the consequent method of the allocation of resources. The first two provide highly centralized solutions whilst the other two represent decentralized approaches.

1. THE BUREAUCRATIC CENTRALIZED MODEL

In this model, economic processes are dominated by the hierarchical system of planning and management, the Central Planning Authority (CPA) constituting the peak of the pyramid. There is no scope for independence of decision-making at the operational level, as all economic calculation is carried out at the time of the construction of the national plan. Producing units are bound by directive targets and a large number of other directive plan indicators. Economic accounting is done exclusively in physical units, and allocative decisions are not based on prices but on material balances.

The advantage of this model is that it ensures the structure of production according to the priorities postulated by the Party and the internal feasibility of the plan. However, the system is wasteful and it lacks flexibility. Resources are not allocated in the most efficient patterns. Errors in planners' judgment lead to bottlenecks, shortages and even rationing of consumer goods.

2. the planometric centralist model

The method of physical balances is replaced by mathematical solutions carried out at the CPA level. The system presupposes a well-developed network of computers for collecting, processing and cross-checking economic data. By solving billions of simultaneous equations an input-minimizing or output-maximizing plan variant is arrived at. The interrelationships in the optimal plan provide the basis for optimal prices which are also established computationally. All production decisions are based on these prices, but the actual methods of plan fulfilment at the operational level are left to individual producing units.

In theory, this system provides a considerable degree of flexibility and it can ensure the optimum utilization of resources. However, it is still beyond practical possibility, owing to the insufficiently developed network of computers and the shortage of trained personnel. Furthermore, enforcement of the computational prices in individual enterprises would be a formidable task.

3. a selectively decentralized model

Under this system, central planning and the administrative machinery are retained. But some responsibilities are delegated to branch associations or regional bodies and to enterprises, and they are in a position to influence the central plan. The number of directive indicators is reduced and profitability is accepted as the main criterion of enterprise performance. Prices are still centrally planned but they more closely reflect production costs in order to reduce the need for subsidies and to attain the desired levels of profitability for different branches of the economy. There is freedom of consumer's choice, but retail prices may be manipulated by the authorities to ensure equilibrium in the market for consumer goods.

This system provides some freedom of initiative for enterprises, within circumscribed limits, and a better deal for consumers. But the price-setting process is not devoid of arbitrary elements, and the allocation of resources is not necessarily placed on the most efficient basis from the standpoint of scarcity–preference relations.

4. supplemented market model

Economic processes are conditioned by the market mechanism, thus replacing annual plans and directive targets. As a rule, prices are determined in the market reflecting supply and demand conditions, but they are corrected by authorities in accordance with long-run macrosocial cost–benefit considerations. Prices provide a guiding function to enterprises endeavouring to maximize their profits, and consumers' preferences almost entirely determine the allocation of resources to different uses. The role of the greatly reduced body of planners is limited to what Ota Šik (a prominent Czechoslovak economist) calls 'orientation planning'—i.e. to determining certain basic proportions (such as those between consumption and investment and amongst different branches of production) and where necessary to initiating key developmental projects. But to achieve the desired objectives, planners essentially rely on fiscal and monetary measures operating through the market.

There are many obvious advantages of this model. The rigidities and waste of bureaucracy are largely removed. There is a sound system of pricing which is conducive to an efficient utilization of resources.

Of the nine European Socialist countries, only two can be fairly easily fitted into these models—Albania as a bureaucratic centralized case, and Yugoslavia as a supplemented market economy. The remaining countries mostly conformed to the first model up to the late 1950s. Since that time, although still retaining several elements of the centralized system, they have been increasingly inclined to embrace the selectively decentralized model. Two of them, Czechoslovakia and Hungary, have gone further and have incorporated several features typical of the supplemented market model. No country has yet adopted the planometric model, but more theoretical and empirical work has been done in this direction in the German D.R., Hungary and the USSR than in other Socialist countries.

C. ECONOMIC REFORMS

With the exception of Yugoslavia,[3] the economic reforms that were carried out in Eastern Europe and the USSR before 1960 were practically all of the bureaucratic and administrative type. A certain measure of liberalization during 1956–8 in some of them (Poland, the German D.R. and Hungary) was followed by Stalinist-type reactions. A summary of the reforms implemented or initiated since 1960 is presented in Fig. 1. Their general purpose is to increase the efficiency of the Socialist economies which have attained a fairly advanced stage of development. We shall now briefly bring out the significant

[3] Minor changes were initiated in 1949–50, following Yugoslavia's expulsion from Cominform in 1948. The main reform was carried out in 1952 when detailed annual plans were discontinued, substantial independence was granted to enterprises, a greater role was assigned to the price mechanism and a decollectivization of land became permitted. Further reforms along these lines were carried out in 1958.

FIG. 1. *Economic Reforms in the European Socialist Countries since 1960*

Year	Country	Details of reforms[1]
1960	Poland	Reform of producers' prices.
1961	USSR	Domestic revaluation of the ruble.
1963	Hungary	Decentralization of planning and management.
1963	Rumania	Reform of producers' prices.
1963	Poland	Some decentralization of management in industry.
1963	German D.R.	Guidelines on the New System of Economic Planning and Management adopted.
1964	Hungary	Capital charges introduced in industry.
1964	Poland	Greater role assigned to material incentive to labour, interest rates and profits.
1964	Czechoslovakia	Some liberalization of restrictions on private enterprise.
1964	German D.R.	Reform of planning, management, price setting procedures, producers' and retail prices. Wage payments to be related to enterprise profits.
1964–5	USSR	Experiments on profit as a criterion of enterprise performance.
1965	Yugoslavia	A general reform leading to further decentralization. Strengthening of the role of fiscal and monetary policies. Closer orientation to foreign trade. Price reform more favourable to agriculture.
1965	USSR	Liberalization of individual plot farming. Official acceptance of profit as the main indicator of enterprise performance and greater independence granted to enterprises.
1966	Poland	Reform of material incentives and factory prices. Extension of self-financing of enterprises. Bonuses in export industries to be based on net foreign exchange earnings.
1967	Czechoslovakia	Decentralization of planning and management. Flexible price system. Strengthening of economic levers.
1967	Bulgaria	Decentralization of planning and management. Strengthening of material incentives and financial instruments. Banking reform (greater centralization).
1967	USSR	Reform of producers' prices.
1968	Hungary	Flexible price system. Extension of material incentives in agriculture.

1968	{ German D.R. Hungary Rumania	Banking and credit reforms—greater diversification, flexible credit policies, strengthening of financial controls.
1968	Bulgaria	Reform of wholesale industrial and agricultural prices and of the prices of imported goods.
1969	Rumania	Extension of material incentives. Greater independence of enterprises. Decentralization of foreign trade.
1969	German D.R.	Reform of industrial prices.

---

[1] The reforms were generally preceded by discussions and experiments (usually for two or more years) and then implemented over the period of one to two (or more) years.

Sources. Based on the Socialist countries' daily and periodical literature.

elements of the reforms common to all the countries under consideration.

a. *Liberalization of Planning*. Planning is now less prescriptive and detailed. Instead, there is a growing trend to lay down only broad targets expressed in value terms, and there is a shift of emphasis from short-term to long-term (five- to twenty-year) planning. There is closer correspondence between the planning authorities and the enterprises.

b. *A Greater Independence of Enterprises*. Industrial and trading enterprises have been given greater freedom to choose the ways and means of plan fulfilment. The hierarchical system of economic relationships is being partly replaced by horizontal dealings between enterprises based on contracts.

c. *Profit*. This criterion has been accepted as the main indicator of enterprise performance, whilst the number of directive indicators previously regulating enterprise activities has been greatly reduced.

d. *Strengthening of Material Incentives to Labour*. Increased importance is now attached to material, as distinct from moral, incentives. A portion of enterprise profits is distributed individually and collectively to the workers and other employees according to the quantity and quality of the work performed.

e. *Price Reforms*. Producers' prices have been brought closer in line with production costs to reduce the need for State subsidies and to enable average enterprises to be profitable. Similarly, the procure-

27

ment prices payable to the farms have been raised in relation to industrial prices, to encourage agricultural production and to improve living standards in rural areas. In some countries (Bulgaria, Czechoslovakia, Hungary and Yugoslavia) the so-called flexible price systems have been introduced, whereby a large proportion of prices can be determined by the market conditions of supply and demand.

f. *A Greater Role Assigned to Finance and Credit.* Enterprises have been charged with greater and stricter financial responsibility. Capital charges (on capital supplied directly by the State) have been introduced. Instead of directives, the authorities are increasingly relying on a flexible use of interest rates, credit and taxes.

g. *A Closer Link Between Production and Distribution.* There has been some overhaul of the retail and wholesale trade network, designed to improve service to consumers and to enable effective transmission of customers' preferences to producing enterprises. Profit is now generally calculated on the basis of the output sold, not merely produced or handled so that it is in the interest of both industry and trade to supply customers with what they want.

h. *A Stronger Orientation to Foreign Trade.* The monopoly of the ministries of foreign trade and foreign trade corporations has been relaxed in favour of other ministries, branch associations and selected enterprises to provide greater flexibility and efficiency. New systems of incentives have been devised to stimulate foreign trade and in particular to promote a greater effectiveness of exports.

These are the main features of the reforms in brief outline. Further details of the new principles, policies and practices are pursued in the remaining chapters. But some general observations are warranted at this stage. The degree of decentralization achieved so far differs, of course, in each of the eight countries. Arranged in descending order the list looks like this: Yugoslavia; Hungary, Czechoslovakia; Bulgaria, the German D.R., Poland, the USSR, Rumania. Albania has not so far embarked on economic reforms in a liberal spirit.

The reforms have not gone as far as some enthusiastic Western commentators have made them appear. With the exception of Yugoslavia, the authorities have exercised a good deal of caution, lest too much power is handed over to the 'invisible hand' of the anonymous market forces. The reforms have been gradual, consisting in selective engrafting of the elements of the market mechanism rather than in radical departures from central planning. Economic reforms are not merely a question of economics. They inevitably involve ideological, social and political issues. There is no lack of Stalinist hardliners critical of the 'economic revisionism' who still exercise a good deal of restraint on the governments and liberal reformers.

D. THE NEW SOCIALIST ECONOMICS

Up to about the mid-1950s, the science of economics, or 'political economy',[4] in Socialist countries was in a deplorable state. Most thinkers believed that there was little scope for independent study of economics in the context of a Socialist planned economy. Some extremists even denied the existence of economic laws under Socialism. This view was most forcefully expressed by Rosa Luxemburg, who wrote before World War I that 'the victory of the working class constitutes the last act of political economy as a science'.[5] It is not without significance that between 1928 and 1954 no textbook of economics was written and published in the Soviet Union.

The majority of writers were preoccupied with interpreting Marx in order—as was concluded at the Conference of Polish economists in 1967—'to provide apologetic justification of current economic policies'.[6] Yet neither Marx, nor Engels, nor Lenin ever presented a systematic and complete treatment of economic theory, particularly in respect of the allocation of resources, demand analysis, consumer equilibrium and foreign trade.

[4] The term 'political economy' was first used by A. de Monchrétien (*Traité de l'économie politique*) in France in 1615 to indicate that his book was concerned only with the State economic management. In England, the term was established by James Steuart (*Inquiry into the Principles of Political Œconomy*) in 1767. Marx borrowed the term from previous writers (his main work, *Capital*, published in 1867, carried the sub-title *Critique of Political Economy*) and since then the description has been commonly used in Marxist literature.

Since the publication of A. Marshall's *Principles of Economics* (1890), the term 'economics' has become firmly established in English-speaking countries, whilst the phrase 'political economy' has been generally reserved for the classical and Marxist treatment of economics. However, the usage in Eastern Europe has varied. On the one hand, even before the communist takeover the phrase 'political economy' was mostly used to also describe post-classical capitalist economics. On the other, today the term 'economics' is also used in these countries in reference to Socialist economics, and this practice appears to be on the increase (e.g. *Ekonomika konsumpcji*, Warsaw, 1966; *Ekonomika evropeiskikh stranchlenov SEV*, Moscow, 1968).

In the title of this book, the term 'economics' is preferred not only for the sake of brevity, but also to indicate that this study is concerned with modern Socialist economics, not merely an exposition or reinterpretation of Marxist or orthodox Socialist ideas.

[5] Quoted from Oskar Lange, *Ekonomia polityczna* (Political Economy), Warsaw, PWN, 1959, Vol. I, p. 78.   [6] *Ekonomista*, 5/1967, p. 1293.

However, a new era has opened up to the science of Socialist economics since the mid-1950s. Stalin's death (March 1953), growing moderation in ideological fervour, milder censorship and increasing contacts with Western economic thought have largely removed previous crippling constraints on objective discussions and research. At the same time the increasing complexity of the Socialist economies, the slowdown in economic growth and the stagnation of the early 1960s have created an unprecedented need for new solutions. But the most obvious challenge has been provided by the economic reforms in the last decade. The editor of the well-known theoretical organ of the Communist Party of the Soviet Union clearly indicated the direction in which the winds are now blowing in the world of Socialist economics:

'The reform confronts economic science with responsible tasks. The economic scientists must analyse the essence of economic processes more profoundly, discover new trends in the national economy, make evaluations of the operation of the new system and formulate scientifically substantiated recommendations for further progress.'[7]

This remarkable rejuvenation of economics has been stimulated by the increasing application of mathematics to economic thinking and testing. For a long time, the orthodox Socialist economists bitterly opposed the 'mathematization of economics', regarding it as being 'anti-historical' and 'anti-social' because they correctly foresaw a threat to the traditional Marxist political economy. Mathematical models and other important contributions to economics, as for example those put forward by L. V. Kantorovich and V. V. Novozhilov (of the USSR), J. Kornai and T. Liptak (of Hungary) and M. Kalecki and O. Lange (of Poland), recognize the scarcity of non-labour resources and involve marginal analysis. These are in open conflict with the labour theory of value, one of the cornerstones of Marxism. But although there is no lack of opponents even today, especially amongst the older economists, such as M. Kolganov, Y. Kronrod, S. M. Nikitin and K. Ostrovityanov of the USSR,[8] mathe-

---

[7] ('Economics—the Decisive Link in the Struggle for Communism'), *Kommunist*, 11/1968, p. 13.

[8] M. Kolganov, ('Political Economy and Mathematics'), *Voprosy ekonomiki*, 12/1964, pp. 111–25; Ya. Kronrod, ('On the Problems of the Logic of the Political Economy of Socialism'), *Vop. ekon.*, 12/1964, pp. 74–85; S. M. Nikitin, *Kritika ekonometricheskikh teorii 'planirovaniya' kapitalisticheskoi ekonomiki* (Critique of the Econometric Theories of "Planning" in Capitalist Economics), Moscow, Gostatizdat, 1962; K. Ostrovityanov, ('Methodological Problems in the Political Economy of Socialism'), *Vop. ekon.*, 9/1964, pp. 111–28.

matics is now clearly calling the tune in the further development of the science of Socialist economics.

In contrast to the past, the Communist Parties are not unduly interfering in these developments. They are rather staying aloof from the most controversial issues, but on the whole encouraging theoretical research and particularly empirical testing. At the same time the serious thinkers, especially the younger generation of economists, although naturally expressing their thoughts in Marxist terminology, display little inclination for adapting their ideas to the Marxist straitjacket.

In the last few years universities and institutes of economics have been busily engaged in rewriting textbooks of economics to embody the new principles. When asked why he sponsored a new textbook, considering that there were already a dozen recent texts available in Poland, the vice-chancellor of the Advanced School of Social Sciences in Warsaw justified his decision by the 'stormy development of the science of economics in recent years'.[9]

The fields in which Socialist economic thought has made greatest progress in the last fifteen years include optimal planning, econometrics and cybernetics, intensive growth, steering mechanisms, the role of the market mechanism in the context of central planning, criteria of enterprise performance, the effectiveness of investment, and foreign trade efficiency studies. It does not mean that Socialist economists have provided complete solutions, even in these fields. According to the Institute of Economics of the Polish Academy of Sciences, the research effort in the next fifteen years (coinciding with the present perspective plans) should be concentrated on the following problems, in addition to the eight fields stated above: multisectoral models of growth, the reconciliation of microeconomic behaviour with long-run macroeconomic objectives, the operation of economic levers, the application of mathematical methods to management, workers' self-government, economic accounting, wholesale and retail pricing, consumption models, 'unproductive services', regional economics, economic prognoses, and the perfection of intra-Socialist economic integration.[10]

[9] *Życie gospodarcze*, 22/10/1967, p. 9. The textbook in question is M. Pohorille (ed.), *Ekonomia polityczna socjalizmu* (The Political Economy of Socialism), Warsaw, PWE, 1968.
[10] *Ekonomista*, 5/1967, pp. 1285, 1297–1303.

RECOMMENDED REFERENCES AVAILABLE IN ENGLISH

1. Campbell, R., 'Economic Reform in Eastern Europe and the USSR', *Amer. Ec. Rev.*, Papers and Proceedings, May 1968, pp. 547–58.

2. Campbell, R., 'Marx, Kantorovich and Novozhilov: *Stoimost* versus Reality', *Slavic Review*, Oct. 1961, pp. 402–18.

*3. Fedorenko, N., 'Basic Trends in the Development of Economic Science', *Problems of Economics*, April 1966, pp. 3–10.

4. Feiwel, G. R., *New Currents in Soviet-type Economies: A Reader*, Scranton and London, Intern. Textbook Co., 1968.

5. Felker, J. L., *Soviet Economic Controversies. The Emerging Marketing Concept and Changes in Planning 1960–1965*, Cambridge (Mass.), M.I.T. Press, 1966.

*6. Földi, T. (ed.), *For the Progress of Marxist Economics: Selected Studies*, Budapest, Institute of Economics, Hungarian Academy of Sciences, 1967.

7. Gamarnikow, M., *Economic Reforms in Eastern Europe*, Detroit, Wayne State U.P., 1968.

8. Horowitz, D. (ed.), *Marx and Modern Economics*, New York and London, Modern Reader Paperbacks, 1968.

*9. Pavlat, V., 'The Classification of Economic Sciences Under Socialism', *Czechosl. Econ. Papers*, No. 2, 1962, pp. 29–38.

*10. Rakitskii, B., 'In Refutation of Bourgeois Interpretations of the Economic Reform in the USSR', *Problems of Economics*, March 1966, pp. 21–31.

11. Samuelson, P. A., 'Marxian Economics as Economics', *Amer. Ec. Rev.*, Papers and Proceedings, May 1967, pp. 616–23.

12. Schroder, G. E., 'Soviet Economic "Reforms": A Study in Contradictions', *Soviet Studies*, July 1968, pp. 1–21.

*13. Stojanovic, R. (ed.), *Marx and Contemporary Economic Thought*, translated from the Yugoslav, New York, I.A.S.P., 1968.

14. Treml, V. G., 'Revival of Soviet Economics and the New Generation of Soviet Economists', *Studies on the Soviet Union*, Vol. V, No. 2, 1965, pp. 1–22.

15. Zauberman, A., 'Breakthrough to Economics', *Survey*, July 1965, pp. 118–24.

indicates contributions by writers from Socialist countries.

CHAPTER 2

Planning and the Market

The role of planning and of the market under Socialism has been the most fundamental and controversial issue ever since the first Socialist state was established in 1917 and, no doubt, it will continue to be so in the future. All Socialist economies have always embodied elements of both, but the role of each varied in different periods and further differences could be found amongst the countries in question even at a particular time. We shall examine these two mechanisms in some detail because their interrelations decisively condition the functioning of the specific economic processes to be considered in the remaining chapters of this study.

A. BASIC PRINCIPLES OF SOCIALIST PLANNING

The term 'planning' has a very broad meaning in Socialist countries. It is defined in a Socialist textbook as:

'. . . the system of managing economic processes involving production, distribution, investment and consumption. Its essence consists in determining economic targets and methods for their implementation, in particular the allocation of the means of production and of labour to different uses. As such, planning is an instrument of economic strategy to achieve the optimum growth of national income or the maximum satisfaction of social needs.'[1]

The system presupposes the existence of a central planning authority, usually known as the State Planning Commission,[2] whose chairman is (with the exception of Yugoslavia) a member of the cabinet. There are five specific tasks for which the SPC is responsible:

(i) determination of the criteria of economic calculation underlying planning decisions;
(ii) determination and quantification of the targets to be reached in the planned period;

---

[1] R. Chwieduk et al., Ekonomia polityczna (Political Economy), Warsaw, PWN, 1966, Vol. II, p. 172.
[2] In Hungary it is called the 'National Planning Office' and in Yugoslavia the 'Federal Institute for Economic Planning'.

(iii) co-ordination of the targets to ensure the internal consistency of the plan;

(iv) determination of appropriate methods to ensure plan fulfilment;

(v) current revision of targets according to changing conditions.[3]

The SPC has to work within the confines of the overall social goals and priorities laid down by the Party. It is then implicitly assumed that the scale of planners' preferences constitutes a reflection of social needs.

The period for which a given plan is constructed is called the *planning horizon* which largely determines the purpose and content of the plan. Long-term, or 'perspective', plans (fifteen to twenty years) are primarily concerned with long-term problems of structural changes on the national scale, technology, the training of labour and the like. The greatest role is played by medium-term plans, usually covering five (occasionally six or seven) years and concerned mostly with changes in the capacity and rate of production of different industries or enterprises, i.e. mostly with investment. There are also short-term, or 'operational' plans (covering twenty-four, twelve and four months) concerned with current production tasks and problems of equilibrium—e.g. between the wage fund and market supplies, between imports and exports, etc.

In general, the longer the planning horizon the less directive are the targets. In recent years there has been a tendency for the planning commissions to concentrate on medium- and long-term planning, and to make short-term plans less prescriptive or to abolish them altogether (as in Yugoslavia, and virtually in Bulgaria, Czechoslovakia and Hungary). The existence of plans covering different periods creates co-ordination problems. A new approach to this question is contained in *continuous planning*, whereby medium-term plans are not closed within specified periods but are constantly supplemented and extended in the process of their implementation. Most progress along these lines has been achieved in Czechoslovakia.

The details of the plan are naturally worked out in close collaboration with the different ministries. The role played by the operational level (enterprises and branch associations) differs according to the degree of centralization. In the extreme case of 'hierarchical' planning, the plan is simply imposed from above by the SPC, and the different administrative organs and individual economic units have no influence on the plan (beyond supplying basic information to higher authorities). This system has now been largely replaced with 'plan-

---

[3] M. Pohorille, (ed.), *Ekonomia polityczna socjalizmu* (The Political Economy of Socialism), Warsaw, PWE, 1968, p. 362.

ning from below', whereby individual enterprises submit 'counter-plans' to branch (or 'economic') associations and the latter to the SPC.

Under decentralized planning, also known as *horizontal* or *demand planning*, the central plan is based on contracts between virtually independent enterprises. Such contracts are co-ordinated, and in some cases pruned and supplemented by the SPC (or lower-level organs) to provide for developments of long-run macro-economic importance. This system of planning exists in its most liberal form in Yugoslavia and is developing in Bulgaria, Czecho-slovakia, the German D.R. and Hungary.

The national plan is first examined by the Council of Ministers and then submitted to Parliament. The latter lays down the sphere of responsibility of each level of economic administration towards the plan fulfilment and the law becomes a law. After the plan is accepted, the targets are disaggregated and transmitted to their respective executors (ministries, branch associations, enterprises). The plan is put into effect by means of directives and indicators, administrative regulations, orientational guidelines and incentives.

Directives issued to enterprises can be in the form of instructions for producing and delivering specified quantities of products of defined quality to specified recipients by particular dates. Or alternatively, and this form is now assuming increasing importance, the targets may be formulated in terms of a certain level of profit, or financial reserves or net value of production (value added) without specification of the size or structure of production.

The number of products for which there are compulsory targets in the central plan has been greatly reduced in recent years—for example in Czechoslovakia to about sixty (compared with 1,500 in 1966), to eighty in the German D.R. and to 120 in Bulgaria.[4] Similarly, the number of directive indicators issued to enterprises has been substantially pruned. In Bulgaria before 1967 they ran into several dozens, but since then they have been reduced to five—the total value of production, the volume of production of basic products, limits to investments, limits to centrally allocated raw materials and components, and restrictions on transactions involving foreign exchange.[5] The number of directive indicators is largest in Poland, whilst in Yugoslavia they are no longer compulsory.

To be capable of fulfilment, the plan must be above all *internally consistent*. This condition is ensured at the construction stage by the method of *material balances* or of *inter-branch balances*, whereby

[4] *Nowe drogi*, 10/1968, p. 49; *Planovoe khoziaistvo*, 5/1967, p. 73; *Życie gospodarcze*, 1/10/1967, p. 11.
[5] *Życie gosp.*, 1/10/1967, p. 11.

targets are reconciled with the limiting constraints of available resources. The balances, which are normally expressed in physical units, provide a basis for the financial counterpart of the plan. According to the existing practice in most Socialist countries, the overall balance of the national economy comprises the following flows which, naturally, have to be harmonized:

(i) production, consumption and accumulation;
(ii) primary, secondary and final distribution of national income;
(iii) personal money income and expenditure;
(iv) fixed and circulating assets in the productive and unproductive spheres;
(v) utilization of labour resources.

Of the two methods of balancing, that of material balances was commonly used in the past. However, with the growing number of alternatives and the complexity of the production processes, this method has become increasingly cumbersome to handle, and moreover it obscures inter-branch links and the repercussions of economic changes. Although still useful in some respects, it is being replaced with a more sophisticated analysis—the complex method of inter-branch balances, which we shall discuss next.

B. THE COMPLEX METHOD OF INTER-BRANCH BALANCES

This method can be best described as input–output analysis.[6] It consists in working out a matrix of flows which looks like a chessboard. It provides a synthetic and lucid picture of processes directed to production and distribution. The theoretical framework of such a model is represented in Fig. 2. The following discussion of the table should help an understanding of the nature of the method of inter-branch balances.

The table consists of columns i and rows j. The economy is divided into so many branches, and each of them achieves an annual output equal to $Q_1, Q_2, Q_3, \ldots, Q_n$. Each branch uses a certain portion of its own annual output, which is designated $x_{11}, x_{22}, x_{33}, \ldots, x_{nn}$. The

[6] The original inventor of this technique was an American economist (of Russian descent), W. W. Leontief, who undertook after 1931 to work out such a model for the American economy for 1919, 1929 and 1939 (according to Soviet economists, on the inspiration of the first national balance sheet of the Soviet economy for 1923–4). Oskar Lange (see his book translated into English, *Introduction to Econometrics*, Oxford, Pergamon Press, 1959, pp. 218–29) endeavoured to demonstrate that Leontief's analysis can be regarded as an elaboration of Marx's ideas.

FIG. 2. *A Model Table of the National Balances of the Economy*

Receiving branches (j) / Producing branches (i)	Inter-branch flows					Total	Final recipients — of which		Gross output
	1	2	3	$\cdots$	n		Consumers	Investors	
1	x_{11}	x_{12}	x_{13}	$\cdots$	x_{1n}	x_1	C_1	I_1	Q_1
2	x_{21}	x_{22}	x_{23}	$\cdots$	x_{2n}	x_2	C_2	I_2	Q_2
3	x_{31}	x_{32}	x_{33}	$\cdots$	x_{3n}	x_2	C_3	I_3	Q_3
.	.	.	.	.	.	.	.	.	.
.	.	.	.	.	.	.	.	.	.
.	.	.	.	.	.	.	.	.	.
n	x_{n1}	x_{n2}	x_{n3}	$\cdots$	x_{nn}	x_n	C_n	I_n	Q_n
Personal income	P_1	P_2	P_3	$\cdots$	P_n		P		
Surplus product	S_1	S_2	S_3	$\cdots$	S_n		S		
Gross output	Q_1	Q_2	Q_3	$\cdots$	Q_n				

Source: Based on: M. Pohorille (ed.), *Ekonomia polityczna socjalizmu* (Political Economy of Socialism), Warsaw, PWE, 1968, p. 535.

remaining portion of each branch's annual output is to be delivered to other branches.

Thus, coal mines retain a given quantity of coal for their own use (to operate engines, pumps, lifts, locomotives, etc.) and deliver the rest to iron smelting, chemical, railway and thermal power branches. Symbol x_{12} signifies the portion of the output of branch $_1$ for the use of branch $_2$, x_{32} is the portion of output of branch $_3$ for branch $_2$, x_{7n} is the portion of production of branch $_7$ to branch $_n$. To generalize, x_{ij} indicates the flow of production from branch i to branch j, whilst x_{ii} is the portion used up in branch i.

The remaining part of production, i.e. over and above that used up in the branch and other branches during the year, constitutes value added or *net material production* (or *national income* as understood in Socialist countries). This total is devoted to consumption and invest-ment. Wages, expressed of course in money terms, indicate the distribution of labour among the different branches. The vertical columns indicate the gross value structure in each branch—material inputs $(x_{n1}, \ldots, x_{nn})$ on the one hand, and personal income $P_1, \ldots, P_n)$ and 'surplus product' $(S_1, \ldots, S_n)$ on the other.

The table of inter-branch balances falls into four distinct parts:

I	II
III	IV

Part I shows the indirect stages of production, i.e. the actual inter-branch flows, and it is the basic division of the table. It shows the economic and technical relations between different branches of the economy. It is called the *square matrix of inter-branch balances*.

Part II represents *net material production* or simply *national income*, according to the Socialist method of social accounting (see Ch. 4 A), created by the branches and distributed to the final recipients in the form of current consumption and investment. Part III shows the types of incomes generated in the productive branches. Part IV comprises personal expenditure and that out of the State budget.

The *square matrix of inter-branch balances* enables the calculation of *technical coefficients of production* which play a very important part in Socialist economic planning. To produce a given quantity of a particular article, one needs a certain quantity of inputs. The quantity of input used up per unit of output depends on the technological level of production. Thus if, to produce Q_j units of output in branch j, one needs x_{ij} units of the product from branch i, then the technical coefficient of production is:

$$tcp = \frac{x_{ij}}{Q_j} \; (i, j = 1, 2, 3, \ldots, n).$$

This coefficient is also known in different Socialist countries as the *technical norm of production, coefficient of production,* or *coefficient of material utilization.* If the matrix of inter-branch balances is expressed in value terms, then the coefficient becomes the *technical coefficient of costs.* For example, by the Polish matrix for 1962, the technical coefficients of costs in the 'building' branch according to the materials received from different branches were—from 'building': 0·98201, from 'forestry': 0·001058, from 'agriculture': 0·0002538.[7]

The first actual models of inter-branch balances were *ex-post* balances worked out in Hungary and Poland for 1957, in which thirty-eight and twenty branches were distinguished respectively. But in recent years the techniques of construction have been greatly improved, the number of branches dealt with has increased, and some progress has been made towards expressing the matrix in value terms. The number of branches covered in the latest models known is— in Bulgaria: 70×70, in Hungary: 80×80, in the USSR: 125×125, and in Poland: 144×144.[8]

C. THE PROBLEM OF OPTIMAL PLANNING

There may be a large number of plans which are internally consistent and capable of fulfilment. But once a particular criterion is accepted there can be only one *optimal* plan. The problem of optimal planning had not attracted much attention until the late 1950s. On the one hand, in the earlier stages of economic development there were more immediate problems, associated with the utilization of unused resources and capacities and the industrialization 'at all costs'. On the other, the methods of economic accounting and planning were too crude to enable sophisticated analysis of optimization processes.

But the situation has changed since that time. As Socialist countries have been entering higher stages of development, the number of alternative uses for resources and the complexity of economic processes have greatly increased. Consequently, the possibilities of errors have been multiplying, threatening the economies with greater dislocations and waste than before. It also became evident that the 'extensive growth factors' were being rapidly exhausted. If

[7] M. Pohorille, op. cit., p. 540.
[8] *Vestnik statistiki*, 1/1968, pp. 70–4.

the high rates of growth are to be sustained and the economic race with the West is to be won, it is essential to turn to 'intensive growth factors', i.e. to ensure the most efficient allocation of resources.

Optimization of plans is now entering the realm of possibility owing to the remarkable progress made in mathematical methods, including linear and dynamic (non-linear) programming, the theory of games, the theory of probability and cybernetics. The utilization of these methods in the process of finding optimal solutions in planning is made possible by employing high-memory computers. For example, if all data are available in a programmed form, the solution of a planning problem involving 15,000 m. calculations can be carried out in a few hours.[9] The problem of optimization reduces in the ultimate analysis to the minimization of one function of the objective (resource outlay) and the maximization of another (output). In the theory of programming this is known as *duality of programmes*.

As long as balancing is done in physical terms, there is little need for prices in planning. However, although the problem of physical balancing and internal consistency can be solved without prices, the problem of optimization can not. As is well known, the system of pricing in Socialist countries has been in a state of confusion, as a consequence of the absence of the free market mechanism, the ideological commitment to the labour theory of value and the various *ad hoc* pricing policies to suit specific goals (see Ch. 9 A–D). To provide a rational basis for pricing, the supporters of optimal planning advocate computationally determined prices on the macro-economic scale. Applying modern mathematical methods and electronic computers, it is proposed to work out a large number of *plan variants* according to different alternative applications of resources (or opportunity costs). Using the criterion of the minimization of inputs to attain given levels of national income and the criterion of the maximization of national income or of consumption in a given period, it is possible to arrive at the optimal plan. The optimal plan should then itself provide the basis for rational planning (or 'programming') prices. Such prices, or as Kantorovich calls them, 'objectively determined valuations', would represent the relative significance of the different resources to the fulfilment of the optimal plan (for further details, see Ch. 9 E).

Practical effort so far has been limited to the application of the optimization procedures only to selected sectors of the economy, such as investment, the location of specific industries, transport and foreign trade. The most advanced and comprehensive work in this respect has been done in Hungary, where forty-three variants of the 1966–70 five-year plan were worked out. These variants were based

[9] M. Pohorille, op. cit., p. 552.

on a small number of alternative applications of different resources and on different weightings according to selected objectives. Different foreign trade alternatives assumed the focus of the analysis.[10] In the USSR, twenty variants were considered in the drafting of the inter-branch balances for 1970 in terms of costs and fifteen variants in physical units.[11]

The task of complete plan optimization has proved so far to be beyond practical possibility. The main obstacle is the absence of information in suitable forms, as the existing system of collecting, transmitting and processing data is not yet adapted to the requirements of optimal planning. Besides, Socialist countries still lack a sufficiently well developed network of computers.[12] They are well behind the West, especially in the production of high-memory models; and the Western strategic embargo on exports to Socialist countries, although relaxed in recent years, still applies to the most advanced models. But there is no doubt that progress will continue. Theoretical, technical and institutional solutions will be perfected, opening up most promising vistas for optimal planning.[13]

D. THE ROLE OF THE MARKET

Under capitalism, the functioning of the market provides the fundamental mechanism for guiding economic processes. Indeed, 'capitalist' and 'market' economy are normally regarded as synonymous. In practically all capitalist countries nowadays, the authorities intervene in the market in pursuance of various objectives, but they endeavour to work through the market and do not interfere with it as a system.

Under Socialism, the market mechanism is superseded to varying degrees by planning. Markets for the means of production in the

[10] J. Kornai and L. Ujlaki, 'Application of an Aggregate Programming Model in Five-Year Planning', *Acta Oeconomica*, Vol. 2, No. 4, 1967, p. 335.

[11] *Kommunist*, 18/1968, p. 80.

[12] At the beginning of 1965, the USSR had about 3,500 computer installations, including eighty-four computer centres. According to V. Glushkov (Director of the Kiev Institute of Cybernetics) optimal planning and management in the USSR necessitates 10,000 computing centres grouped into forty to fifty major nodal centres, all headed by the central system in Moscow. By the plan covering the 1967–70 period, the USSR is to establish 600 automated control systems and 230 new computer centres. The number of computers in Hungary reported in 1968 was seventy (but none of them up to the latest world standards). The estimated number of computers needed in Poland is over 1,000, compared with less than 100 in existence in 1968. See *Voprosy ekonomiki*, 8/1965, p. 128; *Izvestiya*, 21/8/1966, p. 7; *Figyelo*, 2/10/1968, p. 5; *Życie gosp.*, 18/11/1968, p. 5.

[13] However, many Western economists are sceptical about the feasibility of complete optimization, even in the more advanced Socialist countries, for many years yet to come. See references 20 and 21 at the end of this chapter.

socialized sector have been virtually eliminated. But elsewhere markets have never completely disappeared, and even under Stalinist 'command' planning and administration they had to be tolerated. They have always existed for certain consumer goods and services, such as privately grown produce, fish and wild animals caught privately, articles and services made or rendered by tradesmen in their spare time and sold directly to private users. Such transactions have usually taken place in local markets at (relatively) free prices according to local supply and demand.

The authorities could never, of course, completely disregard the problem of the market for consumer goods even in the socialized sector, if embarrassing shortages or the piling up of stocks were to be avoided. But in their endeavour to prevent such disequilibria, the authorities have usually resorted to *adjusting demand to the postulated supply* by manipulating incomes or prices.

However the question of the market presents itself in a different light altogether in the context of the recent economic reforms. Many more elements of the market mechanism have been incorporated or extended in Socialist economies, such as a greater role assigned to consumers' preferences, considerable independence of enterprises, profit, the strengthening of material incentives to labour, financial instruments (interest, depreciation allowances, taxes, tariffs), and a considerable degree of price flexibility (see Ch. 1 C). Socialist economists now normally assume that three market mechanisms are largely operative in Eastern Europe:

(i) the market for the distribution of consumer goods;
(ii) the financial market;
(iii) the external market.[14]

But more reforms are urged, and some economists, even in the USSR, advocate a market for the means of production, or its extension where it already exists (as in Yugoslavia, Poland, Czechoslovakia and Hungary).[15]

Extension of the role of the market in a planned economy can be justified on three major grounds. First, being based on Marxian ideas, Socialist economies have traditionally concentrated on macro-

---

[14] E.g., L. Leontyev, ('Selling Processes in a Socialist Economy'), *Kommunist*, 3/1967, p. 71; I. Dvornik, ('The Money Market and the Capital Market'), *Finansije*, Sept.–Oct., 1968, pp. 542–51; B. Blass, ('Some Controversial Questions on the Theory of Money in a Socialist Economy'), *Finanse*, 6/1967, pp. 18–19; Ota Šik, *Plan and Market under Socialism*, Prague, Czechoslovak Academy of Sciences, 1967, esp. p. 192; *Muszaki Elet* (Technical Life, Budapest), 9/8/1968, p. 4.

[15] E.g., see W. Przelaskowski, ('Plan, Economic Accounting and the Socialist Market'), *Życie gosp.*, 19/1/1969, p. 8.

economic issues, but they have failed at the microeconomic level. A substantially free operation of the market mechanism is a device to overcome the undesirable consequences of central planning in the micro sphere of production and consumption not lending itself to remote central control in order to produce the best results. The delegation to the market of the working out of microeconomic details also relieves central planners of unnecessary routine work, so that they can concentrate on long-run macro problems.[16]

Second, the operation of the market mechanism is necessary for the continuous verification and correction of planned decisions. 'Even under Socialism', a well-known Czechoslovak economist concluded, 'it is therefore essential for a real market to function as a continual criterion and correction of erroneous decisions in planning.'[17]

Third, the market provides a salutary discipline in the form of competition, so that production and distribution are constantly being adapted to buyers' preferences, and so that this is done in the most efficient manner. Lack of competition has contributed to the persistence of sellers' markets noted for shortages and inflationary pressure, a low quality of products and of service, a weakening of incentives, speculation and various other abuses. In brief, the extension of the role of the market could improve the performance of the Socialist economy by contributing to the minimization of costs and the maximization of desired effects.

The Socialist economic system which is almost completely governed by the market mechanism is known as *market socialism*. The idea was first put forward by Oskar Lange in the 1930s, but its details have been developed and improved more recently by such economists as W. Brus (of Poland), P. Erdös (of Hungary), E. D. Kaganov (of the USSR), Ota Šik (of Czechoslovakia) and J. Sirotkovich (of Yugoslavia).

It is now widely agreed amongst Socialist theoretical and practising economists that, as a Soviet writer put it, 'There is no real justification for treating plan and market under Socialism as mutually exclusive.'[18] Market socialism may assume diverse forms, but in essence it

[16] As explained by V. Glushkov, a Soviet authority on planning mentioned before, under the existing set-up the volume of planning work increases at least as the square of the output. Compared with 1928, Soviet planning in 1963 was 1,600 times more complex, employing over six million persons. At that rate, by 1980 the whole adult population of the USSR would have to be employed in planning (quoted from: J. Prybyla, 'Patterns of Economic Reforms in East Europe', East Europe, 11/1968, p. 11).

[17] Ota Šik, op. cit., p. 272.

[18] V. A. Volkonskii, *Model optimalnogo planirovaniya i vzaimnosviazi ekonomicheskikh pokazatelei* (A Model of Optimal Planning and the Interdependence of Economic Indicators), Moscow, Nauka, 1967, p. 68.

represents peaceful co-existence, and indeed the complementary and harmonious co-operation of these two mechanisms. Social ownership of the means of production and central planning are still retained. The basic proportions and directions of development of macrosocial importance are centrally determined—such as the division of national income between investment and consumption, the division of consumption between private and social, basic investments and the ensuring of overall financial equilibrium. But otherwise, the operation of the economy is left to the market forces. Some extremists, such as the Czechoslovak financial expert E. Löbl, whilst supporting public ownership of the basic means of production, advocate market Socialism without planning, entrusting all economic decisions to the market.[19]

Whilst it is not difficult to put forward abstract models linking planning and the market, it is a different matter to devise practical and workable models of the interaction and organic coalescence of the two under specific socio-economic conditions. So far only Yugoslavia has adopted a type of market Socialism. But in other Socialist countries there is still a strong reluctance to commit the economy too much to the anonymous and 'anarchical' market forces. The opposition is led, on the one hand, by Stalinist diehards who are against any form of 'economic revisionism', and on the other, by mathematical economists who believe that modern centralized planometric techniques and computers can provide better solutions than the market can.

E. RELEVANCE OF THE STAGE OF ECONOMIC DEVELOPMENT

It is customary to distinguish between two stages in the economic development of the European Socialist countries (Albania excepted). The first stage, which lasted up to about the mid-1960s, consisted in laying down basic foundations for rapid industrialization and in increasing the sheer volume of production. This was the period of extensive growth when the main reliance was placed on increasing the size of employment and investment and making structural shifts to tap 'hidden reserves'. In the second stage, economic development has to be concerned primarily with the intensification of productive processes so that high rates of growth are sustained mainly by the rapidly rising productivity of labour and capital.

It is widely believed in Socialist countries that the highly centra-

---

[19] E. Löbl, ('Economic Democracy, But Of What Sort?'), *Plánované Hospodářství*, 6/1968, pp. 67–72.

lized system of economic planning and management is a historical necessity in the early stages of Socialist economic development. Swift and profound changes in the structure of the economy to utilize underemployed resources and to create new sources of raw materials, capital and skilled labour are imperative. Oskar Lange, a brilliant Polish economist and statesman, bluntly compared this stage to a 'siege economy' in capitalist countries, and justified it on similar national emergency grounds.[20] Owing to the inherited mentality and institutional set-up such changes cannot be easily carried out without drastic measures imposed from above. The market mechanism had had ample time to prove itself under the pre-Socialist regimes, yet it had sadly failed to get these countries out of the vicious circle of stagnation, backwardness and poverty.

Centralized planning and management also enable the concentration of resources in key industries for the initial take-off, crucial to subsequent balanced development. The initial backwardness also means that there is a lack of competent managers, so that the centralized detailed tutelage provides practical management assistance to enterprises.[21] As at that stage quantity is more important than quality, the absence of the market is not a great apparent loss.

However, there is no general agreement on the validity of the centralized approach. Some Socialist thinkers believe that, although historically speaking this approach was followed, it must not be regarded as a necessary feature peculiar to the Socialist road to development. It is pointed out that the tremendous social cost was not commensurate with the results achieved. Overburdened with a mass of unnecessary details, central planners cannot help committing errors of judgment, which are then magnified on a national scale in the course of the plan implementation. In a sense, this produces dissipation, not concentration, of resources.[22] This question has received a good deal of attention from a number of Western economists, notably A. Nove and G. W. Nutter (see references 22 and 24 at the end of this chapter).

As far as the advanced stage of the Socialist economic development is concerned, the majority of economists agree that whilst economic planning must be retained, an extension of the role of the market is possible, and indeed imperative. The operation of the market forces can:

[20] O. Lange, *O socjaliźmie i gospodarce socjalistycznej* (On Socialism and the Socialist Economy), Warsaw, PWN, 1966, pp. 210–11.
[21] ibid., p. 212.
[22] E.g., W. Brus, *Ogólne problemy funkcjonowania gospodarki socjalistycznej* (General Problems of the Functioning of the Socialist Economy), Warsaw, PWN, 1961, pp. 147–57.

(i) ensure adaptation of production to buyers' needs and thus lead to the development of buyers' markets;

(ii) evolve and maintain rational price structures conducive to the optimization of production and distribution;

(iii) create conditions for rapid technological progress;

(iv) accelerate growth in labour productivity.

These are precisely the spheres in which centralized planning and management have failed. It was concluded in a recent major work on the functioning of the modern Socialist economy that '... an organic synthesis of planning and the market mechanism should provide that vital link between macroeconomic and microeconomic rationality'.[23]

However, there is also dissident opinion on this approach. Quite apart from the lingering Stalinist opposition, Socialist economists believe that the extension of the role of the market must be paralleled with the strengthening of central control ('democratic centralism') to prevent the worst features of the market mechanism from raising their ugly heads (for example fluctuations, speculation, unemployment, misleading advertising).

But many mathematical economists would go further, and restrict the working of the market. They argue that the higher stages of economic development also enable the perfection of advanced planning and accounting techniques. Armed with modern mathematical methods and computers, central planners can simulate ideal economic processes in the so-called *shadow markets*, which in many respects can provide better solutions than the traditional markets can.[24] The actual developments in the near future will most likely follow a compromise between market Socialists, democratic centralizers and planometricians.

[23] J. Pajestka and K. Secomski, *Doskonalenie planowania i funkcjonowania gospodarki w Polsce Ludowej* (The Perfection of Planning and of the Functioning of the Economy in Socialist Poland), Warsaw, PWE, 1968, p. 96.

[24] E.g., see L. V. Kantorovich, *The Best Use of Economic Resources*, Harvard U.P., 1965, *passim*, esp. p. 151. Also see Ch. 9 E.

RECOMMENDED REFERENCES AVAILABLE IN ENGLISH

*1. Berg, A., 'Economic Cybernetics: Yesterday and Today', *Problems of Economics*, June 1968, pp. 25–8.

2. Bergson, A., *Planning and Productivity under Soviet Socialism*, Columbia U.P., 1968.

*3. Bor, M., *Aims and Methods of Soviet Planning*, translated from the Russian, London, Lawrence & Wishart, 1967.

*4. Dadaian, V., 'The Principles and Criteria of Optimum Planning', *Problems of Economics*, Nov. 1966, pp. 16–29.

*5. Dorovskikh, A., 'Some Problems in the Theory and Practice of the Interbranch Balance', *Problems of Economics*, Aug. 1968, pp. 12–20.

6. Ellman, M., 'Optimal Planning', *Soviet Studies*, July 1968, pp. 112–36.

7. Ewing, D. W., *The Practice of Planning*, New York, Harper & Row, 1968.

8. Hardt, J. P., Hoffenberg, M., Kaplan, N., and Levine, H. S. (eds.), *Mathematics and Computers in Soviet Economic Planning*, London, Yale U.P., 1967.

*9. Horvat, B., *Towards a Theory of Planned Economy*, translated from the Yugoslav, New York, Intern. Arts and Sciences Press, 1968.

10. Johansen, L., 'Soviet Mathematical Economics', *Econ. Journal*, Sept. 1966, pp. 593–601.

*11. Kantorovich, L. V., *The Best Use of Economic Resources*, translated from the Russian, Harvard U.P., 1965.

*12. Kohlmey, G., 'From Extensive to Intensive Economic Growth', *Czechosl. Econ. Papers*, No. 6, 1966, pp. 23–30.

*13. Konnik, I., 'Plan and Market in the Socialist Economy', *Problems of Economics*, Dec. 1966, pp. 24–35.

*14. Kornai, J., *Mathematical Planning of Structural Decisions*, translated from the Hungarian, Amsterdam, North Holland Publ. Co., 1967.

*15. Kornai, J., and Liptak, T., 'Two-level Planning', *Econometrica*, Jan. 1965, pp. 141–69.

*16. Kotov, I., 'Some Problems in Applying Mathematical Methods to Economics, and the Political Economy of Socialism', *Problems of Economics*, Aug. 1966, pp. 3–14.

*17. Kozma, F., 'On the International Comparison of Input–Output Tables', *Acta Oeconomica*, Vol. 1, No. 1–2, 1966, pp. 107–18.

*18. Lur'e, A. L., 'Mathematical Methods in the Study of the Economics of the Socialist Economy and the Economic Theory', *Problems of Economics*, Feb. 1968, pp. 3–11.

*19. Nemchinov, V. S., *The Use of Mathematics in Economics*, Edinburgh, Oliver & Boyd, 1964.

20. Neuberger, E., 'Libermanism, Computopia, and Visible Hand: The Question of Informational Efficiency', *Amer. Ec. Rev.*, Papers and Proceedings, May 1966, pp. 131–44.

21. Nove, A., 'Planners' Preferences, Priorities and Reforms', *Econ. Journal*, June 1966, pp. 267–77.

22. Nove, A., *Was Stalin Really Necessary? Some Problems of Soviet Political Economy*, London, Allen & Unwin, 1964 (it also appeared in the USA under the title: *Economic Rationality and Soviet Politics*, New York, Praeger, 1964).

*23. Novozhilov, V. V., *Problems of Measuring Outlays and Results Under Optimal Planning*, Translated from the Russian, New York, Intern. Arts and Science Press, 1969.

24. Nutter, G. W., *Growth of Industrial Production in the Soviet Union*, Princeton U.P., 1962; and 'Some Reflections on the Growth of the Soviet Economy', *Studies on the Soviet Union*, Vol. VII, No. 1, 1967, pp. 144–50.

25. Olgin, C., 'Cybernetics and the Political Economy of Communism', *Bulletin*, Munich, Oct. 1966, pp. 3–21.

26. Pejovich, S., *The Market-Planned Economy of Yugoslavia*, Minneapolis, Univ. of Minnesota Press, 1966.

*27. Porwit, K., *Central Planning: Evaluation and Variants*, translated from the Polish, Oxford, Pergamon, 1967.

*28. Rakovskii, M., 'Introducing Economic–Mathematical Methods in Planning Practice', *Problems of Economics*, Jan. 1968, pp. 14–21.

*29. Šik, O., *Plan and Market Under Socialism*, translated from the Czech, New York, Intern. Arts and Sciences Press, 1967.

30. Sirkin, G., *The Visible Hand: The Fundamentals of Economic Planning*, New York, McGraw-Hill, 1968.

*31. Volkonskii, V., 'Methods of Mathematical Economics and the Theory of Planning and Administering the Economy', *Problems of Economics*, Nov. 1967, pp. 3–10.

32. Zaleski, E., *Planning Reforms in the Soviet Union 1962–1966. An Analysis of Trends in Economic Organization and Management*, University of North Carolina Press, 1967.

33. Zauberman, A., 'Soviet Attempts to Dynamize Interindustry Analysis: A Survey', *Economia Internazionale*, May 1968, pp. 258–77.

34. Zauberman, A., Bergstrom, A., Kronsjö, T. and Mishan, E. J., *Aspects of Planometrics*, Yale U.P., 1967.

*35. Zielinski, J. G., *On the Theory of Socialist Planning*, Oxford U.P., 1968.

*indicates contributions by writers from Socialist countries.

CHAPTER 3

Profit

Of all the economic reforms in Socialist countries, the question of profit has aroused the greatest sensation in the West. Ever since Marx wrote his *Theories of Surplus Value*, his followers have looked upon profit as the hallmark of capitalism, under which 'the pursuit of profit inexorably increases the exploitation of workers, leads to wars and distorts the lives of hundreds of millions of people'.[1]

After prolonged discussions, initiated by Evsei G. Liberman,[2] and experiments extending over some three years, profit was officially accepted in the USSR in 1965 as the main criterion of enterprise performance. Although differing in the details of application, other European Socialist countries (except Albania) have followed; Yugoslavia, of course, had adopted it much earlier—after the reforms of 1952. In this chapter we shall examine the function and determination of profit under modern Socialism, its distribution and its relation to prices. We shall conclude by examining some misconceptions, common in capitalist countries, on Socialist profit.

A. THE FUNCTION AND DETERMINATION OF PROFIT

It must be observed that profit as an economic category has always existed in Socialist countries. But before the reforms it was treated merely as an accounting device to ensure that enterprises endeavoured to cover their costs out of their own resources where possible, and to hand over the surplus to the State. To promote enterprise performance (which is not the same thing as efficiency), in addition to directive targets several criteria had been in use on which bonuses to workers and 'employees' (the white-collar personnel, including the manage-

[1] A. Birman, ('Profit Today'), *Kommunist*, 10/1967, p. 100.
[2] Liberman, professor of economics at the Kharkov Technical University, now retired, put forward his idea first at a meeting of economists in Moscow in 1948 and then again in the mid-1950s, but did not succeed in arousing any significant interest. It is only his articles in 1962 in *Voprosy ekonomiki* (August 1962) and in *Pravda* (9/9/1962), followed by other writings that have produced a widespread impact.

ment) were based. But their inadequacy became apparent to the reformers.

Thus when incentives were based on the volume of output, producing enterprises were interested merely in the quantity produced; if on the value of output, they strove to concentrate on the articles containing the most expensive raw materials and components; if on the net value of production (value added), they tended to be extravagant with labour. Similarly in the case of trade. When incentives were calculated on the basis of the value of trade turnover, trading enterprises were mostly interested in supplying high-priced articles, often paradoxically because the State may have fixed high prices to discourage consumption of such items.

Liberman and his followers came to the conclusion that even under Socialism the only all-embracing ('synthetic') criterion that could ensure the growth, suitability, quality and efficiency of production was the maximization of enterprise profit. One wonders what Marx would say if he saw such words in praise of profits in the organ of the Central Committee of the Communist Party of the Soviet Union:

'Every achievement or breakthrough in the organization of production, in the use of fixed and circulating assets, in the observance of financial discipline, in the quality and variety of products, in brief, any move in the work of the enterprise is inevitably reflected in profit—positively or negatively'.[3]

The significance and success of the profit criterion consist mainly in the fact that a direct link has been established between profit and incentive payments, so that it is in the interest of the enterprise personnel—and at the same time of society—to strive to maximize enterprise profits. But profit can achieve more than merely a better utilization of resources at the operational level. Trends in the levels of profitability of different branches of the economy provide guidance to central planners in their endeavour to optimize the allocation of resources on the macrosocial scale. Thus profit provides that unique bond of union between micro and macroeconomic interest—the missing link from which Socialist economies had traditionally suffered.

Increases in the profitability of the enterprise, within the power of the management and workers, can be achieved by producing exactly what consumers and other enterprises want, on the one hand, and by reducing costs on the other. In contrast to previous practice, fixed capital allocated by the State to enterprises is no longer free, but is subject to capital charges now representing cost (see Ch. 5 C). These

[3] A. Birman, loc. cit.

50

relationships are shown in the index of profitability or, as it is commonly called in Socialist countries, 'rentability':[4]

$$R = \frac{Q(P-C)}{F+V}\,100;$$

R = rentability, or profit rate;
Q = quantity of output actually sold by the enterprise;
P = price at which the output delivered is sold;
C = average prime cost;
F = average annual value of fixed assets;
V = average annual value of variable (circulating) assets.

To give the same basic chance to all enterprises in the industry, those enjoying special advantages in respect of location, the quality of natural resources, their type of equipment, etc., are subject to special charges reminiscent of differential rent. Profits are now generally calculated on the basis of the output actually sold, not merely produced. Moreover, improved systems of penalties are being introduced whereby fines are deducted from profits, or receipts, for non-fulfilment of contracts, delays, poor quality, faulty specifications and negligence.

B. THE DISTRIBUTION OF PROFITS

The function of profits in specific respects depends on the manner in which profits are shared. The rules governing the distribution of enterprise profits differ widely from country to country, and they are still in the process of being tested and improved. Taking the example of the Soviet Union, enterprise profits are distributed as represented in Fig. 3.

The first claimant on the enterprise profits is usually the State.[5] These deductions are calculated on the basis of fixed and circulating assets held by the enterprise, differential advantages, and loans directly received from the State budget. In other countries deductions may also be made in the form of payroll tax and a charge on stocks held. The proportion of gross profit on the national scale absorbed directly by the State normally varies in different countries according to the degree of financial decentralization. It is highest in

---

[4] Adapted from, J. Popkiewicz, *Stopa zysku w gospodarce socjalistycznej* (Profit Rate in the Socialist Economy), Warsaw, PWE, 1968, p. 68. This formula was first proposed by a Soviet economist, Z. Atlas, ('Economic Accounting and Profitability'), *Vop. ekon.*, 8/1961, pp. 114–15.

[5] In some Socialist countries, as in Hungary, deductions from profits are made only after gross profits are divided into different funds, including the wage fund and the bonus fund.

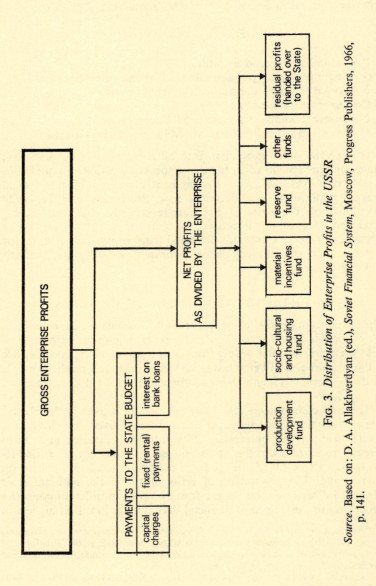

FIG. 3. *Distribution of Enterprise Profits in the USSR*

Source. Based on: D. A. Allakhverdyan (ed.), *Soviet Financial System*, Moscow, Progress Publishers, 1966, p. 141.

Poland—nearly 80 per cent; in the USSR the proportion is about 70 per cent, in Hungary about 60 per cent, whilst in Yugoslavia it is only about 35 per cent.[6] This proportion tends to fall owing to the increasing acceptance of the principle of self-financing (see Ch. 5 D). However, the absolute size of profits attained by enterprises is now very large compared with the past, and it is rapidly increasing, so that profits are now becoming the main source of State revenue, displacing turnover taxes.[7]

The remaining portion of the profits is divided by the enterprise into a number of funds. This is done in accordance with strict rules laid down by the State, and further supplemented by other bodies (branch associations, economic associations, regional authorities, enterprise workers' councils). Thus the *production development fund* is to provide for the financing of cost-saving processes or new products, on the enterprise's own initiative, likely to increase profits in the future. The *sociocultural and housing fund* is used for the provision of collective benefits for the enterprise personnel, reading and rest rooms, entertainment and factory housing for those in greatest need.

As far as the individual members of the enterprise personnel are concerned, the *material incentives fund* is of greatest interest. The proportion of the enterprise profits channelled into this fund varies in different countries. In the USSR in 1968 on the average it was 6 per cent, and in Hungary 15 per cent, of *gross profits*, whilst in the German D.R. 20 per cent of *net profits* (i.e. after State deductions) can be placed in the fund.[8] In the German D.R., Poland and Rumania the size of the fund is based on complicated formulae in which a distinction is made between planned and above-plan profits, and further between profits made by exceeding production targets and those achieved by reductions in prime costs.

In most countries under consideration incentives payable to individuals are proportional to their basic pay, but the amount of working time and work discipline are also taken into account. In the USSR about 10 per cent of workers' earnings in industry is derived from the enterprise profits distributed in the form of incentives. In Hungary, the proportion is about 20 per cent, and furthermore the participation in enterprise profits is roughly proportional to the influence of the different groups of personnel on the size of the

[6] *Finanse*, 1/1969, p. 5; *Kommunist*, 3/1968, p. 47; *Życie gospodarcze*, 30/3/1969, p. 11; *Ekonomista*, 4/1968, p. 917 (respectively).

[7] E.g., in the USSR in 1960, profit constituted 24 per cent of the State budget revenue, whilst turnover taxes represented 41 per cent. By 1969, the respective proportions had changed to 36 per cent and 32 per cent. For further details, see Ch. 11 B, esp. Fig. 12, p. 157.

[8] *Kommunist*, 3/1968, p. 51; *Figyelo*, 29/1/1969, p. 5.

profits created; thus up to 80 per cent of the basic pay of the persons in managerial positions may be supplemented from the incentive fund, up to 50 per cent in the case of intermediate administrative staff, and 15 per cent in the case of blue-collar workers.[9]

In addition to the three crucial funds considered above there may be other funds as well. In each enterprise there is usually a *reserve fund* to provide for unexpected contingencies. There may also be a *sinking fund* (for the repayment of long-term loans), a *trade risk fund* and a *fund for the regulation of retail prices* (in trading enterprises), a *crop failure fund* (in farms) and others. Residual profits, i.e. those which remain after the division is carried out according to the rules, as well as windfall profits (e.g. due to changes in prices) are normally handed over to the State.

C. PROFITS AND PRICES

As has been explained in Part A of this chapter, the enterprise gross profit can be increased by increasing the production of those articles which meet buyers' preferences (i.e. can be sold) and by reducing unit costs. But there is another obvious factor relevant to the size of profits, viz. prices—*producers' prices* (received by producing enterprises) and *retail prices* (received by retail trading enterprises). In contrast to the former two determinants, prices cannot as a rule be manipulated by enterprises, but are set by the State (however, see Ch. 9 D). Thus it must be realized that the profitability of enterprises can be completely reshuffled in the whole economy merely by the State modifying prices. The problem of pricing will be considered in detail in Ch. 9 so that here we shall concentrate only on the relevance of producers' prices to profits.

Acceptance of profit as a criterion of enterprise performance and efficiency necessitates the rationalization of the prices payable to producing enterprises. Until recently these prices bore a haphazard relation to production costs and the need for enterprises' profitability. Thus in the USSR in 1965 (before the wholesale price reform of 1967) the profitability of different *industries* (not to mention different enterprises) ranged from −17 per cent in coal mining to +30 per cent in light industry, the average having been +13 per cent.[10]

All European Socialist countries, except Albania, carried out far-reaching reforms of producers' prices over the period 1962–8 (Poland partly in 1960). The main purpose of these reforms was to

[9] *Finanse*, 9/1968, p. 62.
[10] Y. M. Zinoviev, *Pribil i povyshenie effektivnosti sotsialisticheskogo proizvodstva* (Profit and the Increase in the Efficiency of Socialist Production), Moscow, Mysl, 1968, p. 102.

make all industries and most enterprises reasonably profitable and thus, as far as possible, to eliminate the need for State subsidies. In general, producers' prices are based on the average branch-of-industry (or zonal) all-embracing production costs, plus a profit margin differentiated according to the quality and other desirable features of the article in question. The margin may include a reward for novelty, which is not unlike the capitalist 'innovation profit'.

Thus according to the Soviet reform, effective since July 1967, the gross (before State deductions) profitability of the different major branches of the industry is planned to range from +8 per cent (coal mining) to +16 per cent (the iron and steel industry). On the whole, the level of producers' prices has been raised, but the increases have not been passed on in retail prices but absorbed by the State (in the form of lower turnover taxes).[11] Within each branch there are bound to be differences in gross profitability, depending on the conditions under which different enterprises operate. Thus according to an investigation carried out for the third quarter of 1966 the ratio of the highest to the lowest unit cost of production in Soviet enterprises in respect of selected products was as follows (1·0 is taken as the unit cost of production in the most efficient enterprise in the branch of industry):[12]

crude alcohol	1·3
lumber	2·1
cement	7·9
coal	16·1
electric power	37·0
natural gas	96·1

Two devices are employed in Socialist countries in an endeavour to equalize the net profitability of different enterprises in the same branch of industry. On the one hand, charges are made in the form of differential rent according to the degree of advantage not created by the enterprise. On the other, there is a system of differentiated computational prices payable by the State to enterprises roughly in proportion to those production costs which are beyond the control of the enterprises.

D. PROFIT UNDER CAPITALISM AND UNDER SOCIALISM

Under capitalism profit is the mainspring of economic activity. Private enterprises are set up in search of profit, and in pursuing this

[11] Ibid., p. 103.

[12] E. Kuprinov, ('Calculated Prices and Enterprise Profitability'), *Vop. ekon.*, 3/1968, p. 46.

objective production becomes a means whereby employment is provided to labour in conjunction with other resources. In the absence of competition, a firm can increase its profits by actually restricting production to the point where marginal cost is equal to marginal revenue. Profits are distributed, in the form of dividends, to the shareholders, most of whom do not work in the enterprise in question. Even where profits are not distributed, they remain the property of the shareholders. Profit is the main source of private capital, and thus indirectly is largely responsible for social class differences. The rate of profit earned determines the flow of investment between different firms, industries and even countries.

Upon reflection it is not difficult to see that the similarity between capitalist and Socialist profit is more in name than in the actual functions it performs in economic processes. The role of profit under Socialism differs in seven significant respects from that under capitalism.

a. *Profit is not an objective but a means.* Profit is basically treated not as an end in itself but as a criterion of enterprise performance and, up to a point, of the efficiency of production.

b. *Profits cannot be increased by restricting production.* As prices cannot (as a rule) be freely manipulated by enterprises, they have to be taken for granted. The equilibrium size of production of the enterprise is established where average (or marginal) cost is equated with the given price. This production may be further increased if incentives are payable for exceeding targets.

c. *Profits are not owned by private persons.* On ideological, as well as practical, grounds profits cannot accrue to private individuals (except to a limited extent in the private sector if it exists). Profits can be earned only by enterprises and so they accrue in the first instance to society. Part of the profits is handed over to the State; most of the remainder is retained by the (socialized) enterprise; a portion is distributed to the personnel working in the enterprise in question in the form of incentives, thus constituting a component of total *wage earnings*. Profits cannot lead to social stratification.

d. *Profit is only one of several driving forces behind Socialist production.* Planning must still be regarded as the main driving force (with substantial qualifications in application to Yugoslavia). Overall profitability itself (of the economy and its different branches) is planned by the State, and besides enterprises are still subject to a number of more or less directive indicators supplementing and overriding profit considerations (see Ch. 2 A). The regimes are committed to continuous full employment irrespective of the profitability of some branches of the economy, and losses do not usually lead to the closing down of enterprises. Non-profitable production is still widely carried on, under subsidization or other concessions, on macrosocial grounds considered to outweigh microeconomic losses.

e. *Profit is not necessarily an objective measure of efficiency.* This is so because, to start with, the prices of the factors of production and of the articles produced are not usually determined freely in the market, to reflect scarcity–preference relations. For a variety of reasons, the State fixes prices (or assumes them to be) above or below production costs (however the latter may be understood). By the very act of changing prices, the State may make some products profitable and others unprofitable, even though the methods of production have not changed.

f. *Differences in the profit rate do not necessarily determine the distribution of investment.* Basic investments are still centrally determined by reference to a variety of considerations, of which the profitability of the different enterprises, or even branches of the economy, is only one of the factors taken into account. Even if private individuals happened to have large amounts of capital, they could not purchase the means of production (disregarding the private sector where it is tolerated) to invest in ventures, however profitable these might appear.

g. *Flows of capital to foreign countries are not determined by profit.* On ideological grounds, Socialist countries are against foreign investments for profit. In reality they do send capital abroad—to other Socialist and to underdeveloped capitalist countries. But this is done in the form of repayable loans or gifts, motivated either by political considerations or by a genuine desire to aid the recipient countries.[13] Where interest is charged, it is nominal (usually ranging from 1 to 3 per cent p.a.), to cover administrative costs rather than to make financial gains.

It should be obvious from the preceding discussion that there is a world of difference between capitalist and Socialist profit. At the time of the experiments and reforms involving profit in Eastern Europe, a good deal of nonsense filled the Western daily and periodical press on this subject. Many enthusiastic observers, some

[13] Capitalist countries (or rather governments) also extend foreign aid on similar grounds. Nevertheless, most capital movements are private, motivated by financial gain.

fiercely anti-communist, others misinformed and naive, hailed the Socialist acceptance of profit as a return to capitalism.

There is little evidence so far in support of these expectations. Even Liberman himself most emphatically denied such a possibility. Replying to Western critics he stated:

'Rivers do not flow backward. And if, at high water, rivers make turns, they are simply cutting better and shorter channels for themselves. They are not looking for a way to go back.'[14]

[14] E. Liberman, 'Are We Flirting with Capitalism?', *Soviet Life*, Soviet Embassy in Washington, July 1965, p. 39. Also see his letters to *Time*, 5/3/1965, p. 3, and *The Economist*, 31/10/1964, p. 459 and 26/2/1966, pp. 873–4.

RECOMMENDED REFERENCES AVAILABLE
IN ENGLISH

*1. Birman, A., 'Profit Today', *Problems of Economics*, Jan. 1968, pp. 3–13.

2. Bush, K., 'Liberman Prods the Bureaucrats', *Bulletin*, Munich, May 1968, pp. 23–5.

3. Ivanov, V., 'Bulgaria's Pursuit of "Profitability" ', *East Europe*, Dec. 1968, pp. 26–30.

*4. Kalecki, M., 'Remarks on Factory Prices, Production Indicators and Quality Control', *Eastern Europ. Econ.*, Fall 1967, pp. 28–30.

*5. Komin, A., 'Problems of Improving Industrial Wholesale Prices', *Problems of Economics*, Nov. 1967, pp. 22–7.

*6. Liberman, E. G., 'Profitability and Socialist Enterprises', *Problems of Economics*, March 1966, pp. 3–10.

*7. Liberman, E. G., 'The Plan, Direct Ties and Profitability', *Problems of Economics*, Jan. 1966, pp. 27–31.

*8. Liberman, E. G., 'The Role of Profits in the Industrial Incentive System of the USSR', *Intern. Labour Rev.*, Jan. 1968, pp. 1–14.

*9. Liberman, E. G., and Zhitnitskii, Z., 'Economic and Administrative Methods of Managing the Economy', *Problems of Economics*, Aug. 1968, pp. 3–11.

*10. Révész, G., 'Regulation of Enterprise Profits under the New System of Control and Management', *Acta Oeconomica*, Vol. 3, No. 1, 1968, pp. 23–40.

*11. Sukharevskii, B., 'The Enterprise and Material Stimulation', *Problems of Economics*, Aug. 1966, pp. 42–9.

*12. Turetskii, Sh., 'Price and Its Role in the System of Economic Methods of Management', *Problems of Economics*, May 1967, pp. 3–14.

*13. Wilcsek, J., 'The Role of Profit in the Management of Enterprises', *Acta Oeconomica*, Vol. 2, No. 1–2, 1967, pp. 63–75.

*14. Zieliński, J. G., 'On the theory of success indicators', *Econ. of Planning*, Vol. 7, No. 1, 1967, pp. 1–29.

15. Zybenko, R., 'The Reform of Wholesale Prices', *Bulletin*, Munich, Nov. 1967, pp 41–7.

* indicates contributions by writers from Socialist countries.

CHAPTER 4

Production and Growth

A. NATIONAL INCOME ACCOUNTING

As one would expect, national income accounts play a much greater role in a centrally planned economy than under free enterprise. But the Socialist concepts underlying national income accounting, both in regard to scope and valuation, are fundamentally different from those accepted in the West. They are based on the Marxist (or classical) theory of value, according to which production, or 'value', can be generated by *productive labour*. Productive labour is defined as 'labour expended in the sphere of material production, which is directed to the control and transformation of the means of production to satisfy human wants'.[1] We shall now examine the nature of 'material production', the production and distribution phases of the national income flow, the problem of valuation and the international comparability of the Socialist national income figures.

1. THE SPHERE OF MATERIAL PRODUCTION

This sphere covers those activities which create material goods or help in productive processes, viz. gathering, extracting or growing raw materials, processing the latter into finished products, and delivering them to the intermediate or final users. According to the official classification, material production falls into six major divisions:

  (i) Industry.
 (ii) Construction.
(iii) Agriculture.
(iv) Transport.
 (v) Trade.
(vi) Other material production.

This list indicates the descending order of importance attached to the different branches of the economy. The classification 'industry' is very broadly understood in Socialist countries—it includes mining, quarrying and the crude treatment of primary products as well as manufacturing. Forestry, fishing, hunting and gathering are also 'productive'; they may be included under 'industry' or 'agriculture',

[1] *Mała encyklopedia ekonomiczna* (Concise Encyclopedia of Economics), Warsaw, PWE, 1962, p. 500.

or are sometimes treated as separate divisions, or included in the last (residual) division.

The remaining forms of activities constitute the 'unproductive sphere'. These are usually classified under eight groupings:

   (i) Public administration and justice.
  (ii) Education, science and culture.
 (iii) Health, social welfare and sport.
 (iv) Finance and insurance.
  (v) Local government and housing administration.
 (vi) Defence.
(vii) Political, social and religious activities.
(viii) Other services.

Although these activities are classed as 'unproductive', it does not mean that they are not considered useful. Their indispensability is, of course, officially accepted, and their increasing importance in the higher stages of economic development is commonly recognized.

The methodology of national income accounting in Socialist countries is still in the process of evolution, and there is still disagreement on a number of services. But efforts to promote a uniformity of classifications among the CMEA countries are making progress.

The proportion of the working population engaged in the sphere of material production ranges from 70 per cent in the more developed European CMEA countries (Czechoslovakia, the German D.R.) to 85 per cent in the less developed ones (Bulgaria, Rumania). The range in Western countries is from 55 per cent to 70 per cent. The higher proportion in the Socialist countries is due partly to deliberate policies favouring material production as this is considered 'productive', and partly to their less advanced stage of development and lower living standards.

As can be concluded from the preceding discussion, the Socialist concept of national income includes material production only. The concept of national income normally implied in Socialist countries is that of *national income produced*. If 'losses to the economy' are deducted and 'foreign balance' (the balance of payments on current account) is added, the total obtained is called *national income distributed*. If the value of output of all enterprises (including farms) engaging in material production is added, then the total arrived at is called *social product* (or *gross social product*, or *global product*); it includes 'materials used' at each stage of production, so that the total is unduly high due to double-counting. The two related concepts frequently used, *gross industrial output* and *gross agricultural output*, are similarly inflated by double-counting.

The designation 'national income' is used in both Socialist and capitalist countries. Sometimes, to avoid confusion with the national income figures calculated by the Western method, the description 'net material product' (NMP) is applied to Socialist figures. This description can be found in United Nations sources (to distinguish it from the 'net national product' applying to capitalist countries) but it is not used in Socialist literature.

2. VALUATION

In Western practice, national income totals can be calculated on different bases, according to the purpose to be served—'gross' or 'net', 'domestic' or 'received', 'at market prices' or 'at factor cost'. The Socialist approach is more rigid and the basis is clearly defined, allowing for fewer alternative coverages.

Thus national income calculated by the Socialist method, in addition to comprising material production only, is based on:

(i) *net* value of production, i.e. excluding depreciation;
(ii) *domestic* production, i.e. as attained within the country, irrespective of who ultimately receives it;[2]
(iii) *realized* prices (not factor cost), i.e. including indirect taxes (called 'turnover taxes') but disregarding subsidies.[3]

The fact that national income is calculated at the prices at which transactions in final products actually take place raises several problems, deriving from the uneven incidence of turnover taxes. On the production side of national income, the share of agricultural production is understated in relation to industrial production. In contrast to the latter, agricultural production is not usually subject to turnover taxes, and in addition it is sometimes priced below production costs (see Ch. 8 C). Thus at realized prices (recorded in statistics), the shares of agriculture and industry in the Hungarian national income in 1963 were 20 per cent and 57 per cent respectively; but if the same price basis is applied to both, the shares work out to be 35 per cent and 38 per cent respectively.[4] On the distribution side, the share of accumulation is understated whilst consumption is exaggerated because the former does not generally carry turnover taxes, whilst the latter does.

There are also other structural distortions. The rates of turnover

[2] In practice, this is of little significance as Income Payable To, or Receivable From, Other Countries is of small magnitude (except in Yugoslavia).

[3] It is better to avoid using 'market prices' because realized prices, on the one hand, also cover producer goods transmitted from one State enterprise to another (where there is no market) whilst, on the other, black market prices are not taken into account.

[4] *Życie gospodarcze*, 5/5/1968, p. 11.

taxes are not uniform, so that even within the taxed group of commodities the degree of upward bias varies. In fact, one and the same article may carry different rates of turnover tax according to its use. Different valuations of exports and imports (see Ch. 13 C) also produce distorting results; the weight of such distortions is greater in the case of those countries where foreign trade constitutes a large proportion of national income (e.g. in Bulgaria 65 per cent, compared with 8 per cent in the USSR).

It can be thus concluded that the value structure of Socialist national accounts is not indicative, even to Socialist authorities, of factor cost or of social utility. Of the two standards that may be applied to national income accounting—'efficiency' or 'welfare', neither is consistently followed in Socialist countries.

In spite of these obvious structural distortions, the use of realized prices is defended by Socialist economists on the grounds that such prices 'reflect the actual economic processes and they indicate the financial resources available in different sectors of the economy'.[5]

3. PRODUCTION AND DISTRIBUTION PHASES OF THE NATIONAL INCOME FLOW

Fig. 4 represents different phases of the national income flow as understood in Socialist countries. The national income total is taken as 100, and the figure in each division roughly indicates the share of each component in the total, taking the European Socialist countries as a whole.

A few explanatory notes may be helpful. Department I production includes means of production (producer goods) whilst Department II covers objects of consumption (consumer goods). Group A represents industrial producer goods, Group B—industrial consumer goods. The socialized sector consists of State and of cooperative (collective) productive units. The Social Requirements Fund is that part of production which is not distributed in wages but is used for social (collective) consumption and for accumulation (investment and increase in stocks and reserves). Accumulation is usually higher than the Department I production because the former also includes durable final consumer goods.

4. INTERNATIONAL COMPARABILITY

Owing to the peculiarities of the valuation of the different components of production and the disequilibrium exchange rates, it is obvious that the comparability of the national income figures, even amongst Socialist countries, is greatly impaired. But the problem is of greater

[5] L. Zienkowski, *Jak oblicza się dochód narodowy* (How National Income is Calculated), Warsaw, PWE, 3rd ed., 1966, p. 109.

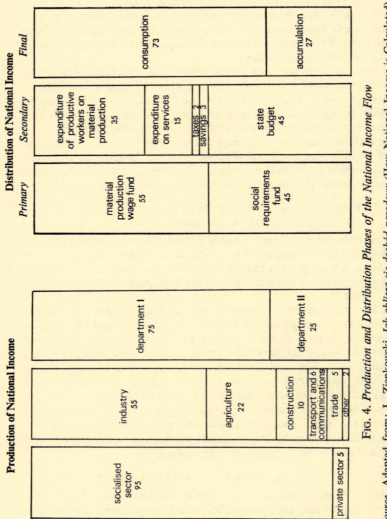

FIG. 4. *Production and Distribution Phases of the National Income Flow*

Source. Adapted from: L. Zienkowski, *Jak oblicza się dochód narodowy* (How National Income is Calculated), Warsaw, PWE, 3rd ed., 1966, p. 102.

magnitude if we want to bring Socialist figures to a Western basis, and *vice versa*. Three major adjustments are involved—'unproductive' services, the price structure, and exchange rates.

A study of 'unproductive' services shows that they may constitute up to 40 per cent of the national income calculated by the Western method, but in most cases the proportion is about 20 per cent.[6] Thus to bring a Western national income figure to the Socialist basis, as a rough approximation, reduce the former by one-fifth (e.g. from $125 m. to $100 m.). Similarly, to place a Socialist figure on the Western basis, add one-quarter to the former (e.g. 100 m. rubles to 125 m. rubles). It must, however, be realized that many services appearing in capitalist national income figures, such as professional services, travel, entertainment, if rendered to 'productive' enterprises would also form a part of the Socialist material production (but they would appear as produced by the enterprises in question). The higher the level of turnover taxes in the Socialist country the smaller the disparity between the national income figures by the two methods.[7] In fact, if the total of turnover taxes exceeds the value of 'unproductive' services, the figure by the Socialist method will be *higher* than by the Western method.[8]

Now to the question of the national price structure. As we have already demonstrated, the prices of agricultural products in Socialist countries are depressed in relation to the prices of industrial consumer goods. At the same time, compared with the industrialized West, the volume of agricultural production constitutes a relatively high proportion of total production in Socialist countries. Consequently national income calculated on the basis of the Socialist

[6] E.g., according to the calculations made by a Czechoslovak economist, the national income of the USA in 1961 was $427,829 m. by the Western method, whilst by the Socialist method the figure was $305,051 m., i.e. 'unproductive' services represented 28·7 per cent of the total. In the economically less advanced nations service industries are less developed, so that the proportion can be expected to be lower. As a rule, 'unproductive' services tend to grow faster in capitalist countries than material production, and thus the percentage gap tends to increase. The percentage difference for the US figure for 1950 was only 21·5 per cent. See, A. Brůžek, 'Recalculation of the National Income of the USA for the Period 1951–1961 According to the Conception Used in the Socialist Countries', *Czechosl. Econ. Papers*, No. 4, 1964, p. 99.

[7] National income by the Western method is calculated at factor cost (i.e. net indirect taxes are deducted from market values) whilst by the Socialist method indirect taxes (turnover taxes) are included.

[8] This can be illustrated by figures calculated in Hungary (noted for a very high level of turnover taxes). The Hungarian national income in 1965 was 166,800 m. forints if calculated on the Socialist basis, but only 155,500 m. forints (i.e. 7 per cent lower) by the Western method. See A. Csernok, 'Hungary's National Income Established on the Basis of the System of National Accounts', *Acta Oeconomica*, Vol. 3, No. 3, 1968, p. 407.

country's own price structure gives a lower figure than by applying a Western country's price structure.

Thus according to calculations carried out by Morris Bornstein in 1959, the Gross National Product of the USSR expressed in the Soviet price structure represented 26·8 per cent of the US GNP, but the proportion was 53·4 per cent when the US price weights were applied.[9] A Soviet economist, S. Strumilin, by applying the standardized world prices of a sample basket of goods, estimated the national income of the USSR for 1962 to be 62·8 per cent of the US total.[10]

By the official exchange rate, the Socialist currency is overvalued in relation to convertible Western currencies, so that if this rate is applied the Socialist national income figure expressed in dollars, francs, pounds, etc., is exaggerated. The degree of upward bias will be smaller if the *tourist* rate is applied, this being closer to the equilibrium rate than the official rate applicable to visible trade (see Ch. 13 C). To overcome this problem we would have to establish a rate indicating the purchasing power of the Socialist currency in relation to the Western monetary unit, for example in terms of internationally traded goods. This is sometimes done by individual researchers. Thus the Polish official exchange rate is 4·00 złotys = US $1·00, the tourist rate is 24·00 z. = $1·00, but in a study involving international comparisons of the Polish national income the rate of 30·00 z. = $1·00 was used.[11]

B. THE ORGANIZATION OF PRODUCTION

In spite of considerable decentralization associated with the reforms in the last decade, the economic administration in Socialist countries, with the exception of Yugoslavia is still substantially centralized. Typically, there are five levels of administration:

  (i) the Council of Ministers;
 (ii) the State Planning Commission;
(iii) economic ministries;
 (iv) 'intermediate' administrative bodies (branch, or economic, associations, regional authorities);
  (v) enterprises (including workshops, farms, etc.).

The pyramid is headed by the *Council of Ministers* (the Government) which is responsible for carrying out the general goals laid down by the Communist Party. The *State Planning Commission*, in

[9] US Congress, Joint Economic Committee, *Comparisons of the United States and Soviet Economies*, Washington, GPO, 1959, Pt. II, p. 385.
[10] *Voprosy ekonomiki*, 7/1963, p. 114.
[11] *Życie gosp.*, 13/11/1966, p. 7.

addition to working out the national plan (see Ch. 2 A), is also responsible for determining the channels of its implementation, and the rest is then largely left to the respective economic ministries.

Government involvement in economic administration in a Socialist country is, of course, much greater than in a market economy. Thus in the USSR there are 50 ministries, plus 10 commissions which can be classed as 'economic' (of the 70 members of the Council of Ministers only 12 have no administrative responsibilities of an economic nature).[12] The United States, a capitalist country comparable in size to the USSR, has only 6 ministries (called Departments), out of a total of 12, clearly concerned with economic administration. The number of economic ministries is, naturally, smaller in other Socialist countries under consideration—the German D.R.: 22; Rumania: 22; Poland: 18; Bulgaria: 14; Czechoslovakia: 13; Hungary: 12; Yugoslavia: 5; compared with 13 in Britain.

Intermediate administrative agencies assume different forms— 'industrial branch associations' (in Czechoslovakia, the German D.R., Hungary, Poland, the USSR), 'industrial associations' (in Rumania) or 'economic associations' (in Bulgaria and the German D.R.). In Yugoslavia there are very active chambers of industry, commerce, transport, etc., and in Poland 'agricultural circles' play an important part in the countryside. In addition, there are republican (in the USSR and Yugoslavia), provincial and local bodies which participate in economic administration. The hierarchical ladder of economic organization and administration is best developed in industry and least in agriculture.

Productive enterprises can be conveniently divided into six categories.

  (i) State industrial and trading enterprises.
 (ii) Co-operative enterprises.
(iii) State farms.
 (v) Agro-industrial undertakings.
(vi) The private sector.

Of these, the last two warrant separate comment. The *agro-industrial* entities represent a form of vertical integration where agricultural and industrial activities are combined. Such activities may be carried on by industrial or trading enterprises in addition to their main pursuits or jointly with State or collective farms. They usually combine agricultural activities with food processing, building, transport, repair work, storage, etc. Their highest form is represented by fully

---

[12] Between 1957 and 1965 the Soviet economic administration was organized on a territorial basis, and it was exercised by over 100 regional economic councils, so that there were only about ten economic ministries at the Union level.

integrated and independent 'agro-industrial kombinats', most developed in the USSR and Yugoslavia.

Taking the European Socialist countries as a whole, the private sector plays only a minor role, contributing about 5 per cent of total production. But it is of considerable importance in some countries, notably Poland and Yugoslavia, where the private sector produces 24 per cent of national income; the proportion in Bulgaria is 10 per cent, in the German D.R.—6 per cent, in Czechoslovakia and Rumania—5 per cent, in the USSR—4 per cent and Hungary—3 per cent.[13] Private enterprise is almost exclusively limited to agriculture, small-scale industry, trade and services. In addition to private farms, which are found in all European Socialist countries except the USSR, there are 'personal' plots cultivated by the members of State and collective farms, rural intelligentsia (officials, teachers) and even urban workers (see Ch. 8 A for further details).

Private producers in the small-scale industry are mostly joiners, locksmiths, shoemakers, tailors, weavers and some (except in the USSR) may own sizeable workshops. Laundries, fashion shops, small retail shops, kiosks, service stations, restaurants and boarding houses are also fairly commonly run by private persons, especially in Yugoslavia, Poland, Hungary, Bulgaria and Czechoslovakia. Privately owned undertakings are subject to discriminatory taxes (see Ch. 11 B), and they usually have no assurance of materials allocations from the State.

C. THE STRUCTURE OF PRODUCTION

Taking the European Socialist countries as a whole, the composition of production, based on official statistics, is indicated by the following percentage figures:[14]

	%
Industry	55
Agriculture	22
Construction	10
Transport and communication	6
Trade	5
Other material production	2
	100

As the official figures are based on 'realized' prices, not on factor

[13] Based on the statistical yearbooks of the countries concerned.
[14] Based on *Vop. ekon.*, 9/1968, p. 101, and supplemented with the statistical yearbooks of the countries concerned.

or social cost, the above proportions overstate the share of industrial production especially in relation to that contributed by agriculture. If price distortions were eliminated, the respective proportions would be closer to 45 per cent and 35 per cent.[15]

From the point of view of the immediate purpose, Socialist production is divided into Department I (means of production) and Department II (objects of consumption). This classification, based on Marx's model of growth, is of great importance when planning economic development. To ensure high rates of economic growth, it is essential that a high proportion of national income should be planned to consist of the means of production, and moreover their output should rise faster than that of consumer goods.[16] For example, in the USSR over the period 1950–67, Department I production averaged 25 per cent of national income (by Socialist definition) and it increased 6·2 times, whilst Department II production rose only 4·2 times.[17]

Although originally Marxism was a protest against the Industrial Revolution, upon the formation of the Socialist States, the communist regimes became champions of industrialization for several practical reasons. Apart from a natural reaction against social conditions based on semi-feudal and backward agriculture, industrialization offers the promise of social emancipation, a cornucopia for the masses and a solid defence base against real or imagined capitalist aggression.

In relatively short periods of time, and with virtually no assistance from the capitalist world, the European Socialist countries have attained most impressive levels of industrial development. They now

[15] According to calculations made by S. H. Cohn for 1964, if total production in the USSR were brought to the *Western GNP basis*, then the proportions represented by industry, agriculture and unproductive services would be (compared with the UK and USA) expressed as percentages:

	Industry	Agriculture	Services	Other
USSR	34	25	17	24
UK	40	4	30	26
USA	32	4	36	28

See S. H. Cohn, 'Soviet Growth Retardation: Trends in Resource Availability and Efficiency', US Congress, Joint Economic Committee, *New Directions in the Soviet Economy*, Washington, GPO, 1966, Pt. II-H, p. 110.

[16] However, this traditionally accepted view is being increasingly questioned by a number of Socialist economists today. They maintain that expanded reproduction (a positive rate of growth) is possible without the Department I production having to rise faster than Department II. A falling capital–output ratio may ensure high rates of growth in national income even if Department I production does not rise faster than Department II. E.g. see M. Usiyevich, ('Leninist Doctrine on the Two Departments of Social Production and the Experience of Socialist Development in the CMEA Countries'), *Vop. ekon.*, 1/1969, pp. 111–22.

[17] ibid., p. 120.

claim about 30 per cent of the world's industrial output, compared with 15 per cent in 1937.[18]

The degree of industrialization attained, of course, differs amongst these countries. The least industrialized are Bulgaria and Rumania, and the most are Czechoslovakia and the German D.R., the USSR occupying an intermediate position. Comparative figures for the eight European Socialist countries are given for 1950 and 1965–7 in Fig. 5.

The relative importance of the European CMEA members (Yugoslavia excluded) in the grouping's total industrial output is indicated by the following percentages:

	%
USSR	69·5
German D.R.	8·9
Poland	8·0
Czechoslovakia	6·4
Hungary	2·8
Rumania	2·8
Bulgaria	1·5
	100·0

Source. D. Fikus, *RWPG Fakty* (Facts on CMEA), Warsaw, PWE, 1966 p. 49, (the figures add up to 99·9 per cent owing to rounding).

FIG. 5. *Differences in the Industrialization of the European Socialist Countries*

Country	Industrial production as a percentage of national income		Industrial production per head (USSR = 10)	
	1950	1966	1950	1965
Bulgaria	37	45	4	7
Czechoslovakia	63	66	15	12
German D.R.	56	64	—	15
Hungary	48	57	8	8
Poland	47	52	7	8
Rumania	43	49	3	5
USSR	58	51	10	10
Yugoslavia	52	46	7	6

Source: *Voprosy ekonomiki*, 9/1968, p. 101, and the statistical yearbooks of the countries concerned.

[18] B. Vladimirov, ('Fifty Years of Economic Competition between the Two Systems'), *Kommunist*, 1/1968, p. 41.

Within the sphere of *industrial* production, Socialist countries have traditionally attached greater importance to *producer goods* (Group A) than to *consumer goods* (Group B).[19] As a rule, parallel to the treatment of Departments I and II, not only is Group A production planned to rise faster, but also priority is given to it in reaching and exceeding targets in the course of plan implementation. This is illustrated by the following average annual rates of growth—planned and actually attained:

	Group A		Group B	
	Planned	*Actual*	*Planned*	*Actual*
Poland (1961–5)	8·6	9·7	8·3	6·7
USSR (1959–65)	9·3	10·1	7·3	6·9

Source. United Nations, *Incomes in Postwar Europe*, Geneva, ECE, 1967, Ch. 7. p. 1.

The proportion of Group A in total industrial output is rising. Taking the European Socialist countries as a whole, it constituted only 45 per cent before World War II, by 1950 it had risen to 60 per cent, and today its share is 70 per cent.[20]

Within Group A, preferred treatment is accorded to those producer goods which will subsequently be used to produce other producer goods, rather than to those which will produce consumer goods; the former are termed Group A1 (mostly heavy industries) and the latter Group A2 (mostly light industries). A generalization may be ventured that, historically speaking, industrialization in capitalist nations usually proceeds from light to heavy industries, whilst in Socialist countries the sequence is reversed.

As a consequence of the priorities assigned to heavy and machine-building industries, other branches of the economy have suffered, especially agriculture, light industries and trade. They have been neglected in respect of investment allocations, working conditions and the quality of labour. However, in recent years the official attitude has been slowly changing in favour of these industries (see Chs 6 C and 12).

D. RATES OF GROWTH

Figure 6 shows official rates of growth in national income, industrial

[19] Slightly different classifications are used in the German D.R., Hungary and Yugoslavia, so that the descriptions, Group A and B do not appear in official statistics.

[20] N. G. Klimko (ed.), *Problemy razvitiya ekonomiki sotsialisticheskikh stran Evropy* (Problems of the Economic Development of the European Socialist Countries), Kiev, Izd. Pol. Lit. Ukrainy, 1968, p. 129; I Oleinik, ('Economic Tendencies in Socialist Countries'), *Vop. ekon.*, 9/1968, p. 102.

output and agricultural output. The rates for selected capitalist countries are also given. As can be deduced from the discussion in Part A of this chapter, the comparability of figures in a table of this nature is limited. This problem is of lesser magnitude with regard to

FIG. 6. *Average Annual Rates of Growth in Socialist and Capitalist Countries, 1950–68*
(Official rates at constant prices)

Country	National income[1]	Industrial output			Agricultural output
		Total	Group A	Group B	
Bulgaria	10	13	16	12	4
Czechoslovakia	6	7	8	6	2
German D.R.	8	9	12[2]	7[3]	3
Hungary	7	9	10[4]	8[5]	4
Poland	7	9	10	8	2
Rumania	10	13	15	11	5
USSR	8	10	11	9	4
Yugoslavia	7	10	—	—	5
AVERAGE (8 countries)	8	10	11	9	4
Japan	10	15	—	—	2
United Kingdom	3	3	—	—	3
United States	4	5	—	—	2
EEC	6	8	—	—	4
ALL CAPITALIST COUNTRIES	5	6	—	—	4

[1] Net Material Product of the Socialist countries, Net National Product at Factor Cost of the capitalist countries.
[2] Metal processing industry.
[3] Light industry.
[4] Heavy industry in the State sector.
[5] Light industry in the State sector.

Sources. Based on: *Voprosy ekonomiki*, 1/1969, p. 119; *Gospodarka planowa*, 12/1968, p. 11; *United Nations Yearbook of National Accounts Statistics* (various issues) and the statistical yearbooks of the countries concerned.

the rates applying to the same country than in respect of comparison with other Socialist, and more so with capitalist, countries. Nevertheless, the table provides an interesting and useful basis for broad comparisons.

The Socialist rates of growth are likely to embody an upward bias. First, as the success of the enterprises is largely judged by the targets attained and overfulfilled, the management in providing statistical returns has a vested interest in overstating production achievements. Secondly, as in the past targets were usually defined in quantitative terms, the poor quality or even sheer uselessness of some production was not reflected in the rates.[21] This upward bias may be partly matched in capitalist rates. The fastest growth in Western countries is usually recorded in 'unproductive' services. As this component forms part of the Western, but not Socialist, national income, it may be assumed that to this extent the rates of growth in capitalist (especially advanced) countries embody an upward bias, too.

Socialist rates of growth, particularly those of the USSR, have been subjected to thorough critical examination by a number of Western (mostly American) economists, notably A. Bergson, R. W. Campbell, S. H. Cohn, R. Greenslade, J. P. Hardt, D. Hodgman, N. Kaplan and R. Moorsteen, S. Kuznets, A. Nove and G. W. Nutter.

There is general agreement amongst them that the official Socialist rates are exaggerated. Thus S. H. Cohn, testifying before the US Congress in 1966, gave the annual growth rate in the Soviet GNP as 7·1 for the period 1950–8, and 5·3 for 1958–64, i.e. an average rate of 6·4 per cent compared with the official Soviet rate of 9 per cent p.a.[22] Some experts arrived at lower figures: G. W. Nutter produced an average long-range rate for the USSR up to 1963 of about 3 per cent.[23]

Most Socialist economists react strongly against the Western estimates, as being biased misrepresentations designed to belittle Socialist economic achievements. Thus a Soviet economist, I. Kotkovskii, argued that Cohn had understated Soviet economic growth over the six-year period, 1959–64, by a quarter—instead of 36 per cent, the total growth was in fact 48 per cent.[24] On the other hand, some Soviet statisticians, viz. B. N. Mikhalevskii and Yu. P. Solovev, believe that the Soviet official average rate of 9·1 per cent for the

[21] The rates for industrial and agricultural output (as the term 'output' indicates) are based on *global* returns, in which there is a good deal of double-counting, i.e. the final product, as well as its components obtained from outside the enterprise or farm (and in some cases also those produced internally), are counted as production. However, this in itself does not necessarily bias the *rate* of growth from year to year provided there is no change in the pattern of overlap. On the whole, the degree of double-counting appears to be decreasing owing to the increasing concentration and integration of processes.

[22] S. H. Cohn, op. cit., p. 105.

[23] G. W. Nutter, 'The Effects of Economic Growth on Sino-Soviet Strategy', in D. M. Abshire and R. W. Allen (eds.), *National Security: Political, Military, and Economic Strategies in the Decade Ahead*, New York, Praeger, 1963, p. 166.

[24] I. Kotkovskii, ('Present Conditions of Economic Competition between the USSR and the USA'), *Vop. ekon.*, 4/1967, p. 75.

period 1951–63 is too high; instead they arrived at a rate of 7·0 per cent, which is not far from Cohn's figure of 6·4 per cent.[25]

All in all, there are many good reasons for believing that Socialist rates of growth are higher than those in the capitalist world, or even the West, as a whole, although probably by less than the gap on paper would imply. The high rates attained in Socialist countries in the past can be partly explained by their accelerated early economic development. The *absolute* rise in production was not as large as the high *rates* would suggest—they are typical of countries starting from low absolute figures of national income. The relatively high rates achieved by Bulgaria and Rumania, as compared with Czechoslovakia and the German D.R., can be largely explained on these grounds.

This fact is further illustrated by the following figures showing the average annual rates of growth (in national income) attained by the European CMEA countries:

1951–5	10·7
1956–60	8·4
1961–5	6·0
1966–8	7·5

Sources. Gospodarka planowa, 7/1968, p. 19; *Życie gospodarcze*, 11/5/1969, p. 11.

The 'recession' of the early 1960s clearly stands out. In reality the drop was greater, but owing to the relative undervaluation of agricultural production, the disastrous failures in agriculture are not fully reflected in this rate.

It is generally assumed in the West that, as Socialist countries achieve mature stages of economic development, the rates will gradually decline and settle at levels typical of Western countries. This possibility is strongly discounted by most Socialist economists, such as E. Gorbunov of the USSR and K. Łaski of Poland. It is argued that compared with the past, Socialist economies now command new sources of growth. The perfection of economic planning (see Ch. 2 C), a greater economy in the use of resources consequent upon the systematic application of capital charges (Ch. 5 C) and differential rent (Ch. 8 B), improving microeconomic efficiency (Chs 3 and 7 C), and an increasing participation in the international division of labour (Ch. 13 A, B) are likely to arrest a decline in the rates of growth.[26]

[25] B. N. Mikhalevskii and Y. P. Solovev, ('The Growth Function of the Soviet Economy over the Period 1951–1963'), *Ekonomika i matematicheskie metody*, No. 6, 1966, pp. 823–40 (quoted from G. F. Denton, 'A Recent Soviet Study of Economic Growth 1951–63', *Soviet Studies*, April 1968, p. 503).

[26] E. Gorbunov, ('The Efficiency of Accumulation and Economic Growth'),

It is further pointed out that in contrast to capitalist countries, under Socialism lagging effective demand is not a limiting factor, and besides the authorities can determine such levels of investment as will ensure continued high growth. The low rates prevalent in the 1960s were due to natural calamities and to the dislocations caused by the transition to the new economic system. Since that time the rates have already increased, and they will improve further once the new system is in full operation.[27] It is generally assumed by Socialist economists that, on the whole, the long-run rate of growth will settle at the level of 50–70 per cent higher than in the developed capitalist countries.[28]

Kommunist, 8/1967, pp. 88–97; K. Łaski ('The Question of Economic Growth in Socialist Countries'), *Nowe drogi*, 1/1968, pp. 85–93.

[27] ibid.

[28] J. Kleer, J. Zawadzki and J. Górski, *Socalizm–Kapitalizm* (Socialism *v.* Capitalism), Warsaw, KiW, 1967, p. 98.

RECOMMENDED REFERENCES AVAILABLE IN ENGLISH

1. Alton, T. P., Korbonski, A., Mieczkowski, B., and Smolinski, L., *Polish National Income and Product in 1954, 1955 and 1956*, New York, Columbia U.P., 1965.

2. Campbell, R. W., *Accounting in Soviet Planning and Management*, Harvard U.P., 1963.

3. Campbell, R. W., *Soviet Economic Power: Its Organization, Growth and Challenge*, 2nd ed., Boston, Houghton Mifflin, 1966.

4. Denton, F. G., 'A Recent Soviet Study of Economic Growth 1951–63', *Soviet Studies*, April 1968, pp. 501–9.

5. Dobb, M., *Soviet Economic Development Since 1917*, 6th ed., London, Routledge, 1966.

6. Gamarnikow, M., 'The New Role of Private Enterprise', *East Europe*, Aug. 1967, pp. 2–9; and 'Another Step Toward Private Enterprise', *East Europe*, Jan. 1968, pp. 2–9.

*7. Gervai, B., 'The Role and Situation of Private Artisans in Hungary', *Acta Oeconomica*, Vol. 3, No. 4, 1968, pp. 441–8.

*8. Goldmann, J., and Kouba, K., *Economic Growth in Czechoslovakia*, translated from the Czech, New York, Intern. Arts and Sciences Press, 1968.

9. Hardt, J. P., 'Soviet Economic Development and Policy Alternatives', *Studies on the Soviet Union*, Vol. VI, No. 4, 1967, pp. 1–25.

*10. Horvat, B., 'An Integrated System of Social Accounts for an Economy of the Yugoslav Type', *Reivew of Income and Wealth*, March 1968, pp. 19–36.

11. Kaser, M. (ed.), *Economic Development for Eastern Europe*, London, Macmillan, 1968.

*12. Kheinman, S. A., 'Structural Improvement and the Intensification of Industrial Production', *Problems of Economics*, Jan.–Feb.–March 1967, pp. 105–48.

*13. Laptev, I., 'Rates and Proportions in the Development of Industry and Agriculture', *Problems of Economics*, May 1966, pp. 23–33.

14. Moykowski, A., 'The Perils of Private Enterprise in Poland', *East Europe*, Sept. 1968, pp. 19–23.

15. Nutter, G. W., *The Growth of Industrial Production in the Soviet Union*, Princeton U.P., 1962.

16. Rosovsky, H. (ed.), *Industrialization in Two Systems*, New York, London, Sydney, John Wiley, 1966, Part II.

*17. Schmidt, A., 'Some Problems Concerning the Calculation of Socialist National Income', *Acta Oeconomica*, Vol. 3, No. 2, 1968, pp. 221–8.

*18. Šestáková, M., 'The Firm in the Czechoslovak Economy', *Journal of Industrial Relations*, Nov. 1967, pp. 23–33.

*19. Silar, J., 'Considering the Question of the "Accuracy" of Measurements of the Share of Agriculture in National Income', *Eastern Europ. Econ.*, Winter 1967–8, pp. 3–12.

*20. Strnad, V., and Yershov, E., 'Some Mathematical Problems Arising in the International Comparison of Economic Indicators', *Czechosl. Econ. Papers*, No. 5, 1965, pp. 91–106.

  21. Tarn, A., 'A Comparison of Dollar and Ruble Values of the Industrial Output of the USSR', *Soviet Studies*, April 1968, pp. 482–500.

*22. Tsvetkov, G., 'The Proportion Between Industry and Agriculture', *Eastern Europ. Econ.*, Fall 1964, pp. 26–36.

  23. US Congress, Joint Economic Committee, *New Directions in the Soviet Economy*, Washington, GPO, 1966.

  24. US Congress, Joint Economic Committee, *Soviet Economic Performance 1966–67*, Washington, GPO, 1968.

  25. Ward, B. N., *The Socialist Economy—A Study of Organizational Alternatives*, New York, Random House, 1967.

  indicates contributions by writers from Socialist countries.

CHAPTER 5

Accumulation

A. ACCUMULATION *v.* CURRENT CONSUMPTION

Accumulation is a Marxian term corresponding to the Western concept of investment in its broadest sense. It is that part of national income which is produced but not consumed during the year in question ($A = NY - C$). According to the official classification, it consists of:

(i) the stock of added fixed assets in the sphere of material production;
(ii) the stock of added fixed assets in the non-productive sphere;[1]
(iii) net additions to the stocks of circulating assets in the process of production;
(iv) net additions to reserves (held idle as an insurance against unexpected contingencies);
(v) the foreign trade balance.[2]

As in Western practice, depreciation ('amortization' in Socialist terminology) is deducted from gross investment so that only net investment is included in accumulation.

Under capitalism, the division of national income between investment and consumption is overwhelmingly determined by private producers and consumers. Private firms base their investment decisions on expected profitability (determined by the marginal efficiency of capital and the rate of interest). Savings (on the macro scale) accommodate themselves to investment, and are conditioned by the inequalities in the distribution of national income and wealth. Although governments endeavour to influence and supplement the private sector, the intervention is not on a comprehensive and

---

[1] In the German D.R. non-productive investment is excluded from the concept of accumulation altogether.

[2] In some Socialist countries (e.g. in Poland) the foreign trade balance is not treated as part of accumulation but (in addition to the 'national income losses' and the 'balancing item') constitutes the difference between the national income *produced* and *distributed*.

systematic basis, and the proportion between investment and consumption is not consciously determined.

In the Socialist economy, accumulation is centrally fixed on a planned basis. Neither interest nor profit is allowed to interfere with the size and broad distribution of accumulation at the macroeconomic level. However, interest and profit are now important instruments for promoting the most economical implementation of investment undertakings at the operational level. As accumulation is centrally planned, and for a number of years ahead, it is much more stable from year to year than is normally the case in capitalist countries (where the proportion may range from a negative figure to some 40 per cent of national income).

The decision on the proportion between accumulation and consumption is largely political. It is governed by the available resources and long-run macrosocial objectives, such as industrialization, defence preparedness and the postulated rate of growth.[3] The proportion of national income ('net material product') devoted to accumulation is usually fixed within the range of 20–30 per cent.[4] These officially given proportions are in fact understated, because in the Socialist national income valuation producer goods are relatively undervalued (as, in contrast to most consumer goods, they are not subject to turnover taxes, see Ch. 4 A). In the capitalist economies at about the same stage of development as the European Socialist countries, the proportions normally range from 10 to 25 per cent of national income as estimated by the Socialist method.

Although the precise degree of difference may be disputed, there is little doubt that Socialist countries devote a higher proportion of their national income to accumulation than, *ceteris paribus*, capitalist countries do.[5] This is made possible by the mono-party system of government, central planning and the social ownership of the means of production. Current consumption is restricted by manipulating

[3] In search of the optimal plan, usually a number of plans is worked out, in which the proportion of accumulation is one of the variables. Thus in the USSR for the 1966–70 plan, *Gosplan* worked out five structural plan variants, in which the proportions of accumulation ranged from 24·8 per cent (enabling a planned rate of growth of national income of 5·6 p.a.) and 30·4 per cent (corresponding to the growth rate of 7·5 p.a.). *Voprosy ekonomiki*, 11/1967, p. 86.

[4] *Ekonomista*, 6/1968, p. 1453. In the German D.R., where investment in the non-productive sphere is not treated as part of accumulation, the proportion has ranged from 10 to 20 per cent.

[5] This is illustrated by comparative studies in Hungary and Poland. Before World War II, accumulation averaged 7 per cent and 11 per cent respectively. In the 1960s, the proportion for Hungary ranged from 24 to 30 per cent, and for Poland over the period 1956–60 it was 25–26 per cent. *Statisztikai Szemle*, Jan. 1969, p. 6; L. Zienkowski, *Jak oblicza się dochód narodowy* (How National Income Is Calculated), Warsaw, PWE, 1966, 3rd ed., p. 223.

the wage fund and social consumption on the one hand, and retail prices on the other. It is assumed by the authorities that this sacrifice is warranted, and indeed essential, in the early stages of industrialization, when it is necessary to develop industries noted for high capital absorption, such as mining, heavy industry and transport.

B. INVESTMENT AND SOCIALIST REPRODUCTION

In Socialist economics a distinction is made between 'productive' and 'non-productive' accumulation. The former comprises additions to fixed and variable assets in the sphere of material production, and it is referred to as 'productive investment', or simply investment. The balance of accumulation consists of durable consumer goods for individual as well as for collective consumption, such as private housing and household effects, public buildings and equipment, educational, social, cultural and sporting facilities, and defence installations and materials.

In general, productive investment constitutes about three-quarters of the total, the remaining one-quarter being classed as non-productive. The proportions represented by productive investment in the countries publishing such statistics are shown below for 1950 and 1965:

	1950	1965
Bulgaria	78	86
Czechoslovakia	73	77
Hungary	74	78
Poland	74	73
Rumania	87	85
USSR	68	67

Sources. W. Iskra, *Rozwój przemysłowy krajów RWPG* (Industrial Development of the CMEA Countries), Warsaw, PWE, 1967, p. 297; and statistical yearbooks of the countries concerned.

As Socialist countries proceed to higher stages of economic development, it can be expected that the share of productive investment will decline in favour of 'non-productive' ones more directly relevant to the improvement in living standards.[6]

Productive investment is directly related to Socialist 'reproduction', a concept which was first introduced by Marx. It denotes a continuous process of production where resources are used up, partly to meet current consumption needs, and partly to recreate resources to enable continued production in the future. Reproduction can be

[6] W. Iskra, *Rozwój przemysłowy krajów RWPG* (Industrial Development of the CMEA Countries), Warsaw, PWE, 1967, pp. 291–4.

simple—when the scale of production is unchanged; *extended*—when the scale is increased with the aid of additional investment (unless the efficiency of investment increases); and *contracting*—when the scale is declining, which is normally associated with negative investment (i.e. 'disinvestment').

The rate of economic growth in a given period depends on the investment made in the preceding period, and its efficiency. This applies equally to Socialist and capitalist countries. However, the criteria and methods of determining the rate of investment (I/Y, i.e. the proportion of investment in national income) are different under each system.

In the capitalist economy, a crucial role is played by effective demand and surplus production capacity. Extra investment is made only in anticipation of increased demand beyond the existing idle capacity. This becomes obvious by referring to the well-known 'Harrod–Domar' model of growth. Investment in a given year increases production capacity. But the increase in the money income of the population needed to absorb the extra production depends on *net* investment, as only the latter can produce the multiplier effect. The extent of the increase in money income (ΔY) brought about by the increment in investment (ΔI) is determined by the multiplier (k).[7] Investment that creates production capacity for which there is subsequently insufficient demand leads to losses. If the equilibrium size of investment is known then, given the size of national income, the investment rate can be arrived at—it is equal to the saving rate or the reciprocal of the multiplier.

Under Socialism, the role of investment in economic growth is much greater and more direct. The investment rate is not a product of micro decisions dependent on anticipated demand and profitability, but is determined by the central planning authority in advance. The size of investment is never limited by an insufficiency of demand, because the latter can be easily adjusted to the required level (in fact, it tends to outrun effective supply).

In the best-known model of Socialist growth, developed by M. Kalecki in Poland, the determinants of economic growth in fact reduce to those affecting investment as indicated by the following formula:[8]

$$Rg = \frac{1}{ci} \cdot \frac{I}{Y} - Yo + Ye;$$

[7] The relation between these variables is shown in the following formula: $I/(I/\Delta Y) = \Delta Ik$, in which the left side of the equation indicates the output produced with the aid of the investment, whilst the latter indicates the income generated by the increment in investment.

[8] Adapted to English terminology and concepts from: M. Kalecki, *Zarys teorii*

F

Rg = rate of growth of national income;

ci = coefficient of capital intensity (its reciprocal denotes the coefficient of capital efficiency);

I/Y = share of productive investment in national income;

Yo = reduction of national income caused by the withdrawal of worn-out resources;

Ye = increase in national income brought about by greater efficiency.

It does not, of course, mean that the investment rate under Socialism can be fixed at arbitrarily high levels. Central planners are bound by three constraints. First, if the investment rate is fixed too high in relation to current consumption, the work effort may deteriorate, which might actually lead to a decline in the rate of growth.

Second, in contrast to capitalist countries there is normally continuous full employment (however, see the case of Yugoslavia, Ch. 8 A) so that excessive investment produces immediate strains on labour resources. Third, the implementation and subsequent operation of certain types of investment may be hampered by a lack or shortages of domestically produced equipment and materials. To overcome this, substantial readjustments to imports and exports may be necessary, to which there are usually limitations imposed by conditions at home as well as abroad.

C. THE EFFICIENCY OF INVESTMENT

The rate of growth of national income depends not only on the size of investment but also on the effectiveness of its installation and subsequent utilization. In the earlier stages of economic development, dominated by the goal 'industrialization at any cost', Socialist countries paid little attention to the problem of efficiency. When efficiency declined, to maintain high rates of growth, usually the rate of accumulation was simply increased.[9]

However, as the Socialist countries were approaching more developed stages, the problem was not sorting itself out, but was in fact becoming magnified. Taking the CMEA group of countries as a whole, from the late 1950s to about the mid-1960s, the incremental capital–output ratio was rising alarmingly, i.e. investment was rising

wzrostu gospodarki socjalistycznej (Outline of the Theory of Growth of the Socialist Economy), Warsaw, PWN, 1963, esp. p. 18.

[9] E.g., in the USSR the accumulation rate was increased from 21 per cent in 1927/8 to 27 per cent in 1932 and to 29 per cent in 1940. As a result an average annual rate of growth in national income of 16 was maintained over the period, in spite of sharp deteriorations in the productivity of capital in all major branches of the economy. See E. Gorbunov, ('The Effectiveness of Investment and Economic Growth'), *Kommunist*, 8/1967, p. 90.

at much faster rates than national income. This became most obvious in Czechoslovakia, industrially the most mature Socialist country, where investment cost per 1 koruna of increase in national income (at 1963 prices) was as follows:

	korunas
1950	1.33
1960	2.41
1961	3.14
1962	13.90
1963	18.22

Source. Ota Šik, *Plan and Market Under Socialism*, Prague, Czechoslovak Academy of Sciences, 1967, p. 62.

It may be observed that in 1963 Czechoslovakia actually experienced a *negative* rate of growth of national income (-2.2), even though accumulation constituted over 13 per cent of her national income.[10] Even in the USSR the trend was quite strong. To achieve 1 ruble increase in national income (at constant prices) it was essential to spend 1.40 r. in 1950, 2.53 r. in 1960, and 4.67 r. in 1963 on gross investment.[11]

Although the rising capital–output ratio has been partly due to the capital-intensive progress, there is little doubt that, at least up to the mid-1960s, it was largely due to the continued excessive reliance on extensive growth factors, irrespective of efficiency. As Ota Šik summed it up:

'Enterprises and departments, relying on the experience of the previous extensive development, demanded the greatest possible volume of investments, the most manpower and the lowest production targets they could, so that they could fulfil the plans easily.'[12]

Although investment efficiency studies had been carried on before World War II (in the USSR) they have assumed urgency in all Socialist countries only in the last decade. Indexes of investment efficiency have been worked out to aid planners and enterprises in selecting the most 'effective' investment projects. The simplest and most common index is represented by the following formula:[13]

$$Ie = \frac{(1/T)\,I + C}{V};$$

[10] Central Statistical Office of Czechoslovakia, *Statisticka ročenka 1967* (Statistical Yearbook for 1967), Prague, 1967, pp. 132, 136.

[11] Ia. B. Kvasha, 'Capital Intensity', *Problems of Economics*, Jan.–Feb.–March 1967, p. 67.

[12] Ota Šik, *Plan and Market under Socialism*, Czechoslovak Academy of Sciences, Prague, 1967, p. 86.

[13] The two following formulae have been adapted to English terminology and

Ie = index of investment efficiency;

T = time (in years) for the recoupment of the investment outlay; it is either fixed as a uniform number of years for the whole economy (e.g. six years in Poland) or differentiated according to industries (e.g. three to ten years in the USSR);

I = investment outlay;

C = annual regular production cost of operating the project during its useful life; either prime cost (as in Poland) or total cost (as in the USSR) may be taken into account.

V = annual value, or volume, of production during the lifetime of the project.

In the preceding index no account is taken of the construction period of the investment project (during which investment resources are 'frozen'), the period of exploitation and changing production costs during the lifetime of the project. These considerations are reflected in the 'synthetic' index of investment efficiency:

$$sIe = \frac{(1/T)I(1+d \cdot f) + Cn \cdot vc}{Vn \cdot vp}$$

sIe = synthetic index of investment efficiency;

d = coefficient of discount indicating annual losses caused to the economy during the period of construction of the investment undertaking; it is usually fixed for the whole economy (e.g. in Poland it is 0·15, or 6·67 p.a.);

f = the freeze period, i.e. the number of years necessary to complete the investment project;

Cn = total cost of exploitation of the project including maintenance and repairs during the whole period n;

vc = coefficient of cost variation during the period of exploitation;

Vn = total value of production in the entire period n;

vp = coefficient of production variation during the period of exploitation.

There are several reasons to believe that the effectiveness of investment in Socialist countries will be greater in the future than in the past. First, the progress being made towards optimal planning and computerization place planners in a better position to make more effective allocations of investment resources at the macro level.

concepts from: The State Planning Commission of Poland, *Instrukcja ogólna w sprawie metodyki badań ekonomicznej efektywności inwestycji* (General Instruction Concerning the Methodology of the Evaluation of the Economic Efficiency of Investment), Warsaw, PWE, 1962, pp. 30–5, 78–89.

Second, investment banks, whose role and responsibilities have been greatly strengthened by the recent reforms, now systematically evaluate investment efficiency before extending credits (see Part D of this chapter and Ch. 10 B, C). Third, all CMEA countries have embarked on a consistent policy of standardization of capital equipment and processes, systematic exchanges of technological data and specialization on a CMEA-wide basis.

Fourth, since the early 1960s these countries have introduced 'capital charges', which are annual payments made by enterprises to the State on fixed (and circulating, as e.g. in Czechoslovakia) assets in their possession. These charges now range from 1 per cent to 9 per cent p.a. (for further details, see Ch. 10 C, p. 148). Finally, the acceptance of profit as the main criterion of enterprise performance means that enterprises are no longer as extravagant in endeavouring to secure and hoard equipment they cannot profitably utilize.

D. THE FINANCING OF INVESTMENT

In a capitalist economy, most investment is privately financed, and this is done mainly by ploughing back profits, issuing shares and debentures and by borrowing from banks. Public investment in government business undertakings generally follows a similar pattern, although there may be considerable differences regarding the provision of initial capital and the treatment of profits and losses according to the undertaking's relation to the public authority budget.

In Socialist countries there is, of course, no capital market and virtually all providers and users of capital are socialized entities.[14] There are three sources of investment finance for enterprises—the State budget, banks and the enterprises' own resources. As a result of the economic reforms, the role of direct State financing has been declining in all these countries in favour of bank credits and the

[14] Some interesting exceptions may be mentioned. In most Socialist countries, especially in Czechoslovakia, the German D.R. and Yugoslavia, there is a number of companies with limited liability, with shares and occasionally debentures owned by other socialized enterprises. There are privately financed enterprises (especially in Yugoslavia), but the earnings on such investments are limited to the level of the current bank long-term interest. The private sector in all these countries (except the USSR) can obtain finance from banks, but usually on discriminatory terms. In most of these countries (especially in Bulgaria, Czechoslovakia, Hungary and Yugoslavia), under certain conditions foreign investors can have minority shareholding in local enterprises. Besides, there is a number of joint East–West trading and co-production enterprises in which Socialist countries usually have majority shareholdings. For further details see J. Wilczynski, *The Economics and Politics of East–West Trade*, London, Macmillan, 1969, Ch. 15 D.

enterprises' own funds. The case of Poland, which is typical in this respect, illustrates the role of each, and the prevailing tendency:

	Percentages		
	1963	*1968*	*1969* (*planned*)
State budget	48	28	24
Bank credits	8	20	30
Enterprises' own funds	44	52	46

Sources. Finanse, 12/1967, p. 35, and 1/1969, p. 6.

We shall now examine each source of finance in turn.

1. THE STATE BUDGET

Investment and credit policy still basically rests on broad plans centrally laid down. The investments allocated directly by the State are those which are of key importance to the socioeconomic progress of the country, and they are usually designed to change the structure of the economy.

The initiative originates from the State, and the projects are clearly defined by central planners as to the type, location and size, and the date of completion. The initial capital expenditure may be partly repayable by the enterprise to the State.

The State-provided investments are financed out of capital charges, differential levies, depreciation and other payments made by enterprises to the State budget. But their total may be insufficient, so that the balance may be financed out of the revenue from turnover taxes. These taxes are mostly imposed on consumer goods, and their proceeds have been traditionally directed to industry rather than agriculture. Besides, procurement prices payable by the State to farms have often been set deliberately at very low levels, to provide the State with cheap foodstuffs and industrial raw materials.

In effect, on the macroeconomic scale, the development of industry has been partly financed by agriculture. Thus it is the peasant, as a consumer of high-priced industrial consumer goods and a producer of under-priced agricultural commodities who has borne the main brunt of Socialist industrialization. However, this is slowly changing, as the prices of agricultural products are being raised in relation to industrial articles, and the allocation of investment resources is becoming less discriminatory to agriculture than in the past.

2. BANK CREDITS

These are extended by investment, agriculture, commerce and foreign trade banks, under the overall control of the State central bank, for the purchase of fixed and circulating assets. Credits are granted to enterprises under the condition that the contemplated investment is consistent with the economic plan and that the project is likely to be profitable.

Banks, in conjunction with branch associations and the enterprises concerned, participate in working out operational plans and the efficiency of individual projects. In each country, banks have a scale of interest rates differentiated according to the purpose and length of the credit (for further details, see Ch. 10 C).

3. ENTERPRISES' OWN FUNDS

These resources are used to finance smaller investments, including repairs and the modernization of the existing plant. As a result of decentralization, individual enterprises now have a good deal of freedom to initiate and implement ventures which promise high profitability.

The financial resources for such purposes are now held in the Enterprise Development Fund. There is generally no direct central control over the ways in which the Fund is to be applied. But the State exercises substantial influence through various financial incentives and disincentives, whereby the size of the Fund can be increased or decreased. The finance in this Fund is derived mainly from the retained portions of depreciation allowances and profits, and also from the sale of surplus fixed assets.[15]

[15] According to a recent report, in the USSR these three sources represented the following proportions: 65 : 30 : 5 respectively. *Życie gospodarcze*, 11/7/1968, p. 8.

RECOMMENDED REFERENCES AVAILABLE IN ENGLISH

*1. Bartl, W., and Luck, H., 'Optimum Proportions Among National Income, Accumulation and Consumption', *Eastern Europ. Economics*, Winter 1964, pp. 7–25.

*2. Belik, Iu., 'Planning the Relationship between Consumption and Accumulation', *Problems of Economics*, May 1966, pp. 3–12.

*3. Deak, J., 'New Tasks in Foreign Trade in Connection with Investments', *Soviet and Eastern Europ. For. Trade*, July–Aug. 1967, pp. 27–32.

 4. Fallenbuchl, Z. M., 'Some Structural Aspects of Soviet-type Investment Policy', *Soviet Studies*, April 1965, pp. 432–47.

*5. Horvat, B., 'The Rule of Accumulation in a Planned Economy', *Kyklos*, Vol. XXI, No. 2, 1968, pp. 239–68.

*6. Khachaturov, T., 'The Economic Reform and Problems of the Effectiveness of Capital Investments', *Problems of Economics*, March 1968, pp. 12–24.

*7. Kvasha, Ia. B., 'Capital Intensity', *Problems of Economics*, Jan.–Feb.–March 1967, pp. 66–104.

*8. Rakowski, M. (ed.), *Efficiency of Investment in a Socialist Economy*, translated from the Polish, New York and London, Pergamon, 1966.

*9. Sitarian, S., Gusarov, A., and Senchagov, V., 'Principles of Establishing Norms of Payment for Productive Capital', *Problems of Economics*, July 1967, pp. 26–33.

*10. Szakolczai, G., 'The Pattern of Investments and the Rate of Growth', *Acta Oeconomica*, Vol. 2, No. 3, 1967, pp. 189–210.

* indicates contributions by writers from Socialist countries.

CHAPTER 6

Consumption

A. THE PLANNED CONSUMPTION MODEL

As with other important facets of economic life under Socialism, consumption is planned centrally. The extent and degree of detail, of course, differ from one country to another, and are certainly smaller now than before the reforms. Consumption has to be planned in advance because it constitutes an integral part of the national economic plan, which cannot be constructed and balanced unless the size and structure of consumption are laid down.

In working out the consumption model, the central planning authority (CPA) makes a distinction between the preferences of consumers in their capacity as private individuals and as members of society. The CPA endeavours to meet consumers' private preferences up to the point where they do not interfere with the interest of society. When that conflict arises, the CPA makes value judgments, usually in favour of the long-run interest of society as a whole, in accordance with the principle known as the *primacy of macrosocial preferences*.

Thus the CPA is confronted with such basic alternatives as: current or future consumption, individual or collective consumption, necessities or luxuries, variety or standardization, quality or quantity. The planning of the consumption model at the same time necessitates the planning of the incomes of the population and of the retail prices of consumer goods.

When it comes to the realization of the consumption plan, the CPA may find either that it had gauged consumers' preferences incorrectly, or that some unexpected developments have occurred on the production side. In such cases, three courses are open to the authorities:

(i) No attempt is made to restore equilibrium in the consumer goods market by changing either demand or supply. This leads to shortages (or, less likely, piling up stocks), and perhaps rationing.

(ii) Steps are taken to adjust demand to the existing supply by the process called *consumption steering*. This is done by manipulating the size of the wage fund, increasing or decreasing the prices of relevant articles including their substitutes, tightening up or liberalizing the terms of consumer credit, and by propaganda which may include persuasive advertising. A sort of equilibrium is restored without production responding to demand.

(iii) Supply is adjusted to demand, by the CPA providing for larger stocks of finished goods and raw materials, creating excess capacity through additional investments and perhaps allowing more imports of consumer goods.

All these courses may be followed at the same time but, to generalize, the first two are typical of the short-run and of the earlier stages of the economic development of a country. For a variety of reasons, there is a growing inclination to allow the market to shape production in response to consumers' preferences.

Largely as a consequence of planned consumption, Socialist countries have traditionally suffered from seller's markets, noted for an excess of aggregate demand over supply. The overriding consideration behind the planning of consumption is the curtailment of current consumption in favour of accumulation to ensure high rates of growth of national income. In practice, nominal incomes tend to rise faster than envisaged in the plan. At the same time, priority is given to the fulfilment (and over-fulfilment) of targets for producer goods, if necessary at the expense of consumer goods production (see Ch. 4 C), and the imports of consumer goods are strictly controlled.[1]

But the excess demand is bottled up by price controls. Although formal rationing has been abolished in the European Socialist countries since the mid-1950s, there is still, in effect, rationing of housing, cars and certain other consumer durables and of foreign travel (especially to non-Socialist countries) in the form of long waiting lists.

However, several developments in recent years have tended to remove the worse abuses of seller's markets and the consumer, for long an insignificant pawn on the economic chessboard, is being accorded a new deal. First, in the new approach to planning 'by demand' the consumer is allowed to perform a useful function in relieving the CPA of unnecessary details of planning in the sphere noted for a great variety of preferences and changing tastes. Second, there is a growing assertiveness of the consuming public, tired of past promises and continued sacrifices, a trend which is now called 'consumerism'.

Third, the increased role that is being assigned to material incen-

---

[1] E.g. in 1963 consumer goods constituted the following proportions of total imports: Rumania: 4 per cent, Bulgaria: 7 per cent, Hungary: 10 per cent, Poland: 15 per cent, Czechoslovakia: 21 per cent, the German D.R.: 23 per cent. In the case of most capitalist countries the proportion falls within the range 20–40 per cent. *Ekonomika sotsialisticheskikh stran v tsyfrakh 1964* (The Economies of Socialist Countries in Figures for 1964), Moscow, Mysl, 1965, p. 61.

tives to labour necessitates more and a wider range of consumer goods, particularly luxury items (see Part C of this chapter). Fourth, profit has been accepted as the main indicator of enterprise success, and it is now calculated on the basis of production actually sold, not merely produced. Fifth, closer links are being established between distribution and production to make commerce an effective transmitter of consumers' preferences to producing enterprises.

Finally, as the basic foundations for industrialization have been laid down, the improving capacities now enable more attention to be given to the production of consumer goods. Thus in the USSR in 1968 and in 1969, for the first time since 1946, the rate of growth of industrial consumer goods (Group B) was planned to be higher than for industrial producer goods (Group A).[2] Symbolic of the new official attitude is the decision to develop the mass production of passenger cars not only in Czechoslovakia and the German D.R. but also in Bulgaria, Hungary, Poland, Rumania, the USSR and Yugoslavia, where big contracts with Western companies, viz. Daimler–Benz, Fiat, Renault, Volkswagen and Volvo, are playing a prominent part. Thus in the USSR it is planned that by 1971 the output of cars will exceed that of lorries, for the first time ever, to reach 800,000 annually, as compared with 200,000 in 1965.[3] (For further details on the developments from seller's to buyer's markets, see Ch. 12 C.)

B. PRIVATE AND SOCIAL CONSUMPTION

Under Socialism a good deal of importance is attached to the distinction between 'private' (also called 'individual') and 'social' (also described as 'collective', 'residual', or 'other') consumption. Private consumption still plays the basic role, constituting about three-quarters of total consumption. It consists of those goods and services which are purchased out of the consumer's own earnings on the basis of his *free choice*.

Social consumption includes public child care, education at all levels, health benefits, pensions, housing, communal feeding, special holidays, transport, entertainment and cultural services. These benefits are provided completely free or at charges well below costs on a far wider scale than even in the most affluent Western countries.

[2] Between 1928 (when the first five-year plan began) and 1968, only in three years (1937, 1945, 1946) did Group B output increase faster than Group A. Over the whole period, Group B was increasing at an average annual rate of 4, whilst Group A showed a rate of 11. The planned rates for 1968 were 8·6 and 7·9, and for 1969 7·5 and 7·2 respectively. See *Kommunist*, 11/1967, p. 90; *Pravda*, 11/12/1968, pp. 1–3.

[3] *Izvestiya*, 10/1/1968, p. 2.

Social consumption is financed from the State budget, social insurance funds, communal resources and enterprises' and farms' profits earmarked for the purpose.

The share of social in total consumption in Socialist countries ranges from 20 to 30 per cent, Bulgaria, Hungary and Poland usually being at the lower, and Czechoslovakia, the German D.R. and the USSR at the higher margin of the range.[4] In capitalist countries, the proportion usually falls within the range 5–15 per cent, and for underdeveloped regions it may be less.[5]

In the past, social consumption was rising on the whole faster than private consumption,[6] and the Communist Parties are as a rule committed to maintaining this growth.[7] As put by a Socialist authority on the subject, it is a form of distribution 'transitional from the principle "to each according to the quantity and quality of work" to that based on "to each according to rationally justified needs" '.[8]

Under certain conditions collective goods and services can be an ideal means of satisfying the wants of the consumers most economically and in accordance with their legitimate preferences irrespective of their earned-income disability. Under Socialism, earnings are still based on the value of work performed, not on needs, so that there is a considerable differentiation of incomes. These disparities tend to be accentuated by the new role assigned to material incentives (for details, see the next section). In the case of optional social goods and services, such as non-compulsory education, certain health services and medicines, travel and recreation, the consumer can exercise his choice of whether to use them or not. The provision of such benefits also releases women for paid employment and thus, with family incomes increased, many more consumers' needs of a private nature can be satisfied.

On the other hand, the ability of the consumer to exercise influence in the sphere of social consumption is nil or remote. As far as he is

[4] R. Krzyżewski, *Konsumpcja społeczna w gospodarce socjalistycznej* (Social Consumption in the Socialist Economy), Warsaw, PWN, 1968, pp. 115–20; *Voprosy ekonomiki*, 1/1968, pp. 120–1.

[5] See United Nations, European Commission for Europe, *Incomes in Postwar Europe*, Geneva, 1967, esp. Ch. 6, p. 12.

[6] Over the five years 1960–5, the average annual growth of social (private in parentheses) consumption at constant prices was as follows: Bulgaria: 11 (6), Czechoslovakia: 5 (3), the German D.R.: 3 (2), Hungary: 7 (4), Poland: 7 (5). Based on: *Incomes in Postwar Europe*, op. cit., Ch. 7, pp. 67–8.

[7] E.g. in the USSR, social consumption is to represent one-half of the total real income of the population by 1980. For details see, *The Road to Communism*, Documents of the 22nd Congress of the CPSU, Moscow, FLPH, 1961, pp. 513–79.

[8] K. Szwemberg, *Społeczny fundusz spożycia w Polsce* (The Social Consumption Fund in Poland), Warsaw, 1965, p. 110 (quoted from R. Krzyżewski, op. cit., p. 25).

concerned, the market is completely by-passed, and the continued expansion of this form of consumption means a decline in the role of the individual consumer. Collective goods and services may be of insufficient variety and quality to accommodate individual consumers' preferences, yet they cannot be resold or exchanged for something else that is desired—in a sense not unlike rationing. In the case of compulsory goods and services (such as secular education, inoculations) there is no choice at all, whilst most of the remaining ones are provided under conditions restricting the consumer's freedom of choice as to the quantity, variety, place and time.

The ideal of continued expansion of social consumption, to over one-half of total consumption, is in conflict with the recent reformulation and extension of material incentives. We shall examine this problem next.

C. CONSUMPTION AND THE OPERATION OF MATERIAL INCENTIVES

To ensure the effective operation of material incentives to labour, they must be organically linked to an appropriate consumption model. Until the early 1960s, the importance of this interconnection was not fully appreciated by the authorities. As is discussed elsewhere in this book (Chs 3 C, 4 and 7 C), the recent economic reforms *inter alia* include extension and strengthening of material incentives to labour and the acceptance of profit as the chief criterion of enterprise performance.

Experience had shown in the past only too well that material incentives do not produce the desired result if they consist merely of monetary rewards for more and better work. Their operation, intensity and direction depend on the workers' needs, the ways in which such needs are satisfied and, in the ultimate analysis, on the availability of the exact goods and services the labour force wants in its capacity as consumers. It can easily be seen that private consumption must now receive the focus of attention from the CPA. It ensures the satisfaction of wants on the basis of free choice, and thus it activates the operation of material incentives, contributes to the growth of productivity and thus 'constitutes a dynamic element of economic growth'.[9]

On these grounds, the authorities are now adopting a more favourable attitude to consumer credit, because it has been demonstrated that not only does it provide an incentive to more and better work, but it may actually lead to higher accumulation. In the more market-oriented economies, such as Czechoslovakia, Hungary and Yugo-

[9] R. Krzyżewski, op. cit., p. 15.

slavia, about one-quarter of consumer goods is now sold on hire purchase (see Ch. 10 C for further details).

The introduction of profit as the main indicator of enterprise success provides the basis for a new deal for the consumer. As profit is calculated on the basis of the value of production actually sold (not merely produced), and as this in turn determines bonuses to the personnel, it is now in the interest of the enterprises to adapt their production to consumers' preferences. Of special relevance are incentives applicable to trading enterprises. In the past, the criterion of success for incentive payments was usually the value of trade turnover, so that enterprises were mostly interested in supplying high-priced items. This, again, tended to produce paradoxical results; high prices were often due to high turnover taxes intended to discourage consumption of such items (e.g. alcoholic beverages, tobacco) whilst articles untaxed or subsidized and in common demand were neglected.

It is generally agreed amongst the planners and political leaders in Eastern Europe that response to consumers' pressure for better living is most desirable and likely in respect of industrial consumer goods, especially textiles, footwear, metalware, chemical products and electrical appliances. Such goods, generally being luxuries, have a strong incentive effect to greater effort. Besides, investment outlays involved in expanding their production are two to three times lower than in agriculture and, unlike most necessities, being subject to turnover taxes they are a handy source of accumulation for the State.[10] The trend towards reducing the rates of turnover taxes should further enable consumption to extend in the desirable direction.[11]

But there are many restraints which will continue to limit the scope and operation of material incentives in favour of the consumer. The profit criterion for incentives spurs the enterprises to monopolistic practices, such as limiting production (where they are free to fix their own prices, see Ch. 9 D) increasing prices and concentrating on items which are profitable but not necessarily in the consumers' best interest. Furthermore, the authorities may still insulate or distort the

[10] S. Kuziński, ('The Structure of Consumption and the Market Problem'), *Nowe drogi*, 1/1968, pp. 37–46; G. Pisarski, ('Ways and Means of Expanding Consumption'), *Zycie gospodarcze*, 11/8/1968, p. 4.

[11] In the past, paradoxically, agricultural products were often sold to consumers at prices well below production costs (i.e. produced under subsidization), whilst industrial consumer goods were subject to heavy and arbitrary turnover taxes. In effect, the consumption and waste of the high-cost but low-priced articles were unwittingly encouraged (e.g. grain and even bread was fed to cattle in spite of the critical food situation) whilst unjustified brakes were applied on the consumption of the low-cost but high-priced consumer durables.

effect of incentives on production by planned consumption steering, by manipulating prices, by adjusting the wage fund and by resorting to propaganda. In many cases, material incentives are so designed as to give priority to production and sale for export, rather than domestic consumption, especially to the developed capitalist countries where hard currency can be earned. For a variety of reasons, the Socialist export effort is concentrated on consumer goods and, moreover, to be able to compete in the capitalist buyer's markets such goods have to be of higher quality than for domestic consumers.

D. THE QUESTION OF CONSUMER'S SOVEREIGNTY

The role of the consumer in the economy can be judged by the extent to which he can influence production. In an extreme case of centralized planning, consumption patterns are simply imposed on the consumer from above by means of specific, non-transferable, fixed-period validity rationing. Under such conditions, there is no consumer's choice and it is the planners who are sovereign.

Where production of consumer goods is determined by planners but there is no rationing, so that consumers are free to determine their own patterns of consumption from what is available, the situation is known as 'freedom of consumer's choice'. The economic regime under which production responds to consumption, and thus the producers allocate resources according to consumers' preferences, is known as 'consumer's sovereignty'.

Absence of consumer's free choice is usually associated with tight, centralized command planning (or total war in a capitalist economy). This situation existed in the European Socialist countries up to the early 1950s, and in the USSR during War Communism (1917–21), the early Plan Era (1928–36) and World War II (1940–5). On the other hand, complete consumer's sovereignty exists only in a competitive free market economy, the nearest example of which prevailed in the nineteenth century.

The condition existing in the European Socialist countries today can be described as a liberal form of consumer's free choice. On the one hand, total consumption and its broad structure are laid down by the CPA. The long-term investment programme for major developments in consumer goods industries is also determined centrally. On the other hand, the precise composition and distribution of the output in the consumer goods sector are determined by individual consumers registering their preferences in the market.

Under this set-up, to ensure the fulfilment of the consumption plan on the production and consumption sides, the CPA has to exercise a dual system of control. This assumes the form of a two-tier price system, whereby producers' and retail prices of consumer goods can move independently. Thus the prices received by producing enterprises can be manipulated to regulate profitability, and consequently production, whilst retail prices are regulated to influence consumption.

By this insulation, production does not necessarily have to respond to consumers' preferences, unless the CPA decides otherwise. Using these devices, planners can ensure equilibrium on the market. The deviations of retail from producers' prices so managed (apart from trade margins to cover distribution costs) is an indication of the extent to which the CPA controls consumption by manipulating retail prices rather than allowing production to respond to consumers' changing preferences. These disparities also indicate to the CPA how production should be adjusted in the long run if the authority decides to acknowledge consumers' wishes.

However, it must be added that there are some prices of consumer goods which are 'free' prices, determined in the market according to supply and demand, and the range of articles in this category is gradually increasing (see Ch. 9 D). To this extent, the insulation effect is removed, and consumers can influence production more effectively.

In a centrally planned economy, absolute consumer's sovereignty is not feasible. Nor is it desirable. As a result of prejudice, habit and imperfect knowledge, many consumers' preferences are irrational, such as an excessive preference for drugs, alcohol and luxuries which the economy cannot afford, a lack of appreciation of external economies and diseconomies, and a predilection for immediate consumption. Instead of allowing the consumer to shape production, and consequently the allocation of resources, the CPA intervenes whenever there is conflict between private and social interest. Additionally, or alternatively, it endeavours to appropriately shape the conditions under which consumption takes place. Thus we can conclude that a planned economy—whether of a centralized or decentralized type—cannot, and should not, permit *absolute consumer's sovereignty*, but it is in a good position to ensure *rationalized consumer's sovereignty*.

Whether it does in fact, depends on the extent to which the CPA's preferences really reflect those of the consumers as members of society. In practice, the CPA is more likely to follow the Party's rather than consumers' preferences, and what is good for the Party and the perpetuation of communism is not necessarily in the consumers' best interest. Furthermore, there have been no free elections to prove that the Communist Parties (particularly in Czechoslovakia, Hungary and Poland) really represent all or even the majority of consumers.

It must be pointed out that the better deal that is being accorded the consumer in Eastern Europe is no proof of the restoration of the consumer to the economic throne and that sovereignty over the allocation of resources is handed over to him. It merely indicates that firstly, the consumer is allowed to perform useful functions in perfecting economic planning and secondly, the capacity of the more developed Socialist economies has sufficiently improved to allow higher standards of living.

In Western textbooks of economics the proposition is sometimes advanced with pride that under capitalism 'the consumer is king', and that consumer's sovereignty ensures the most rational allocation of resources. These assertions belong more to fiction than to reality. This is particularly so in the developed Western countries which are noted for strong monopoly elements and large inequalities in the distribution of national income.

In the search for profit maximization, powerful private interests subject the consumer through modern mass media to a constant battery of sales promotion so that consumption patterns are largely imposed upon him and he is deprived of rational choice. The size and structure of demand are further distorted by the socially unjustified extremes in the distribution of incomes. Besides, some consumers' preferences are inherently irrational, which in the absence of government intervention produces adverse long-run effects on the consumers themselves, as well as on society in general. In the Socialist economy, either such irregularities do not exist, or otherwise there is a unique machinery to counteract such tendencies, which is conducive to higher levels of social welfare.

RECOMMENDED REFERENCES AVAILABLE IN ENGLISH

1. Hanson, P., *The Consumer in the Soviet Economy*, London, Macmillan, 1968.

*2. Kresta, J., 'Problems of Exchanging Consumer Goods with the Comecon Countries', *Soviet and Eastern Europ. For. Trade*, Fall 1968, pp. 44–57.

*3. Lengyel, L., 'Living Standard: Facts and Opinions', *Acta Oeconomica*, Vol. 1, No. 3–4, 1966, pp. 327–43.

*4. Parfenova, A. and Rumantsev, V., 'Budgets of the Population and the Study of Demand', *Problems of Economics*, Sept. 1967, pp. 33–6.

*5. Pervushin, S. P., 'Production and Consumption at a New Stage', *Problems of Economics*, Jan.–Feb.–March 1967, pp. 1–21.

*6. Raitsin, V. I., 'Planning the Standard of Living According to Consumption Norms', *Problems of Economics*, Oct.–Nov. 1968 (the whole issue).

7. Robinson, Joan, 'Consumer's Sovereignty in a Planned Economy', in *On Political Economy and Econometrics*, Essays in Honour of Oskar Lange, Warsaw, Polish Scientific Publishers, and Oxford, New York, Pergamon Press, 1965, pp. 513–22.

*8. Sova, V., and Teichman, V., 'Observations on the Forecasting of Long-term Trends in Living Standards', *Czechosl. Econ. Papers*, No. 8, 1967, pp. 19–38.

*9. Stadukhin, D., and Khaverson, M., 'Social Consumption Funds and Living Standards', *Problems of Economics*, Aug. 1968, pp. 21–5.

10. United Nations, Economic Commission for Europe, *Incomes in Postwar Europe*, Geneva, 1967, Chs 6–12.

* indicates contributions by writers from Socialist countries.

CHAPTER 7

Labour

A. CONDITIONS AND ORGANIZATION OF LABOUR

The position of labour is fundamentally different under Socialism from that under capitalism. Political power rests in the hands of the Communist Party representing the interests of working people, the only social class. Labour is the only factor of production credited with the capability of creating value, so that it alone can be remunerated (to the exclusion of land, capital and enterprise). As the means of production are (to generalize) socialized, owners and workers are the same people, so that there is no basic antagonism between the interest of the employer (the State) and the employees (the workers).[1]

All able-bodied persons are guaranteed the right to work. As labour is the only source of personal income (apart from social services) there is in fact a general obligation to work, in accordance with the principle 'he who does not work shall not eat' (Article 12 of the Soviet Constitution). These facts influence the organization of labour, wages and other conditions of work in ways distinct from those under capitalism.

Labour is less subject to directive planning than other facets of the Socialist economy. Economic planning, even of the centralized version, is compatible with the individual *freedom of the choice of occupation and of the place of work*. This principle is now followed in all European Socialist countries,[2] with some minor exceptions. Professional people, especially new graduates of technical colleges and universities, may be assigned to particular places of employment, and labour recruiting in the countryside for work in specified industries and regions is common. The possibility of being directed to particular responsibilities anywhere in the country is implicit in the

[1] Although exceptional, the private hiring of labour still exists in the private sector and in domestic service. E.g. in Poland in 1966, the total numbered nearly 200,000 people (2 per cent of the total working population), of whom 38,000 were domestic servants. There is special heavy taxation of incomes derived from hired labour, and the employers are legally bound to work with their employees. The figures are from: *Rocznik statystyczny 1967* (Statistical Yearbook of Poland for 1967), p. 55.

[2] Between 1940 and 1956 in the USSR, it was prohibited to leave one's place of work without permission (punishable by imprisonment or forced labour).

99

membership of the Communist Party and of its youth organizations. The labour discipline code has been substantially liberalized since the mid-1950s, and the labour turnover now appears to approximate that in Western countries.

Socialist countries have traditionally been committed to continuous *full employment*. It may be observed that the work force constitutes about 55 per cent of the total population, compared with about 45 per cent in Western countries. The higher proportion in Socialist countries is accounted for by a higher proportion of women in paid employment,[3] and by the absence of non-working owners of businesses, shares, bonds, patents and land.

The concept of full employment under Socialism still lacks precise definition. In the past it was generally assumed that the only unemployment that can be tolerated is of the frictional type, which owing to economic planning should not exceed 1 per cent of the total work force (compared with 2–3 per cent under free enterprise). However, in recent years many economists, especially in Poland and Yugoslavia, have argued that optimal employment is in fact below maximum employment as the latter may in fact lead to lower national income.[4] However, the majority of economists still supports the officially accepted line, as was demonstrated at the CMEA Conference on the Use of Labour Resources in Budapest in 1968.[5] For a variety of reasons, Czechoslovakia, the German D.R. and Hungary have suffered in recent years from over-full employment (and from 'hoarding of labour'), whilst Yugoslavia, and to a minor extent Poland, have experienced unemployment.[6]

Trade unions in Socialist countries are a curious mixture of survivals from the past and modern adaptations to the needs of the State. In some respects, they are reminiscent of medieval guilds in that they embody the employer (representative of the State) and the employees (workers), they organize educational and recreational activities, and

---

[3] About 50 per cent in the USSR, and about 40 per cent in other Socialist countries, of the work force consists of women (compared with about 30 per cent in the West). Women are employed even in such capacities as truck drivers, carpenters, bricklayers, foundry workers and miners. This is regarded as evidence of the equality of the sexes.

[4] E.g. see Z. Łaski, ('Economic Accounting and the Optimization of Employment'), *Życie gospodarcze*, 11/9/1966, p. 3; B. Fick, ('Incentives and Disincentives Relevant to the Planned Optimization of Employment and the Wage Fund'), *Finanse*, 3/1969, p. 41.

[5] *Voprosy ekonomiki*, 1/1969, p. 152.

[6] Unemployment has become a problem in Yugoslavia, where in the 1960s it averaged 250,000 and ranged from 5 to 10 per cent of the working population. Besides, about 300,000 Yugoslav workers are employed in Western Europe. See *Statistički godišnjak Jugoslavije 1968* (Statistical Yearbook of Yugoslavia for 1968), p. 102; *Ekonomski pregled*, 10/1968, p. 539.

in some countries (as in the USSR) they administer social insurance funds. In some ways they are like the unions of the advanced capitalist countries, in that they endeavour to safeguard the interest of the workers against the management, send elected representatives to the national trade union congresses and are affiliated to the World Federation of Trade Unions (with its head office in Prague). But their most distinctive feature is that, whilst providing protection against the management and bureaucracy, they co-operate with the employer, the State, and assist in the implementation of the economic plan on the labour front.

The unions are organized on a vertical, industrial basis, i.e. according to the branches of industry, although there is also regional co-ordination. The pyramid in each country is headed by the Central Council of Trade Unions consisting of representatives who, like other trade union leaders, are elected. The membership of unions is voluntary and it includes both workers and persons of managerial status. The union funds are derived partly from members' contributions and partly from State grants. The work of the local trade union typically includes the following vital responsibilities:

(i) They cultivate the Socialist attitude to work, devise rules for work discipline and teach the workers how to protect socialized property.

(ii) They organize meetings to discuss ways and means of reaching and exceeding targets, quality improvement and the rationalization of work.

(iii) They participate with the management in working out the details of output norms, work incentives and the distribution of various enterprise funds (especially the 'material incentive fund' and the 'sociocultural and housing fund').

(iv) They make sure that various facilities for workers and safety devices are provided and maintained in good condition.

(v) They take up individual members' grievances against the management concerning such matters as qualifications allowances, bonus payments, dismissals, etc.

The State control of trade unions is assured. The election of union officials is usually arranged by the Communist Party and higher positions at least are mostly occupied by Party members. Lenin himself described trade unions as a 'school for communism' and 'transmission belts' for the Party economic programme to the working masses. Strikes are essentially considered illegal in all Socialist countries, except in a qualified sense in Yugoslavia.[7]

[7] E.g., in 1964 and 1965 there were 504 'protest work stoppages' in Yugoslavia, involving some 20,000 workers (quoted from *East Europe*, Jan. 1967, p. 26).

The recent economic reforms appear to be providing a new challenge to Socialist trade unions. The profit criterion, the growing power of technocracy and the strengthened position of the managers are creating new conflicts, such as the threat of dismissal of inefficient and redundant labour, the closing down of unprofitable factories and the need for stricter work discipline. This tends to reduce ordinary workers to a similar position in some respects as in capitalist countreis. There is evidence to suggest that some Socialist leaders would like to see the Party divorced from industrial conflicts, and instead they think that trade unions should take over the responsibility and become genuine guardians of workers' interests at the enterprise level (see reference 5 at the end of this chapter).

The degree of workers' participation in the management of enterprises differs from one Socialist country to another. In the USSR, soon after the Bolshevik Revolution, industrial management was handed over to the factory workers' committees, but the idea was soon scrapped as wasteful and unworkable. Today the system of workers' participation is best developed in Yugoslavia, where it is described as 'workers' self-management'. It is in the hands of Workers' Councils, in existence since 1950.

A Workers' Council in Yugoslavia is elected from among the workers and the managerial staff of each enterprise, and in many ways it resembles the 'board of directors' of a company in a capitalist country. Within the rules laid down by the State, the Council adopts a 'constitution' providing a basis for the management of the enterprise to suit local conditions. Since 1964 the Council has been vested with the power of appointing the enterprise director (general manager). Besides, it makes other crucial decisions with regard to the use of funds, the distribution of profits, major developments, the prices and marketing of the articles produced. The director can suspend the Council's decisions, but only if they are not consistent with the State law.

Many observers in other Socialist countries, and even elsewhere, believe that the Yugoslav system is an ideal basis for the management of enterprises, because it is in the hands of those who actually work there, and there is little direct interference from the State, the Party and trade unions. A similar system was introduced in Poland in 1956 and in Czechoslovakia in 1968, but the powers of their Workers' Councils are much smaller than in Yugoslavia. In other Socialist countries, there are factory committees, usually consisting of the local trade union and management representatives, but their influence is more of an advisory than an executive nature.

B. THE SIZE AND STRUCTURE OF WAGES

Although labour enjoys considerable freedom from directive planning, there is a high degree of centralization and control over the determination of wages. The total amount of wages to be paid, and the production counterpart to support the wage fund, depends on the division of the national income between accumulation and consumption and, further, of consumption between the 'social consumption fund' and the 'wage fund'.[8] The tendencies in the wage fund, together with those in employment, and in nominal and real wages in the seven CMEA countries are shown in Fig. 7.

The overall occupational and industrial standard structure of wages is also centrally laid down. The degree of State control over the wage funds at the microeconomic level is smaller, although naturally there are national differences in this respect. In some of them (e.g. Bulgaria and the USSR) enterprises have less freedom in the division of profits and the payment of incentives, but the enterprise wage fund is guaranteed. In others (as in Czechoslovakia and Yugoslavia) enterprises have more freedom but their wage funds are not fully guaranteed.

The wage structure in each Socialist country today embodies considerable differentiation according to occupations, industries and regions. The aim is, first of all, to encourage greater performance. But in addition, in the absence of the direction of labour, wage differentials have to perform an allocative function. They are used to promote vertical (from less to more skilled jobs) and horizontal (between enterprises, industries and regions) mobility of labour, according to planned priorities.

The well-known Marxian principle, 'from each according to his ability, to each according to his needs', was put into practice when the first Socialist State was established in 1917. But soon the effects proved disastrous, and on the initiative of Lenin the second part of the principle was modified to '. . . to each according to his work'. The Leninist principle has been accepted ever since as being applicable to the transitional stage called 'lower phase of communism', or 'socialism', whilst the Marxian ideal is still considered valid in the long run under 'full communism'.

Wage differentiation reached its peak in the mid-1950s, when the ratio of wages between the most and least skilled workers was 4 : 1, which was higher than in most Western countries. However, since

[8] The wage fund may be further subdivided between 'personal' and 'impersonal' funds, the latter including benefits to the enterprise workers concerned in the form of group amenities. However, this division is usually determined not centrally but by the enterprise workers themselves.

FIG 7. *Trends in the Wage Fund, Employment and Wages in the European CMEA Countries*

(Index Numbers, 1955 = 100)				
Country	1950	1955	1960	1965
BULGARIA				
Wage fund	48	100	179	259
Employment	66	100	144	179
Average nominal wages	74	100	124	145
Average real wages	—	100	135	148
CZECHOSLOVAKIA				
Wage fund	68	100	128	159
Employment	86	100	113	129
Average nominal wages	79	100	114	123
Average real wages	91	100	125	132
GERMAN D.R.				
Wage fund	60	100	133	153
Employment	83	100	103	104
Average nominal wages	72	100	129	146
Average real wages	44	100	143	162
HUNGARY				
Wage fund	46	100	167	213
Employment	76	100	112	128
Average nominal wages	60	100	149	167
Average real wages	96	100	147	160
POLAND				
Wage fund	41	100	164	236
Employment	76	100	111	135
Average nominal wages	54	100	148	176
Average real wages	91	100	128	138
RUMANIA				
Wage fund	49	100	176	310
Employment	72	100	110	148
Average nominal wages	68	100	160	210
Average real wages	80	100	148	180
SOVIET UNION				
Wage fund	72	100	144	211
Employment	80	100	128	159
Average nominal wages	89	100	112	133
Average real wages	72	100	115	135

Source. Based on: United Nations, *Incomes in Postwar Europe*, ECE, Geneva 1967, Ch. 7, p. 34. The indexes were worked out by the Secretariat of the Economic Commission for Europe on the basis of the official statistics of the countries concerned. Their conparability between countries is less reliable than between years applying to a particular country.

that time the gap has been gradually narrowed down to about 2 : 1, mostly by uplifting the wages of the least skilled workers (a similar trend can be observed in the developed capitalist countries). The earnings of the managerial personnel, including those with professional training, are generally higher than those of the workers.

The differences in standard pay rates, i.e. wages and salaries without bonuses, overtime, etc., amongst different occupations in selected Socialist and capitalist countries are demonstrated in Fig. 8. The pay spread is indicated by ratios, the wage of a foreman being taken as 1·0. It can be concluded that the spread in most Socialist countries in a complex industry is 5 : 1. The spread is, of course, smaller in less complex industries and in those which rate lower priorities in overall development. In general, the pay spread is smallest in Bulgaria and Poland, where the regimes find it expedient to court the support of manual workers against the intelligentsia.[9]

All in all, the occupational structure of wage and salary rates in Socialist countries at present is not much different from that prevailing in the West, provided two exceptions are borne in mind. On the one hand, successful managers and professional people in large firms, and persons with special skills in temporarily short supply earn relatively more in capitalist than in Socialist countries. On the other, in most capitalist countries there are no minimum wage legislations protecting the unskilled worker, whilst in Socialist countries there are laws to this effect (formally adopted or reviewed during 1956–7). Besides, the rule of 'equal pay for equal work' is applied in Socialist, but only exceptionally in capitalist, countries. This means that the lower deviation of wages from the average is greater in most capitalist countries.[10]

In addition to occupational pay differentials, there are also industrial differences. As one would expect, average wages are higher in those industries where higher skills are required and work is difficult. But in addition, the State fixes higher wages for industries or regions

[9] In an investigation carried out in Poland on the impact of the communist regime on the earnings of manual and non-manual workers, it was demonstrated that in 1960, as compared with 1937, the real earnings of the former were 45 per cent higher whilst those of the latter were 25 per cent *lower*; J. Kleer, ('Observations on the Principle of Distribution'), *Nowe drogi*, 9/1968, p. 93. The egalitarian principle has been applied to near-extremes in Cuba and China. In the latter country, as a consequence of the 'anti-economism' associated with the Cultural Revolution, not only are pay differentials very small, but in addition managers of enterprises are expected to perform manual work periodically to 'bring them closer to the masses'.

[10] *Income* disparities are, of course, much greater in capitalist countries, where about 10 per cent of the national income is distributed in the form of rent, interests and dividends, mostly received by the upper income groups.

FIG. 8. *Differences in Maximum Standard Pay Rates in the Engineering Industry in the Mid-1960s*
(Pay rate of a foreman = 1·0)

Position	Bulgaria	Czecho-slovakia	German D.R.	Hungary	Poland	Rumania	France[1]	UK[2]
General manager	1·8	2·9	1·9	2·1	1·9	2·0	2·9	2·3
Chief engineer	1·7	2·6	1·9	1·8	1·7	1·9	2·5	—
Production manager	1·5	2·4	1·6	—	1·6	1·5	2·4	—
Chief accountant	1·4	2·1	1·7	—	1·3	1·6	—	—
Department manager	1·5	1·9	1·3	1·4	—	1·5	1·7	1·5
Finance section manager	—	—	1·2	—	1·3	1·3	—	—
Senior foreman	1·3	—	1·2	1·0	1·1	1·1	—	—
Senior engineer	1·1	—	—	—	1·0	1·3	—	—
Legal adviser	1·1	—	1·5	—	—	0·8	—	—
Engineer	1·0	1·5	1·1	1·0	0·9	1·1	2·1	—
Foreman	1·0	1·0	1·0	1·0	1·0	1·0	1·0	1·0
Personnel manager	—	—	—	—	0·9	1·0	1·4	0·8
Economist	0·9	0·9	1·0	—	0·9	0·8	—	—
Technician	0·8	0·9	0·9	0·9	1·0	1·0	1·1	—
Senior accountant	1·0	—	—	—	0·7	0·7	—	—
Experienced unskilled worker	0·9	0·9	0·6	—	0·8	0·8	0·4	0·7
Accountant	0·9	—	—	0·6	—	0·6	0·8	—
Machine operator	0·6	0·6	0·5	—	0·4	0·5	—	—
Charwoman	0·5	0·5	—	—	—	0·3	0·3	0·4

[1] Average standard pay in industry.
[2] Average standard pay in industry in 1960.

Sources. Based on: V. P. Gruzinov. *Materialnoe stimulirovanive truda v stranakh Sotsializma* (Material Incentives to

FIG. 9. *Differences in Average Wages According to the Major Branches of the Economy in Socialist Countries in 1955 and 1965*
(Average wage in industry = 100)

Branch of the economy	Bulgaria		Czechoslovakia		German D.R.		Hungary		Poland		USSR	
	1955	1965	1955	1965	1955	1965	1955	1965	1955	1965	1955	1965
Building and construction	119	119	106	109	97	100	98	104	112	110	111	106
Transport	105	109	99	104	—	—	93	99	—	96	106	103
Industry	100	100	100	100	100	100	100	100	100	100	100	100
Unproductive services[1]	88	92	98	81	—	—	90	—	78	80	84	92
Trade	84	87	77	81	—	—	82	90	77	79	75	74
Communications	76	82	80	85	—	—	75	—	92	—	75	72
Agriculture[2]	76	87	70	84	78	82	75	87	70	77	68	72
NATIONAL AVERAGE	95	98	93	95	94	98	103	99	92	94	89	92

[1] Culture, Education, Health and Public administration.
[2] State farms only, where earnings are generally higher than in collective farms.

Source. Based on: V. P. Gruzinov, op. cit., p. 239.

107

into which a flow of labour is required. Thus building, transport and industry have, as a rule, enjoyed higher wage levels than agriculture, communications and trade. This is demonstrated in Fig. 9. Industrial classification often overrides occupation classification. For example, in Poland a tradesman classed as 'locksmith' earns 3,100 złotys per month in coal-mining but only 1,905 z. in the textile industry.[11] This means in effect that there is not as much wage consistency in Socialist countries as the labour theory of value would imply.

In recent years there has been a tendency for the differences in personal *earnings* to increase as a consequence of the reinforcement of material incentives. We shall deal with this question next.

C. ECONOMIC INCENTIVES

The problem of incentives in a Socialist economy is of a different order from that under capitalism, as there is practically no private ownership of the means of production, little private enterprise, and virtually no unemployment,[12] whilst social security is very well developed and taken for granted. Socialist economists distinguish two types of incentives.

a. *Moral incentives*. The operation of these incentives is based on a worker's social consciousness in contributing to society's welfare, on his interest in his occupation, his sense of satisfaction from the work performed and pride in his status. Political appeals, slogans, boards and books of honour in factories, awards of pennants, badges, medals and orders and the holding of self-criticism sessions are well-known instruments utilizing these sentiments to spur workers to better production performance.

b. *Material incentives*. These appeal to the materialistic cravings of the worker, and consist of rewards in money or kind according to the quantity and quality of work performed or economies achieved. In addition to the differentiation of standard wage and salary rates, they include individual and group bonuses or benefits out of special incentives funds.

Marx, as well as Lenin, believed that after the overthrow of capitalism moral incentives would gradually assume an increasing role in spurring workers to greater effort. On the other hand, material incentives were considered by them to be essentially anti-social, a relic of capitalism that would wither away. Fifty years of experience

---

[11] *Finanse*, 4/1968, p. 14.
[12] Yugoslavia excepted; see footnote 6, p. 100.

in the Soviet Union has shown that this is far from truth in reality. The most radical element of the economic reforms in the USSR and Eastern Europe is in fact the extension and strengthening of material incentives.

In contradiction of Marxian and Leninist views, it is now widely held among Socialist economists that the higher the stage of the Socialist development, the greater should be the differentiation of earnings. In the early stage, soon after the communist takeover, the incomes of the poorer classes must be raised to satisfy the most basic needs, whilst excessive consumption by others must be prevented; the purpose is to create both a healthy social atmosphere and a high rate of saving in order to forge ahead with industrialization. But in the advanced stage, marked by a changeover from extensive to intensive economic development, a wide scale of material incentives must be provided 'if centralized planning, direction of labour and a decline in the rates of growth are to be avoided'.[13]

For a long time in the past incentives were determined on the basis of the reaching and exceeding of planned quantitative targets. They were explicitly applicable to the management personnel and they were implicitly built into the wages of workers. The wages of manual workers were mostly based on piecework (i.e. according to the quantity of output produced). Under such a system enterprises tended to submit unduly low target proposals and then turn out large quantities of output, irrespective of its quality or prospective use. The stimulating effect on the individual members of the enterprise personnel was generally weak because the incentives were too small to make extra effort worthwhile. There was also a large number of 'specialized' incentives to serve particular objectives, often in conflict with each other.[14]

The new system of material incentives to labour is chiefly based on a 'synthetic' criterion, i.e. on enterprise profits. A part of the profits is channelled into the 'material incentives fund', which was recently described in a Socialist periodical as '. . . an essential factor dynamizing the economic activity of the enterprises today'.[15] A portion of the profits is also allocated to the 'socio cultural and housing fund'. The former fund is distributed to the enterprise personnel in the form of individual bonuses and the latter as group welfare amenities and services.

The aim is to spur the management and workers not only to

[13] J. Kleer, op. cit., p. 95.
[14] E.g., there were about fifty specialized incentives in use in Poland in 1960. See J. G. Zielinski, 'Economic Tools of Plan Fulfilment', *Econ. of Planning*, Vol. 4, No. 3, 1964, p. 132.
[15] *Zycie gosp.*, 29/9/1968, p. 10.

greater output but also to reduce waste, improve quality and produce articles for which there is demand. There is an increasing departure from piecework wages in favour of time wages. Thus in the early 1950s, over two-thirds of workers were paid by piecework rates, but the proportion in the late 1960s declined to only one-third—which is not much different from the practice in most Western countries.[16]

The size of material incentives has, as a rule, been increased. Under the old system, incentives generally constituted about 5 per cent of basic pay. The proportion today varies from one country to another —on the average it is lowest in Rumania (about 10 per cent),[17] and it appears to be highest in the Soviet Union (about 33 per cent).[18] Many economists, even outside the USSR, now believe that under modern Socialism the optimum proportion should average between 30 and 40 per cent.[19]

The actual proportions, naturally, vary within each country according to different industries, occupations and responsibilities. For example, in Poland bonuses for the managerial personnel may reach 80 per cent of their basic pay, whilst in the case of the technical and economic staff the proportions usually are 15–20 per cent, or even less.[20] Furthermore, in some countries, such as Bulgaria, Czechoslovakia, Hungary and Yugoslavia, not only incentive margins but also basic pay rates are dependent on enterprise performance. For example in Hungary, the State guarantees only 75–80 per cent of the basic pay of the management personnel, the balance depending on enterprise profits.[21]

The fact that workers' total pay is dependent on enterprise performance produces problems not common in a Socialist economy in the past. It means that personal earnings fluctuate according to enterprise profits, and these vagaries are likely to be magnified as buyer's markets develop. In capitalist countries, divided profits are received by either rich people, who can easily absorb such fluctuations, or those whose main source of income is salary. Moreover, they can spread their risk of fluctuations by owning shares in a number of companies. But a worker in a Socialist country is not in a position to spread his wage risk.

[16] See, B. Minc, *Ekonomia polityczna socjalizmu* (The Political Economy of Socialism), Warsaw, PWN, 1961, p. 429; *Finanse*, 4/1968, p. 45; United Nations, ECE, *Incomes in Postwar Europe*, Geneva, 1967, Ch. 5, p. 23, Ch. 8, p. 23.

[17] G. Stoica, ('Effective Use of Material Incentives in Enterprises'), *Probleme economice*, 4/1968, p. 25.

[18] J. Główczyk, ('Soviet Economic Reforms'), *Życie gosp.*, 13/8/1967, p. 7.

[19] E.g., B. Fick, ('Guidelines to the Perfection of the Incentive System'), *Finanse*, 7/1968, p. 25.

[20] ibid., p. 24.

[21] *Finanse*, 9/1968, p. 62.

D. GROWTH OF LABOUR PRODUCTIVITY AND WAGE INCREASES

One of the traditionally accepted 'laws of socialism' is that the growth of productivity of labour should exceed the rise in (real) wages. Thus over the period 1950–65, labour productivity per person engaged in material production and real wages increased by the following percentages:

	Labour productivity (%)	Real wages (%)
Bulgaria	195	60
Czechoslovakia	115	45
Hungary	104	65
Poland	130	50
Rumania	200	125
USSR	175	88
German D.R.	195	268[22]

Sources. Based on: *Ekonomicheskie nauki*, 11/1968, p. 46; *Incomes in Postwar Europe*, op. cit., Ch. 7, p. 34.

Although for a long time unquestioned, this principle has been subjected to searching criticism in the last decade or so. If this 'law' is applied consistently, then the share of consumption in national income would have to keep on declining, instead of rising. This question has assumed new significance in the context of the change-over to 'intensive growth', where increases in the productivity of labour are almost wholly responsible for economic growth.[23]

The prevailing attitude to the problem is now as follows. In the earlier stages of the industrialization drive, increases in wages should lag behind the growth in labour productivity to provide a rising rate of accumulation. However, once this stage is over (which now applies to all European Socialist countries except Albania), from the *macro-economic* standpoint the growth of labour productivity should be matched by a proportional rise in wages. But this is not necessarily valid for each micro-unit, and as far as each enterprise is concerned

[22] The case of the German D.R. is exceptional; her wages in 1950 were artificially depressed to provide extra resources for postwar reconstruction and large reparations to the USSR.

[23] Thus the Soviet Five-Year Plan, 1966–70, provides for a 38–41 per cent increase in the national income. 90 per cent of this increase was planned to be achieved by the growth in labour productivity and only 10 per cent by the expansion in the size of productive resources. In the preceding plan period (1959–65), intensive growth was responsible for 74 per cent and extensive growth for 26 per cent of the increase in the national income. See *Mirovaya ekonomika i mezhdunarodnye otnosheniya*, 12/1967, p. 84.

the old law still applies in practice.[24] There are two sources of the growth of labour productivity:

(i) that within the power of the workers concerned, consisting in improved qualifications, greater intensity of application and better local organization of work;

(ii) that external to the workers concerned, deriving from technological progress, greater specialization and favourable natural developments.

In the long run, factors external to the workers are a more important source of the growth of labour productivity. But this growth is not uniform. Some forms of production lend themselves to the application of technological advancement better than others. Besides, owing to State priorities, some branches of the economy benefit more from the allocation of investment than others. Thus even if workers were equally qualified and inclined to improve their efficiency, labour productivity would not rise uniformly in all enterprises.

Now, if gains in labour productivity are achieved by the workers' own exertion, then their wages should increase proportionally. But if such gains accrue independently of the workers' effort, there must be no automatic increases in their wages. Instead, there should be a revision of norms and incentive payments to keep workers' exertion at the same level as in other enterprises.

Is this stand consistent with the now generally accepted principle that on the macroeconomic scale the growth of labour productivity should be passed on *pari passu* in wage increases? Yes, it is—provided that the resources saved as a consequence of the higher labour productivity deriving from external sources are devoted to:

(i) general wage increases, so that all workers in the economy benefit, including those employed in the non-productive service industries;

(ii) reduction of retail prices of consumer goods and services;

(iii) expansion of social consumption provided free by the State.

[24] A. Łukaszuk, ('Growth of Labour Productivity and Wages'), *Materiały do studiowania ekonomii politycznej socjalizmu* (Source Material for the Study of the Political Economy of Socialism), W. Brus *et al.* (eds.), Warsaw, KiW, 1964, pp. 1043–5.

RECOMMENDED REFERENCES AVAILABLE IN ENGLISH

1. Brown, Emily C., *Soviet Trade Unions and Labour Relations*, Oxford U.P., 1966.

2. Dodge, N. T., *Women in the Soviet Economy. Their Role in Economic, Scientific and Technical Development*, Baltimore, London and Oxford, Johns Hopkins and Oxford U.P., 1967.

3. Dodge, N. D., 'Fifty Years of Soviet Labour', *Studies on the Soviet Union*, Vol. VII, No. 1, 1967, pp. 1–34.

*4. Dubovoi, P., 'Ensuring Interbranch Uniformity in Wage Payments for Work of Equal Complexity', *Problems of Economics*, Jan. 1968, pp. 25–35.

5. Gamarnikow, M., 'New Tasks for Trade Unions', *East Europe*, April 1967, pp. 18–26.

*6. Golov, A., 'Methodology of the Measurement and Planning of Labour Productivity in the USSR', *Intern. Labour Rev.*, May 1968, pp. 447–64.

7. Haienko, F., 'Material and Moral Labor Incentives in the USSR', *Bulletin*, Munich, July 1968, pp. 13–21; and 'The Soviet Wage System', *Bulletin*, Oct. 1968, pp. 25–30.

*8. Kotliar, A., 'The Socialist System and the Length of Labour Activity', *Problems of Economics*, Nov. 1967, pp. 28–34.

*9. Markov, V., 'Pressing Problems in the Utilization of Labour Resources', *Problems of Economics*, June 1966, pp. 37–43.

*10. Osipov, G. V. (ed.), *Industry and Labour in the USSR*, translated from the Russian, London, Tavistock Publications, 1966.

11. Schroeder, Gertrude, 'Industrial Wage Differentials in the USSR', *Soviet Studies*, Jan. 1966, pp. 303–17.

*12. Sonin, M., and Zhiltsov, E., 'Economic Development and Employment in the Soviet Union', *Intern. Labour Rev.*, July 1967, pp. 67–91.

13. Swianiewicz, S., *Forced Labour and Economic Development*, Oxford U.P., 1965.

*14. Timar, J., 'Planning the Labor Force in Hungary', *Eastern European Economics*, Winter–Spring, 1966 (the whole number).

*15. Zielinski, J. G., 'Notes on incentive systems of socialist enterprises', *Econ. of Planning*, Vol. 7, No. 3, 1967, pp. 258–69.

* *indicates contributions by writers from Socialist countries.*

CHAPTER 8

Land

A. THE SOCIALIZATION OF LAND

The nationalization, or socialization, of land[1] was advocated by many thinkers in the nineteenth century (such as David Ricardo, James Mill, Jules Guesde, Henry George) and even earlier, but it is only Karl Marx who raised it to the rank of 'social necessity' and integrated it into an overall scheme for a new social order. In his view, the private ownership of land hindered progress in agriculture and was responsible for the existence and perpetuation of antagonistic social classes in the countryside (landowners, capitalists or tenants and agricultural labourers).

Marx's ideas were further elaborated upon by other communist writers, especially Engels and Lenin, and were put into effect when Socialist States came into existence. However, of the European Socialist countries, only the USSR socialized all land (in 1917).[2] In the remaining countries, practically all non-farming land (forests, water resources, minerals, urban sites) has been socialized, but not all *agricultural* land—owing to a strong, traditional peasant attachment to the soil and the fact that the Communist Parties have been anxious to enlist the peasants' support. However, in each country, the regime has increased the State holdings of land and has promoted collectivization by a variety of inducements and pressures, and the Party is committed to the socialization of all land in the long run. Socialized land is transferred to users free of charge, and it cannot be sold, pawned or re-transferred by them.

The proportion of agricultural land in the socialized sector in the countries under consideration was in the late 1960s as follows:

	%
USSR	100
Bulgaria	99
Hungary	97

[1] Although the terms 'nationalization' and 'socialization' are often used interchangeably, the former is normally associated with a piecemeal process with compensation, whilst the latter implies no compensation to previous owners.

[2] Land nationalization has also been carried out in Mexico, Mongolia and Burma. In Israel, over 90 per cent of land is owned on a communal basis.

Rumania	95
German D.R.	93
Czechoslovakia	91
Poland	14
Yugoslavia	14

Sources. Based on the statistical yearbooks of the countries concerned.

It may be observed that the proportion of socialized land in Yugoslavia reached 22 per cent in 1951 and in Poland 23 per cent in 1955, but owing to the peasants' pressure and the need to increase food production, some of that land has been de-collectivized since.[3]

Socialized agricultural land is farmed as either 'state farms' or 'collective farms'. *State farms* (*sovkhozes* in Russian) are owned, managed and operated directly by the State, and those who work on them are paid wages. They are usually larger than collective farms and they mostly concentrate on extensive farming, or otherwise on experimental work. Although considered ideologically superior and receiving favoured treatment from the State, they are generally less efficient and popular than collective farms.[4]

Collective farms (*kolkhozes* in Russian) are the dominant type of socialized farming, except in Poland and Yugoslavia.[5] They are collectively owned, managed and worked by the members. Each farm has its own constitution and is headed by a chairman elected by the members. Remuneration of the members is based on the success of the farm and the quantity and quality of work contributed by each. Losses cannot, as a rule, be offset by State subsidies.

The commitment of the Communist Parties to the socialization of land and farming has been conditioned by several considerations:

(i) The private ownership of land, as of other means of production, fosters acquisitive ambitions, which is contrary to the ideal of the 'communist man' free of such anti-social instincts.

(ii) At the time of the communist takeover, in all these countries large proportions of land were concentrated in the hands of wealthy landowners, whilst the rural masses either had very small holdings or were labourers working for others. This only perpetuated semi-feudal relations, and of course landowners and

[3] B. Strużek, *Rolnictwo europejskich krajów socjalistycznych* (Agriculture in the European Socialist Countries), Warsaw, PWRL, 1963, p. 125; *Rocznik statystyczny 1960* (Statistical Yearbook of Poland for 1960), p. 191.

[4] E.g. in Poland, more than one-third of the State farms regularly incur deficits, which have to be met by State subsidies constituting about 20 per cent of their gross agricultural output. *Życie gospodarcze*, 20/4/1969, p. 8, and 15/6/1969, p. 9.

[5] E.g., they occupy three-quarters of the agricultural land in Bulgaria, Hungary and Rumania, but only 1 per cent in Poland.

richer peasants (called *kulaks* in Russian) could not be expected to support a communist regime, so that land had to be taken away from them anyway.

(iii) The land which was not in the hands of the larger landowners was farmed in small inefficient holdings. The industrialization drive necessitated the release of peasant labour for the newly established and developing industries. This was feasible only if farms became larger so that they could be mechanized and operated by less, but specialized and trained, labour. Transforming holdings into large State and collective farms made the task easier.

(iv) The socialization of land and the formation of larger farms have also been considered highly desirable for the sake of the integration of agriculture into the overall planned development of the economy.

(v) In addition, several ideological considerations of a broader nature have also played a role. Accepting the principle that labour is the only legitimate source of personal income, only society as a whole is entitled to benefit from natural resources. Furthermore, individual peasant holders have a 'petty bourgeois mentality' (as Lenin put it). Large socialized farms make it easier for the Party to instil a new way of thinking, in harmony with the industrial working class.

B. THE PROBLEM OF GROUND RENT

In his writings on land and value under capitalism, Marx treated ground rent as a part of 'surplus value' (like interest and private profit) unjustifiably appropriated by landowners and capitalists (tenant farmers) taking advantage of the monopoly of land ownership and the differences in the productivity of land. He distinguished three forms of rent:

(i) *Differential rent I* is based on natural differences in the quality of land, i.e. soil fertility, location with regard to climate and proximity to markets.

(ii) *Differential rent II* derives from the differences in the productivity of land brought about by man-made improvements.

(iii) *Absolute rent* is a consequence of the private ownership of land and of a lower 'organic structure of capital' in agriculture than in industry.[6]

[6] The phrase means a ratio between fixed and variable outlays. Owing to the private control over land, the amount of capital equipment per worker is lower in agriculture than in manufacturing so that the profit rate is higher in agriculture. The excess of profit earned in agriculture over the average rate in industry con-

Marx perceived two types of evil associated with the existence of rent in industrial societies. On the one hand, he looked upon rent as unwarranted income from the free gifts of nature, and as such a form of exploitation of agricultural workers and society in general by landowners and capitalists. On the other, he viewed rent as a drag on the modernization and growth of agriculture, because not only does it absorb tenants' liquid resources and discourage land improvement but also (through higher prices) reduces the demand for agricultural products. For these reasons Marx and other Socialist thinkers considered the socialization of land essential under any social system. In such a case, under capitalism absolute rent would cease to exist; differential rent would still occur but it would be absorbed by the State. Under communism not only absolute but also differential rent would disappear.[7]

Marx's views on rent and the official Socialist policies based on them are a logical consequence of the ideological subscription to the labour theory of value. Accepting the Marxian contention, '. . . the earth is not a product of labour and therefore has no value' as valid,[8] land's contribution to production is not a cost and thus land cannot receive remuneration. Rent has been regarded as a capitalist phenomenon—a form of distribution and exploitation.

However, in practice there is ample evidence of land having value in Socialist countries. Except in the USSR, there is still private land ownership, and dealings in land take place not only amongst peasants but also between private and State sectors. The prices at which these transactions take place are quoted in official publications, and they reflect differences in the economic quality of land.[9]

stitutes absolute rent (for details see K. Marx, *Capital*, Moscow, FLPH, 1959, Vol. III, pp. 740–6). Modern Socialist writers on the subject maintain that in the developed capitalist economies of today, agriculture is no longer under-capitalized so that absolute rent has disappeared in such countries. See M. Mieszczankowski, *Teoria renty absolutnej* (Theory of Absolute Rent), Warsaw, PWN, 1964, pp. 140–4, 305–9, 410.

[7] K. Marx, op. cit., Part IV, esp. Ch. XLV. Also see, K. Marx and F. Engels, *Selected Works*, Moscow, FLPH, 1951, Vol. I, p. 50; K. Marx and F. Engels, *Letters to Americans*, New York, International Publishers, 1953, pp. 127–9, 288–9; V. I. Lenin, *Selected Works*, London, Lawrence & Wishart, Vol. XII, pp. 308–10, 321.

[8] K. Marx, *Capital*, op. cit., Vol. III, p. 608.

[9] E.g. in Poland, the average price of one hectare of arable land in 1966 was 26,000 złotys (or 80,400 quintals of rye) with regional variations ranging from 16,000 to 42,000 z. If a socialized enterprise erects buildings on private land, it has to pay from 2,000 to 36,000 z. per hectare in compensation according to the classification of the land. *Rocznik statystyczny 1967*, p. 252; H. Chołaj, *Cena ziemi w rachunku ekonomicznym* (The Price of Land in Economic Accounting), Warsaw, PWE, 1966, p. 280. In Yugoslavia, compensation for private land taken over by the State or other users is determined by arbitration.

Similarly, the existence of differential rent is implicitly acknowledged officially by the administration of levies on the users of land:

(i) differentiated land taxes;[10]
(ii) differentiated procurement prices payable by the State to farms (see Part C of this chapter);
(iii) differentiated turnover taxes on a given article produced in different regions payable by different enterprises (such as mines, timber-cutting undertakings) according to the degree of natural advantage.

It is maintained that 'the principle of the *use of land free of charge* and the principle of the *appropriation of differential rent* are by no means contradictory'.[11]

However, in the traditional preoccupation with rent as a distributive category, Socialist authorities have not neutralized the differences in the income-yielding capacity of varying grades of land. The differential levies mostly intercept differential rent I, but a substantial portion of differential rent II usually remains with the users of better land. The considerable disparities in incomes enjoyed by different persons working under different natural conditions, even in a country like the USSR where land is nationalized, are well known.[12]

From the above discussion it should be evident that the State interception of differential rent is not based on a comprehensive and systematic plan. In most cases socialized users receive land free and its use is not considered as a cost. Consequently, such users as industrial enterprises, urban planning authorities, water-power and mining-development bodies have often appropriated unjustifiably large and fertile areas of land.[13]

This wasteful utilization of land cannot be avoided as long as land

[10] E.g., in Czechoslovakia the tax rates vary from 0 to 930 korunas per hectare according to 145 natural conditions officially acknowledged as relevant to agricultural production. In the USSR, the charges range from 0·4 to 1·8 kopeks per square metre of land according to the six regions into which the country has been divided for the purpose. *Finanse*, 12/1967, pp. 64–65; D. A. Allakhverdyan (ed.), *Soviet Financial System*, Moscow, Progress Publishers, 1966, p. 222.

[11] A. Tsagolov (ed.), *Wykład ekonomii politycznej* (Textbook of Political Economy), Polish ed., Warsaw, KiW, 1965, Vol. II, p. 332 (emphasis in the original).

[12] E.g., it was estimated that in Czechoslovakia differential rent constituted 3–35 per cent of agricultural income (disregarding subsidies) and in practice up to 15 per cent of the rent is retained by better farms. *Ekonomista*, 2/1968, p. 467.

[13] E.g., Soviet economists have estimated that losses caused by irrational use of land in the location of buildings alone in the USSR amount to 1,000 m. rubles annually, or no less than 0·5 per cent of the Net Material Product (quoted from H. Chołaj, op. cit., p. 158).

is considered by planners to have no value and there is no rational basis for its valuation. However, attitudes to land economics have greatly changed in recent years, largely under the impact of economic reforms. Even many well-known Marxist economists, such as H. Chołaj of Poland and S. Strumilin of the USSR, advocate the pricing of land for the purposes of its optimum utilization. It is also widely accepted that differential rent should be applied on a systematic basis and treated by the users of land as cost, because rent is not merely a form of distribution but it can have far-reaching salutary allocative functions. However, it is commonly agreed that there is no justification for absolute rent under Socialism.

As far as the rational basis for land valuation is concerned, it could be provided by either the market or computational method. Where land is socialized the former is impracticable,[14] but the latter is now considered feasible. Several schemes have been proposed, of which two deserve to be singled out here.

Some economists, who are still firm believers in the labour theory of value would establish the value of land by calculating the sum of man-made improvements incorporated in the land. Thus Strumilin, making calculations based on the cost of bringing virgin and fallow land in the USSR under cultivation, arrived at an average price of 177 rubles per hectare for 1966, equivalent to sixty-three labour days; he also worked out adjustments for different qualities of land— e.g. for the Krasnodar Region (noted for very good soil) he produced a figure of 708 rubles per hectare.[15]

A more sophisticated and sounder approach has been advocated by the proponents of optimal planning. L. V. Kantorovich has proposed that the allocation of natural resources to different uses by planners should be governed by the coefficients ('objectively determined valuations') representing the relative contribution of different grades of land to the fulfilment of the optimal plan.[16] A similar method has been put forward by V. Novozhilov, whose procedure consists in calculations of the 'cost of forgone alternative applications of land', or simply opportunity costs.[17]

[14] But the supporters of market socialism, inspired by the 'competitive solution' put forward by Oskar Lange in the 1930s, believe that creating competition on the demand side for land would provide sufficient information for central planners to establish and maintain a rational structure of rents by the 'trial and error' method. See reference 18 at the end of Ch. 9.

[15] S. Strumilin, ('Valuation of the "Free Gifts" of Nature'), *Voprosy ekonomiki*, 8/1967, pp. 61–5.

[16] See his tables and discussion of the alternative uses of land for wheat, barley and oats. L. V. Kantorovich, *The Best Use of Economic Resources*, Harvard U.P., 1965, pp. 92–108.

[17] V. V. Novozhilov, ('The Law of Value and Price Formation'), in *Problemy*

C. PRICES OF AGRICULTURAL PRODUCTS

There are two basic problems involved in the determination of agricultural prices: firstly, the level of such prices as a whole in relation to the prices of industrial products and services, and secondly, the price structure, i.e. relations amongst different agricultural products.

The pricing of land products in Socialist countries has always been governed by a curious mixture of different methods and criteria designed to serve particular objectives. Typically, there are three types of prices received by farms (for the same type of product): for compulsory deliveries to the State, for above-compulsory deliveries to the State, and for privately grown produce sold in local markets directly to consumers. Thus in Poland in 1966, the prices in złotys per quintal of wheat paid by the State on compulsory deliveries ranged (according to different districts) from 221 to 236, and on above-compulsory deliveries from 358 to 376; the free market prices obtained by peasants ranged from 398 to 485.[18]

In working out the delivery prices payable by the State, the cost of production on different grades of land is usually taken into account as only one of several factors. For example, in the USSR the cost of production of wheat ranges from 15 to 150 rubles per ton, but the State procurement prices payable diverge from the average by no more than 47 per cent.[19]

Under capitalism, the prices of agricultural products are normally determined by production costs on marginal land. But under Socialism if the production cost is taken as a criterion, in accordance with the traditional opposition to marginal analysis, it is the average standard that is usually adopted. In practice, production cost is accepted on an average farm (which may not necessarily be situated on average land) in the region or district, plus a reasonable profit rate. The proceeds from differential rent imposed on the farms operating under better-than-average conditions are then meant to subsidize production on poorer land. Thus where this policy is consistently pursued, one would expect a lower level of agricultural prices than under capitalism.

However, State pricing policies are also guided by certain social goals, irrespective of production costs. Such policies may be aimed at

primeneniya matematiki v sotsialisticheskoi ekonomike (Problems of the Application of Mathematics to Socialist Economics), Sbornik II, Leningrad, 1965, esp. p. 19.

[18] *Rocznik statystyczny 1967*, pp. 361, 363.

[19] I. Lukimov, ('Agricultural Production and Prices'), *Kommunist*, 4/1968, p. 65.

encouraging or discouraging particular types of primary production, or at the desired distribution of agricultural income between State, collective and private ('individual') farms, at a proper division of national income between the countryside and towns, and at the provision of accumulation funds for the State.

For some years now, there has been a tendency in all Socialist countries to discard price differentiation as a method for the interception of differential rent by the State in favour of greater uniformity. This is advocated on three major grounds: to simplify the financial management of farms and procurement agencies, to provide a sounder basis for the valuation of agricultural output and to facilitate a transition to planning in value terms. Differential rent can, instead, be absorbed easily by taxation, which is a sounder method. If differential rent is treated as a cost then each farm, to maximize its own profits, will endeavour to apply each grade of land to the most appropriate use.

The prices charged by the State to consumers bear little relation to the differing production costs or the procurement prices paid to farms. The retail prices are naturally more uniform, and their main purposes are to preserve equilibrium in the market and, at the same time, a reasonable stability in the cost of living.

D. THE POSITION OF AGRICULTURE

On economic as well as ideological grounds, the position of agriculture differs according to the stages of development of the Socialist economy. Until a high level of development is attained, agriculture is treated as the main reservoir to draw upon to accelerate industrialization. Typically, this takes several forms.

(i) *The State procurement prices* payable to farms are relatively low and differentiated according to natural conditions so that practically all differential rent is absorbed by the State budget, not agriculture. In some cases such prices are below the farms' production costs.

(ii) *Retail prices* of food are maintained at fairly low levels to ensure a low cost of living for industrial workers. Similarly, industry benefits from *cheap industrial raw materials* such as cotton, flax, oil seeds and skins. On the other hand, the *prices of industrial consumer goods* are subject to heavy turnover taxes.

(iii) These *tax receipts*, together with a large portion of *differential rent proceeds*, are used mostly to finance investment in industry, whilst agriculture is neglected.[20]

[20] E.g., the proportion of capital investment allocated to agriculture in Hungary in the early 1950s was only 14 per cent, although agriculture contributed at least

121

(iv) The *most capable and younger people* are attracted to industry, where the conditions of work and living are generally better than in agriculture.

(v) *Agricultural incomes* are not, as a rule, guaranteed by the State. Similarly, *pensions* are not provided from the State budget but have to be met out of the farms' own resources, in accordance with the 'self-supporting principle'. As a result, the incomes of the people employed in agriculture are only about two-thirds of those in industry (e.g. see Fig. 9, p. 107).

The discriminatory treatment of agriculture is reflected in the structural development of the Socialist economies—the rate of growth of agricultural output is only half the rate of growth of national income, and only one-third of that of industrial output (see Fig. 6, p. 72). It may be observed that incomes in agriculture in capitalist countries, even in the West, are also below those in industry, and agricultural output tends to lag behind industrial output, too.[21] But this is a result of microeconomic forces operating in the market, not an outcome of conscious State policies.

In Socialist countries, the discriminatory treatment of agriculture has been a product of planned decisions made at the central level. This attitude can be explained by several factors. Faced with the urgent need of industrialization on the one hand, and the absence of economic aid from capitalist countries on the other, agriculture becomes the obvious source of accumulation. The rural masses had been used to low income levels even before the communist takeover, and the urban working class (constituting the backbone of the Communist Party) can be expected to have less sympathy for the individualistic and 'petty bourgeois' peasants than for the industrial workers.

However, the agricultural failures which prevailed in Eastern Europe in the early 1960s demonstrated that continued neglect of agriculture was in fact producing disastrous effects on the economy as a whole. Valuable hard currencies had to be spent on large imports of grains, ironically mostly from industrialized capitalist countries (Australia, Canada, France, the USA), and imports of industrial equipment had to suffer correspondingly. Moreover, in the higher

38 per cent of national income; in the late 1950s the proportions were 18 per cent and 28 per cent respectively. In Poland over the period 1956–60, 12 per cent of capital investment was directed to agriculture but agricultural production constituted over 23 per cent of national income; the respective percentages for 1961–5 were 13 per cent and 21 per cent. V. Starodubrovskaya, ('Industry and Agriculture in Socialist Countries'), *Vop. ekon.*, 3/1967, pp. 90–100, esp. p. 95.

[21] E.g. see United Nations, ECE, *Incomes in Postwar Europe*, Geneva, 1967, Ch. 5, p. 16.

stages of development, Socialist economies can afford to accord better treatment to agriculture.

Since the early 1960s, higher shares of investment have been allowed to agriculture, and many industries catering for the needs of agriculture (such as agricultural machinery, fertilizers, food processing) have been assigned higher priority. Several Socialist countries (Czechoslovakia, Hungary and Yugoslavia) have abolished compulsory deliveries to the State.

Furthermore, the level of incomes in agriculture has been gradually raised, not only absolutely but also in relation to industry. This process, the beginning of which goes back to the mid-1950s, has proceeded along three lines: increases in procurement prices payable by the State, some reduction in the prices of industrial goods purchased by agriculture,[22] a liberalization of personal plot farming, and some reduction of the direct tax burden on collective farms.

Even in the countries where over 90 per cent of agricultural land is socialized (Bulgaria, Czechoslovakia, the German D.R., Hungary, Rumania, the USSR), 3–5 per cent of that area is now privately cultivated for personal gain. In Hungary about one-half of collective farmers' income is derived from household plots. In the USSR, personal plots contribute nearly one-fifth of total agricultural output (70 per cent of eggs, 60 per cent of potatoes, 40 per cent of meat, 40 per cent of milk and 40 per cent of vegetables). The proportions are higher in other Socialist countries.[23] As a result of a more lenient official attitude to personal plot farming and reduced taxes, the incomes of the collective farmers in the USSR increased by 50 per cent over the period 1965–7.[24] The officially undertaken long-run goal is to completely eliminate differences in incomes and conditions of life between country and town.[25] This ideal is contained in the concept of *agrotowns*.[26]

[22] In the USSR for a long time agricultural prices were held stable, whilst the prices of industrial products were being gradually increased. Thus a collective farm, to buy one ZIS-5 truck, had to sell the following quantities of wheat in different years: in 1940: 99 tons; 1948: 124 tons; 1949: 238 tons; 1955: 55 tons; 1968: 20 tons. *Kommunist*, 4/1968, p. 68.

[23] *Vop. ekon.*, 10/1966, p. 61; *Acta Oeconomica*, Vol. 2, No. 4, 1967, pp. 349–51; *Życie gosp.*, 25/5/1969, p. 1.

[24] *Kommunist*, 12/1968, p. 76.

[25] E.g. see *The Road to Communism*, Documents of the 22nd Congress of the CPSU, Moscow, FLPH, 1961, pp. 522–32.

[26] This term was first used by N. S. Khrushchev in 1949. The scheme consists in a transformation of agricultural settlements into blocks of flats with all the modern amenities normally available in urban areas. Although this idea has often been discussed, there has been little response from the central authorities in practice. However, in 1968 an ambitious experiment was initiated in the USSR in the Orel Region, whereby in twelve to fifteen years the 4,168 villages are to be

FIG. 10. *The Changing Role of Agriculture*

Country		Agricultural production as a percentage of total material production[1]	Employment in agriculture as a percentage of total employment	Rural population[3]	Urban population
Bulgaria	1950	43	80	72	28
	1965	33	45	55	45
Czechoslovakia	1950	16	39	49	51
	1965	12	20	46	54
German D.R.	1950	12	23	30	70
	1965	11	16	27	73
Hungary	1950	25	54	63	37
	1965	20	32	56	44
Poland	1950	33[2]	57	64	36
	1965	19	44	51	49
Rumania	1950	28	74	75	25
	1965	29	57	66	34
USSR	1950	22	48	61	39
	1965	22	33	47	53
Yugoslavia	1950	25	68[2]	*n.a.*	*n.a.*
	1965	28	53	*n.a.*	*n.a.*
United Kingdom	1950	8	5	21	79
	1965	4	2	23	77
United States	1950	7	13	36	64
	1965	4	6	25	75

[1] Forestry is included in all cases as part of agriculture. Material production (in the case of both the Socialist and capitalist countries) excludes non-productive services. Owing to the peculiarities of the Socialist valuation, agricultural production is understated (especially in relation to industrial production), but this undervaluation was smaller in 1965 than in 1950.

[2] In 1953.

[3] Population living in areas classed as 'rural' (as distinct from 'urban'), irrespective of occupation or employment.

n.a. = not available.

Sources. Yu. N. Beliayev, *Sblizhenie i urovnei ekonomicheskogo razvitiya sotsialisticheskikh stran* (Gradual Levelling off of the Economic Development of Socialist Countries), Moscow, Mysl, 1967, p. 84; and statistical yearbooks of the countries concerned.

Owing to the rapid industrialization, the role of agriculture in Socialist economies has been declining. This is reflected in the falling proportions of the population living in rural areas, employment in agriculture and agricultural output, as shown in Fig. 10. However, in spite of these changes, the place of agriculture is still important in all Socialist countries (with the possible exception of Czechoslovakia and the German D.R.), if we make comparisons with the highly developed capitalist countries. Taking the European Socialist countries as a whole, nearly one-half of the population still lives in rural areas, one-third is employed in farming, and agriculture contributes a quarter of total material production.

replaced by 960 modern urban communities. The scheme is partly financed out of the State budget (reported in *Soviet News*, Soviet Embassy in London, 14/1/1969, p. 22).

RECOMMENDED REFERENCES AVAILABLE IN ENGLISH

*1. Bača, J., 'On the Price of Land Under Socialism', *Eastern Europ. Econ.*, Spring 1968, pp. 34–49.

2. Bornstein, M., 'The Soviet Debate on Agricultural Price and Procurement Reforms', *Soviet Studies*, July 1969, pp. 1–20.

3. Clarke, R. A., 'Soviet Agricultural Reforms since Khrushchev', *Soviet Studies*, Oct. 1968, pp. 159–78.

*4. Fekete, F., and Varga, Gy., 'Household Plot Farming of Co-operative Peasants in Hungary', *Acta Oeconomica*, Vol. 2, No. 4, 1967, pp. 345–60.

5. Karcz, J. F. (ed.), *Soviet and East European Agriculture*, University of California Press, 1967.

*6. Karpov, P., 'What Should Be the Size of Differential Rent?', *Problems of Economics*, April 1968, pp. 31–8.

7. Klatt, W., 'Fifty Years of Soviet Agriculture', *Survey*, Oct. 1967, pp. 84–95.

8. Lewin, M., *Russian Peasants and Soviet Power. A Study of Collectivization*, Allen & Unwin, London, 1968.

*9. Makeenko, M., 'The Economic Role of Personal Subsidiary Husbandry', *Problems of Economics*, May 1967, pp. 35–44.

10. Oi, W. Y., and Clayton, E. M., 'A Peasant's View of a Soviet Collective Farm', *Amer. Econ. Rev.*, March 1968, pp. 37–59.

11. Ploss, S. I., *Conflict and Decision-Making in Soviet Russia: A Case Study of Agricultural Policy 1953–1963*, Princeton U.P. and Oxford U.P., 1967.

*12. Sarkisian, G., 'Approximation of the Living Standard of Workers and Collective Farmers', *Problems of Economics*, April 1967, pp. 15–23.

13. Sirc, L., 'Economics of Collectivization', *Soviet Studies*, Jan. 1967, pp. 362–70.

*14. Strumilin, S., 'On the Price of the "Free Gifts" of Nature', *Problems of Economics*, April 1968, pp. 19–30.

15. Wilczynski, J., 'Towards Rationality in Land Economics under Central Planning', *Economic Journal*, Sept. 1969, pp. 540–59.

indicates contributions by writers from Socialist countries.

CHAPTER 9

Pricing

The problem of pricing in a Socialist economy is of a different order of magnitude from that under capitalism. It is certainly more complex and controversial. Pricing is not merely a question of economics, but also of ideology and politics. Being a value category, price cannot be disassociated from labour, ideologically the only source of value. And yet if pricing is to achieve social objectives, prices must deviate from the amount of labour embodied in particular goods and services. Pricing is also the most important nerve centre on social grounds. In fact, at one stage in the USSR economists were forbidden to discuss the principles of price formation because, as Molotov warned in 1938, 'prices concerned politics not economics'.[1]

The views widely held in capitalist countries, that Socialist prices lack rationality and that under central planning the role of prices is reduced to insignificance, are grossly misleading. Although prices do not determine the allocation of resources to the same extent as in a market economy, in all other respects they play a vital role: they are actively used as an instrument of economic and social policies, and as such they have a rationality of their own. In this chapter, we shall examine the law of value, the institutional framework for price determination, the two-tier (producers' and retail) prices, price stability and flexibility, and we shall conclude with a discussion of optimal prices. Specific aspects of prices are considered elsewhere in this book (see Chs 1 B, 3 C, 8 C, 10 D, 13 C and 14 D).

A. THE LAW OF VALUE

The law of value is the Socialist doctrine of prices. It was first formulated by Marx (who drew heavily on the writings of D. Ricardo and other early classical economists). The operation of this law in a Socialist economy was officially denied in the USSR up to 1941, and it was treated as a peculiarity of capitalist production and distribution. Then in the following decade it was held that the law functioned under Socialism but in a limited 'transformed manner'. This view was passively accepted also in other Socialist countries after World

[1] Reported in *Ekonomicheskaya gazeta*, 13/6/1964.

War II. In his last work, published in 1952, Stalin criticized the existing view and pointed out that if an economic law operates, it does so 'objectively', irrespectively of human will. But he restricted the functioning of the law of value to the sphere of private consumption, i.e. the retail prices of consumer goods should be determined according to the conditions of supply and demand.

Following the growing liberalization since the mid-1950s, there has been a veritable outburst of writings on the law of value in all Socialist countries. The arguments advanced vary enormously, ranging from a complete rejection of the law to its enthusiastic acceptance, both extremists eagerly enlisting suitable quotations from Marx in support of their views. However, most writers adopt varying degrees of compromise, also quoting the ultimate authority. Marx's writings, like the Bible and history, are inexhaustible enough to provide believers with proof to support any arguments, however extravagant and contradictory they may be.

There are three problems inherent in the law of value under Socialism.

(i) How should value be determined?
(ii) How should price be determined?
(iii) Should the law of value determine the allocation of resources?

We shall examine the content of the law by answering these questions.

The Socialist concept of value is steeped in the Marxian labour theory of value. According to this view (shared by some early classical economists), value is determined by the amount of 'socially necessary labour' (i.e. efficient labour operating under normal conditions) embodied in the article in question. The Marxian formula for value is as follows (symbols are derived from German terms):

$$c + v + m;$$

c = constant, or fixed, cost (of capital);
v = variable outlays (wages);
m = surplus product,[2] i.e. an average macrosocial profit mark-up proportional to wages (v).

If m is proportional to constant and variable outlays combined, the category so obtained is called the 'production price'.

The traditional Marxian approach virtually denies the role of demand in the determination of value. The idea of marginal utility is rejected because it is in conflict with the assumption that value is

---

[2] Also known as 'product for society'. If applied to capitalist production relations, it is called 'surplus value', and it would include rent, interest and capitalistic profit constituting the exploitation of labour.

objectively determined by the labour content, not by subjective valuation depending on the amount used. The majority of Socialist economists now believe that pricing should be based not on 'value' but on the 'production price', because only the latter reflects social cost, and is thus more conducive to efficiency.

In practice, little attention is paid to either 'value' or the 'production price'. Price setting is influenced by practical needs to achieve a variety of objectives. In the past, when allocating resources to different uses, central planners usually disregarded prices altogether (under the system of material balances), and the programming prices now being developed are in obvious contradiction with the Marxian labour theory of value (see Part E of this chapter). The existence of the two-tier price system already indicates that there is no one uniform criterion for pricing, and indeed a particular product may have a dozen or more different prices according to its use or the specific objective to be achieved.

Under planned economic conditions of the Socialist type, value (i.e. prices) cannot be allowed to determine the allocation of resources. Major structural proportions, such as those between consumption and accumulation, or between different types of industries, are determined directly, largely on political grounds. In crucial spheres, the law of value is overridden by the 'law of planned proportional development'. In fact, prices themselves may be set at such levels as to promote the desired production or consumption patterns ('target pricing').

However, the law of value does function in the microeconomic sphere, and the recent economic reforms have greatly extended its scope. 'The law of value', a Soviet economist pointed out, 'reflects the most effective ways and means for the development of Socialist production and the achievement of the greatest possible effects with the lowest possible outlays.'[3] The same writer observed that, in contrast to capitalism, there is no need to fear adverse effects of its operation. Owing to the public ownership of the means of production and the planning of development and prices, the law of value cannot operate spontaneously to produce disruptive effects.

B.   THE   INSTITUTIONAL   FRAMEWORK   FOR PRICE DETERMINATION

The actual formation and structure of prices in each Socialist country are not a product of one comprehensive and consistent model, but a consequence of historical development and partial

---

[3] A. Birman, ('Profit Today'), *Kommunist*, 10/1967, p. 106.

reforms, carried out at different times and influenced by *ad hoc* social and economic considerations.

As is well known, Socialism attaches fundamental significance to the distribution of national income not only between different social groups and persons but also between current consumption and accumulation, between different branches of the economy and between different regions. In this process, prices, like wages and social services, are manipulated to perform distributive functions.

The overall price policy is laid down in each Socialist country by the Council of Ministers, which shows how much importance is attached to pricing. The Council's powers include:

  (i) laying down general principles and procedures to govern price determination;

 (ii) defining the functions of different price-setting bodies;

(iii) fixing the prices of products and services of key importance.

The responsibility for the administration of pricing otherwise rests with the State Price Planning Commission, which is empowered to issue directives, regulations and recommendations to subordinate bodies. It co-operates closely with the State Planning Commission on the one hand, and with various ministries on the other. The ministries, before they submit price proposals to the Price Planning Commission, study the data supplied by branch (or economic, or industrial) associations, and regional price committees, each of which is in constant communication with producing and trading enterprises.

Although the price policy is still centralized in each country, there has been considerable decentralization of the price setting functions in most of these countries (least in the German D.R., Poland and Rumania) associated with the recent economic reforms. The prices of the most important raw materials and consumer goods sold in retail markets are still fixed centrally, partly by the Council of Ministers, partly by the State Price Planning Commission. But otherwise, a large number of prices is now negotiated by enterprises in accordance with the rules and procedures handed down by superior authorities. For example, in Hungary about two-thirds and in the USSR about one-third of industrial producers' prices are now determined in this way. In addition, the prices of certain listed articles may be allowed to move within set ranges or be freely determined in the market (see Part C of this chapter).

On present indications, it appears that the existing institutional set-up will be preserved in all these countries for some time at least. But there will be a tendency to free larger proportions of retail prices from central control, whilst planning, or 'programming', prices (see Part E of this chapter) will be computed centrally on a systematic basis.

It must be pointed out that the recent concessions granted to certain bodies, and even enterprises and consumers, to set or influence prices at the microeconomic level, do not impair the centralized price policy. Such concessions are still extended on a planned, selective basis and, as Czechoslovakia's recent experience shows, items can be removed from the free lists and controls reimposed as soon as undesirable tendencies appear.[4] Even in Yugoslavia most prices are still subject to controls.

C. PRODUCERS' AND RETAIL PRICES

An important peculiarity of a planned economy of the Socialist type is the existence of a two-tier price system—the prices paid to the producers by the State and the prices paid by consumers for retail goods. The disparity between the two categories of prices is substantial and it cannot be explained merely by commercial margins and the fiscal needs of the State. Each set of prices is in fact largely independent of the other and it is determined and modified according to different criteria to achieve different objectives.[5]

Before we consider each of these prices, to avoid the terminological confusion common in the West, we must examine their component elements:

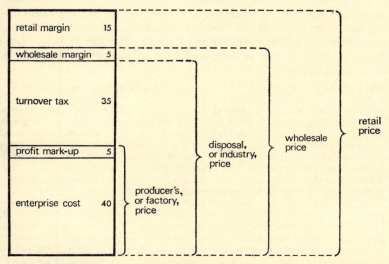

[4] E.g., the State restricted the range of retail prices which could be determined freely in the market from 25 per cent in 1966 to 13 per cent of all retail prices in

131

Although in the past, wholesale prices of consumer goods were usually calculated before turnover taxes, this is no longer a general rule. If we specifically mean the prices obtained by producing enterprises or farms, it is more correct to use the designation 'producers' (or 'factory') prices. In the case of the goods whose wholesale prices do not include turnover taxes and wholesale margins, which applies to most producer goods, wholesale and producers' prices are identical.

Producers' prices are those received by producing enterprises (including farms) from other producing enterprises (in the case of producer goods) and from wholesale trading entities (in the case of the goods channelled for consumption). These prices are set at such levels as to regulate production and to create favourable conditions for the fulfilment of the production plan. The price of each article is normally set at the cost of the average enterprise in the industry, plus a profit mark-up which in the past usually represented 3–5 per cent of the enterprise's average prime cost, but now generally averages 10–15 per cent of the enterprise's average total cost.[6] This means that the differentiated charges levied on the more favourably placed enterprises are meant to subsidize sub-average enterprises.

In the case of some articles, producers' prices may be set below average production costs, so that the industry as a whole operates at a loss, described as a 'planned loss'. For example, before the 1964–6 industrial price reform in the German D.R., the planned loss in the rolled products industry amounted to 55 per cent, and in fuels mining 45 per cent, of total costs.[7] One of the reasons for maintaining the prices of producers' goods at relatively low levels in the past was to encourage the substitution of capital for labour, as by traditional thinking labour is the only factor of production that can be considered scarce.

1967. Similar controls had to be imposed in 1968. *Życie gospodarcze*, 25/2/1968, p. 11.

[5] In a sense, there is a disparity between producers' and retail prices in a capitalist economy, too. Indirect taxes and subsidies usually apply to the goods sold in the retail market for direct consumption, but not to articles for industrial uses—even though they may be the same (e.g. alcohol, drugs, tobacco). The rates of taxes also differ according to the type of goods. However, the discrepancy between the two sets of prices is much smaller, and the main reason for the difference in the two sets of prices is to raise State revenue rather than to control production and consumption by reference to different criteria.

[6] Prime cost includes wages and salaries, social insurance contributions, payments to outsiders for various services, materials (including fuel and power) used, interest on short-term bank loans and depreciation. Total cost, in addition to prime cost, also includes capital charges and differential payments. The precise definition of these components differs from one country to another, and indeed some of them (capital charges and differential payments) may not be considered officially as costs, but represent deductions from enterprise gross profits.

[7] *Gospodarka planowa*, 8–9/1967, p. 103. Also see Ch. 3 C, p. 54.

Where producers' prices are centrally fixed, they usually remain unchanged for about five years (and often longer in the past). As costs do not normally remain unchanged in the meantime, the profitability patterns of different industries and enterprises may change substantially before the next price reform. It should be realized that the short-run responsiveness of enterprises to price changes under planned economic conditions is necessarily pretty limited. If the authorities want major shifts in supply, these are achieved directly by an appropriate investment policy.

As a part of the general economic reforms, all the Socialist countries under consideration have carried out far-reaching reforms of producers' prices. Their average level has been substantially increased, but prices of most raw materials have been increased more than the prices of finished products. Thus by the 1967 reform in the USSR the prices of oil were increased by 230 per cent, coking coal by 93 per cent, cellulose by 46 per cent, rolled metals by 43 per cent and cement by 13 per cent.[8]

Retail prices, which apply only to consumer goods and services, are set at such levels as to ensure equilibrium between the available supply and the existing demand. This is achieved by manipulating the flexible element of the retail price—the turnover tax. In contrast to capitalist countries, where the level of the retail price depends on the indirect tax, under Socialism it is the size of the turnover tax that is determined by the required level of the retail price. The rates of these taxes are highly differentiated, reflecting different elasticities of consumer demand for different products and the macrosocial preferences of the central authorities (see Ch. 11 B). To perform the required functions, retail prices are naturally changed more frequently than producers' prices.

It should be evident from the preceding discussion that there is little correspondence between the two types of prices. That this is so is proved by the radical reforms of producers' prices in recent years, with virtually no effect on retail prices. This dichotomy has been criticized by many economists, especially in recent years. It is advocated that the turnover tax rates should be made reasonably uniform and their level should be reduced (instead, deductions from enterprises' profits should become the major source of State revenue).[9] If this were done, prices would provide reliable guidance to both

[8] *Planovoe khoziaistvo*, 7/1967, pp. 13–18.
[9] E.g. see L. Ząbkowicz, ('Perfection of Retail Prices, Factory Prices and Turnover Taxes'), *Życie gosp.*, 22/9/1968, p. 7. A solution partly along these lines was put forward by Mrs Joan Robinson as early as 1960 in an article written for a leading Polish economic journal, ('Philosophy of Prices'), *Ekonomista*, 3/1960, pp. 530–47.

producers and consumers. The system would be conducive to greater efficiency of production and a higher level of consumer satisfaction. Furthermore, national income accounts would provide a more balanced picture of the national economy and its growth (see Ch. 4 A).

D. PRICE STABILITY AND FLEXIBILITY

The stability of prices over long periods is considered desirable by many Socialist economists on the following grounds. First, Socialism provides a unique system for liberating man from the scourge of uncertainty produced by economic fluctuations. Fixed prices over long periods facilitate economic planning. They are also preferred by producers so that they can plan their commitments and methods of production, knowing that their accounting will not be upset. There is ample evidence that in Socialist countries neither producers[10] nor consumers[11] appreciate or want changes in retail prices.

Second, the use of prices for regulating the distribution of real personal income is clumsy and wasteful. It can be done just as effectively by regulating nominal wages, social services and personal taxes. There is a particularly strong case against frequent changes in the prices of necessities. Such goods constitute a large proportion of the cost of living of the lower income groups, and changes in their prices produce a substantial and haphazard redistribution of real incomes. Third, not only should the authorities refrain from frequent price changes, but they should take active measures to prevent price increases. A planned economy of the Socialist type is noted for an in-built predisposition to inflation (see Ch. 10 D).

On the other hand, flexible prices are not as objectionable now as they were thought to be in the past. Indeed, if the new economic system is to be capable of the desired performance, there must be less rigidity in the price setting and adjustment process. Prices which are centrally fixed and remain unchanged over long periods produce contradictions in the context of changing costs on the one hand and consumers' preferences on the other. If buyer's markets are to be developed, production must be made to respond to demand, and flexible prices (via the profit criterion, see Ch. 3 C) can achieve this more effectively than directives can. As Socialist economies reach

[10] An experiment was tried in Poland in the mid-1960s to change the retail prices of fertilizers seasonally in order to spread sales uniformly throughout the year and to cope with the storage problem in the peak sowing season. The result was that farmers were postponing sowings till prices were reduced and there was a noticeable drop in yields in consequence. *Życie gosp.*, 22/1/1967, p. 8.

[11] E.g., S. Kuziński, ('The Structure of Consumption and the Market Problem'), *Nowe drogi*, 1/1968, p. 44.

more advanced stages, enterprises have a greater capacity and sensitivity to price changes.

It is for these reasons that most Socialist countries (Bulgaria, Czechoslovakia, the German D.R., Hungary and Yugoslavia) have adopted 'flexible price systems'. Thus in Hungary in 1968 (according to the new price system effective since the beginning of that year) there were four categories of prices:

(i) *free prices*—applying mostly to luxuries and certain agricultural products (covering about 23 per cent of the items in domestic trade);

(ii) *free-range prices*—free fluctuation is allowed 5 per cent above and below the levels set by the State, applying mostly to semi-luxuries (27 per cent of domestic trade);

(iii) *ceiling prices*—set by the State for the less essential items of household use (30 per cent of domestic trade);

(iv) *fixed prices*—set by the State, applying to most necessities (20 per cent of domestic trade).[12]

After operating for only six months, the new system produced obvious benefits—'less bureaucratic, more responsive to consumer preferences, and ensuring a better market balance'.[13]

The existence of fixed and variable prices side by side obviously contains elements of incongruence because the latter are likely to rise or fall in relation to the former, which is likely to lead to price distortions. According to the chairman of the Soviet State Planning Committee (attached to *Gosplan*), a reasonable solution to this problem appears to be this. The prices of standardized basic raw materials should be held stable over long periods, but the prices of finished products should be flexible, and should be changed not at one fell swoop as was common in the past, but gradually as the need arises.[14] This may very well prove the pattern for the Socialist price policies in the future.

E. OPTIMAL PRICES

Owing to the public ownership of the means of production and the absence of the free market mechanism, Socialist economies have no automatic or simple mechanism for determining rational prices. Under the system of planning by 'material balances', which pre-

[12] J. Garan, ('The Hungarian Price Reform'), *Życie gosp.*, 18/2/1968, p. 11.
[13] *Figyelo*, 28/8/1968, p. 1.
[14] V. Sitnin, ('The Economic Reform in Action: Producers' Prices—Achievements and Tasks'), *Ekonomicheskaya gazeta*, No. 6, Feb. 1968, pp. 10–11.

vailed in the past (see Ch. 2 B), prices were really irrelevant and they did not perform an allocative function.

However, to ensure the optimum utilization of resources, there must be some rational basis for determining 'programming' prices, i.e. those that could be applied by central planners to work out the overall allocation of resources. Rational prices can be arrived at, in a sense paradoxically: (i) *competitively, on a decentralized basis*, or (ii) *computationally, on a centralized basis*.

The competitive–decentralized solution was already put forward in the 1930s by a Polish economist Oskar Lange, who described it as the 'trial and error' method. Under this system, there would have to be a relatively free market both for inputs (labour, capital, land) and output, in which producers and consumers would be allowed to compete. Starting from the existing structure of prices, and subsequently guided by supply and demand and macrosocial considerations, the central planning authority would be making successive adjustments to prices to ensure equilibrium in the market (see reference 18 at the end of this chapter). Lange's method of 'successive approximations' has never been fully put into practice.

The computational–centralized approach is more suited to Socialist conditions and is gaining increasing acceptance from economists and political leaders. This solution is now becoming feasible owing to the perfection of mathematical programming and the development of high-memory computers. Even Oskar Lange himself, shortly before he died in 1965, conceded that the trial and error procedure was satisfactory only for the pre-computer age.[15] So far, the computational method has been applied only on a limited scale in the more advanced Socialist countries, but it seems certain that it will revolutionize the whole system of planning and reduce the wasteful allocation of resources (see Ch. 2 C).

The founders of the concept of optimal prices are the three Soviet economists, L. V. Kantorovich, N. S. Nemchinov and V. V. Novozhilov. Their ideas can be traced back to the late 1930s, but they had not attracted any real attention till the late 1950s. The advocates of optimal prices differ on the details of approach but they agree on the fundamental issue: the construction of such prices and the optimization of the overall economic plan constitute two aspects of the same problem, and they cannot be disassociated from each other. The essence of the argument is that prices must reflect all social costs, including non-labour costs, i.e. standard capital charges and differential rent. Novozhilov, to placate orthodox Marxists, calls the latter two 'indirect labour costs' because a withdrawal of these resources represents increased (direct) labour costs.

[15] *Życie gosp.*, 24/10/1965.

Furthermore, Novozhilov emphasizes that the application of resources to one particular use involves 'losses' to the economy in some other competing but forgone use. Resources should be allocated in the whole economy in such a pattern that ensures the minimization of what is known in Western terminology as 'opportunity costs'. Novozhilov concludes that it is these all-inclusive valuations (i.e. including direct and indirect labour costs and opportunity cost), which he calls 'social costs', that should provide the basis for programming (or optimal) prices.[16] An approach along similar lines was proposed by Kantorovich, who describes his optimal prices as 'objectively determined valuations'.[17]

The actual prices are arrived at by solving an immense number of simultaneous equations, involving a large number of different plan variants, according to postulated major objectives. This necessitates a comprehensive network of nodal computer centres in each country, capable of storing, up-dating and processing heterogeneous data.

The optimization analysis by-passes the labour theory of value. In fact, at least implicitly, it recognizes the scarcity of resources and involves marginal analysis (the diminishing marginal rate of substitution). Some optimalists, such as the well-known Soviet economist, N. Fedorenko, quite explicitly advocate the application of the marginal principle to costing (i.e. that all enterprises should be made profitable, not only those above average) and the acceptance of relative utility ('social value-in-exchange') as a basis for pricing.[18]

It is widely agreed that optimal prices should be applied only for planning (programming) purposes and should not be allowed to interfere with the socially desirable distribution of national income.[19] In other words, the proponents of optimal prices envisage what is now known as the 'shadow market'. The central planning authority, using modern mathematical methods and electronic computers, simulates supply and demand on a macrosocial scale in the interest of society as a whole in search of the optimal plan. This search, or as Kantorovich describes it 'competition amongst plans', involves the application of *shadow prices* but not actual payments.[20] Consequently such

[16] V. V. Novozhilov, *Izmereniye zatrat i ikh rezultatov v sotsialisticheskom khoziaistve*, Moscow, Akademiya Nauk, 1958 (translation is now available in English: *Problems of Measuring Outlays and Results under Optimal Planning*, New York, IASP, 1969).

[17] L. V. Kantorovich, *Ekonomicheskii raschet nailuchshego ispolzovaniya resursov*, Moscow, Akademizdat, 1959 (there is an English translation: *The Best Use of Economic Resources*, Harvard U.P., 1965).

[18] N. P. Fedorenko, *Ekonomika i matematika* (Economics and Mathematics), Moscow, Znaniye, 1967, esp. pp. 9–25, 41–4, 55–7.

[19] E.g. see M. Pohorille (ed.), *Ekonomia polityczna socjalizmu* (The Political Economy of Socialism), Warsaw, PWE, 1968, p. 452.

[20] *The Best Use of Economic Resources*, p. 150.

prices, although used for the optimal *allocation* of resources, do not perform any distributive functions.

Some optimalists (rightly) believe that the problem of optimization cannot be solved completely until the same principle is applied to all prices, including producers' and retail prices. It is pointed out that the consequent undesirable distributive distortions of such prices could be corrected by the readjustment of wages and social consumption and by taxation and subsidies.

There is little doubt that the mathematical concept of optimal prices is an important milestone in the development of Socialist economics. For a long time, a number of Western economists, notably L. v. Mises, F. A. v. Hayek, J. B. Hoff and A. Bergson, claimed that rational pricing was impossible under Socialism (see references 1, 12 and 20 at the end of this chapter). Although Lange's 'trial and error' method did not convince many Western (and Socialist) economists, the feasibility of the computational optimal prices conclusively refutes any grounds for such claims. Even though much remains to be done on the practical level, there is a sound theoretical basis. In fact, in some respects Socialism provides the possibility of improving on capitalism. There is much to be said in favour of the system of prices which are not distorted by selfish monopolists and myopic consumers, but in which long-run macrosocial cost–benefit considerations can be reflected.

RECOMMENDED REFERENCES AVAILABLE IN ENGLISH

1. Bergson, A., 'Socialist Economics', in Ellis, H. S. (ed.), *Survey of Contemporary Economics*, Philadelphia, Blakiston, 1951, Vol. I, pp. 412–48.

2. Boehme, H., 'East German Price Formation under the New Economic System', *Soviet Studies*, Jan. 1968, pp. 340–58.

3. Bush, K., 'A Comparison of Retail Prices in the USA, USSR and Western Europe', *Bulletin*, Munich, Nov. 1967, pp. 27–40.

*4. Csikos-Nagy, B., *Pricing in Hungary*, London, Institute of Economic Affairs, 1968.

*5. Falkowski, M., and Łukaszewicz, A., *Problems of Economic Theory and Practice in Poland. Studies on the Theory of Reproduction and Prices*, Warsaw, Polish Scientific Publishers, 1964.

*6. Fedorenko, N., 'Price and Optimal Planning', *Problems of Economics*, Nov. 1967, pp. 11–21.

7. Frisch, R., 'Rational price fixing in a socialist society', *Econ. of Planning*, Vol. 6, No. 2, 1966, pp. 97–124.

*8. Ganczer, S., 'Price Calculations and the Analysis of Proportions within the National Economy', *Acta Oeconomica*, Vol. 1, No. 1–2, 1966, pp. 54–67.

9. Gordon, S., 'Why Does the Marxian Exploitation Theory Require a Labour Theory of Value?', *Journal of Pol. Econ.*, Jan.–Feb. 1968, pp. 137–40.

*10. Heil, L., Kýn, O., and Sekerka, B., 'Price Calculations', *Czechosl. Econ. Papers*, No. 8, 1967, pp. 61–82.

*11. Hoch, R., 'Market Equilibrium and Changes in the Price Level in Socialism', *Acta Oeconomica*, Vol. 1, No. 3–4, 1966, pp. 267–83.

12. Hoff, J. B., *Economic Calculation in the Socialist Society*, London, W. Hodge, 1949.

13. Johansen, L., 'Labour Theory of Value and Marginal Utilities', *Econ. of Planning*, Vol. 3, No. 2, 1963, pp. 89–103.

*14. Kalinov, S., and Yordanov, I., 'Some Problems of Price Formation Under the New System of Management of the National Economy', *Eastern Europ. Econ.*, Spring 1967, pp. 9–16.

*15. Kantorovich, L. V., *The Best Use of Economic Resources*, translated from the Russian, Harvard U.P., 1965, Chs I and II.

*16. Komin, A., 'Review of Wholesale Prices and Their Approximation to Socially Necessary Expenditures', *Problems of Economics*, Feb. 1968, pp. 28–39.

*17. Kondrashev, D., 'The Development of Price Formation in the USSR', *Problems of Economics*, March 1968, pp. 30–7.

18. Lange, O., 'On the Economic Theory of Socialism', *Rev. of Econ. Studies*, Vol. IV, No. 1, 1936/7, pp. 53–71; and Lange O., and Taylor, F. M., 'Trial and Error in a Socialist Economy', in Lippincott (ed.), *On the Economic Theory of Socialism*, Minneapolis, 1938, pp. 72–83.

*19. Lure, A., 'Price Formation and a Comparison of Different Variants of Economic Measures (Models of Optimal Development of the National Economy as a Means of Theoretical Analysis of Socialist Economics)', *Problems of Economics*, Aug. 1967, pp. 3–12.

20. Mises, L. v., 'Economic Calculation in the Socialist Commonwealth', in Hayek, F. A. v. (ed.), *Collectivist Economic Planning*, London, Routledge & Kegan Paul, 1935, pp. 87–130.

*21. Petrov, G., 'For a Single Market Price', *Eastern Europ. Econ.*, Spring 1967, pp. 17–26.

*22. Postyshev, A., 'The Labour Theory of Value and Optimal Planning', *Problems of Economics*, Dec. 1967, pp. 3–15.

*23. Reiher, K., and Schierz, E., 'The Relation Between Prices and Production—Financial Planning in the New Economic System', *Eastern Europ. Econ.*, Summer 1967, pp. 40–51.

24. Simon, G., 'Ex post examination of macroeconomic shadow prices', *Econ. of Planning*, Vol. 5, No. 3, 1965, pp. 80–93.

*25. Sztyber, W. B., 'Problems of Setting Prices on New Products (Use Value and Price)', *Eastern Europ. Econ.*, Fall 1967, pp. 38–54.

* *indicates contributions by writers from Socialist countries.*

CHAPTER 10

Money and Banking

A. MONEY AND MONETARY POLICY

Traditionally, the Marxists' views on money have always been negative, largely a reaction against capitalism where money reaches its peak of development and influence. Soon after the Bolshevik Revolution in Russia, steps were taken to replace money with transfers in kind, in accordance with the Marxian long-run ideal of money 'withering away' under communism. In 1920 all settlements in money between State enterprises were abolished and practically all wages were paid in kind. But this practice was soon abandoned, and it was officially conceded that money continues to function in a Socialist economy, the attitude adopted since World War II by other Socialist countries, too. In fact the role of money has been substantially enhanced by the recent economic reforms.

Officially, the currencies of all the Socialist countries under consideration are defined in gold, which is taken as the basis for fixing the official exchange rates applicable to visible trade. But this is of no real consequence, as none of these currencies (with the partial exception of the Yugoslav dinar) is convertible into gold.[1] The amount of currency issue in Socialist countries is not very different from that in capitalist countries, i.e. mostly representing 5–10 per cent of national income, as their requirements for cash are similar.

A large proportion of payments in the advanced capitalist countries is effected through cheques. Cheques are also used in Socialist countries, usually constituting less than 10 per cent of total payments by value.[2] However, most payments between Socialist enterprises are settled not by cheque or cash, but by adjusting the bank accounts. These transfer payments are effected more or less automatically on the basis of delivery documents which perform a similar function to 'not-negotiable' cheques in the West. Transfers of taxes, grants,

---

[1] Yugoslavia is the only Socialist country which is a member of the International Monetary Fund. Czechoslovakia and Poland were foundation members but they withdrew from its membership in 1956 and 1950 respectively. There are several indications now that Czechoslovakia, Hungary, Poland and Rumania may join IMF in the future.

[2] *Finanse*, 2/1968, pp. 31, 34.

subsidies, etc. between the State budget on the one hand and enterprises and institutions on the other are made in a similar way.

Monetary policy under Socialism is much more intimately integrated than under capitalism with wage and fiscal policies, and these are further reinforced by direct controls where necessary. The overall objective of the monetary policy is to provide a financial basis conducive to plan fulfilment and monetary equilibrium in the economy. Before the recent reforms, the scope for monetary policy was pretty limited, as money performed a passive function.

Under the new system, basic proportions in the economy are still centrally determined, but otherwise enterprises have a good deal of freedom in deciding on the details and methods of fulfilling the plan. Directives and prohibitions have been largely replaced with financial incentives and disincentives administered flexibly by monetary authorities. The most important financial instruments consist of differentiated credit terms (considered in Part C of this chapter), which affect enterprises' profits and consequently incentive payments to their personnel (see Ch. 3 A and B). The new system is accentuating inflationary pressure, which provides a new challenge to monetary policy (see Part D of this chapter).

One of the principles adopted in the reforms is the rule of self-financing. This means that enterprises, even in the sphere of investment, have to rely basically on their own resources instead of central allocations from the State budget. This has produced a change in payment flows in the economy. Grants to enterprises are now smaller, and so are their payments to the State budget. Instead, deliveries are now financed mostly horizontally on the enterprises' own initiative. In this process, banks have assumed an active role.

The increasing importance being attached to monetary policy is indicated by the growing number of publications on the role of money, credit and banks. In these discussions Western achievements in the sphere of monetary theory and policy are also analysed with a view to possible adaptations to modern Socialist economic conditions.[3] Two British economists who made a thorough on-the-spot

[3] There are numerous articles in the leading journals of economics and finance. Examples of recent book publications by well-known Socialist writers: S. M. Borisov, *Zoloto v ekonomike sovremennogo kapitalizma* (Gold in the Contemporary Capitalist Economy), Moscow, Finansy, 1968; H. Burg, *Der Staat als Bankier* (The State as a Banker), East Berlin, Dietz Verlag, 1968; K. J. Chizhov, *Mezhdunarodnye valutno-finansoviye organizatsii kapitalizma* (International Foreign-Exchange and Financial Institutions under Capitalism), Moscow, Finansy, 1968; Z. Fedorowicz, *Finanse i kredyt w krajach kapitalistycznych* (Finance and Credit in Capitalist Countries), Warsaw, PWE, 1968; K. Köver, *A tőkés világ valutarendszere* (The Foreign Exchange System of the Capitalist World), Budapest, Közgazdasági és Jogi K., 1967; A. Zwass, *Pieniądz dwóch rynków* (Money under the Two Economic Systems), Warsaw, PWN, 1968.

study of the Yugoslav economy in 1967 concluded that 'Yugoslavia is relying more upon banking policy than is Britain'.[4] Meditating on the modern trends in Socialist countries, a Polish monetary expert concluded:

'... who knows if, in the light of these developments, the theoretical assumption of the withering away of money with the transition to Full Communism is tenable. Perhaps not all paths leading to Communism must deviate from money?'[5]

B. THE BANKING SYSTEM

The banking system in each Socialist country is socialized, highly centralized and operating on a branch (as distinct from an independent unit) basis. Banks collect the means of payment from the State and the public, organize cash and non-cash payments on a planned basis and supervise the use of finance by enterprises and institutions.

The recent economic reforms have affected the Socialist banking system in three major respects.

a. *Increased Role of the Banks.* Socialist banks are no longer mere administrative agencies of the Ministry of Finance carrying out detailed instructions. They can now take some of the initiative in promoting developments of social importance on a sound economic basis. The system is now noted for greater flexibility and adaptability.

b. *A Greater Functional Specialization.* In most Socialist countries new banks have been established in recent years to service the specialized needs of industry, agriculture, foreign trade, etc. The former institutional division between short- and long-term financing has been largely removed and each bank now extends both types of credit. The banks are well equipped with a network of specialized technical, engineering, agricultural and commercial teams to assist them in acting as financial advisers and in controlling the application of funds.

c. *A Greater Financial Centralization.* A stricter control of financial processes from above has proved essential as a consequence of a greater independence of enterprises, and the fact that finance has

[4] (T. Wilson and G. R. Denton), 'Economic Reform in Yugoslavia,' *Planning*, P.E.P., July 1968, p. 225.
[5] Z. Grabowski, ('Money Today'), *Życie gospodarcze*, 4/12/1968, p. 2.

become a more influential factor at the operational level. This development is interpreted as an expression of the Leninist principle of 'democratic centralism'. On the one hand, banks have been given greater powers over enterprises. On the other, the activities of the banks at the operational level are now subject to stricter supervision and control by the intermediate agencies of economic administration (branch associations, regional authorities) and by the central bank. The strengthened control at the central level is exercised in two different ways, as exemplified by the banking reforms in the USSR and the German D.R. By the 1959 reform in the USSR, the *Gosbank* and the Investment Bank took over the Agricultural Bank and Communal Banks to administer credits directly. According to the 1968 reform in the German D.R., the State Bank dropped its general banking activities and has retained only those functions which are essential to its central bank responsibilities, so that it can concentrate on the overall control of (as they are now called) 'business banks'. The reduction in the number of banks in Yugoslavia (from 200 in the early 1960s) to about eighty today can also be interpreted as a move towards centralization.

The overall banking policy in each Socialist country is laid down by the Ministry of Finance in close co-operation with the State Planning Commission and the State Bank. The latter is the central bank and it performs similar functions to those in a capitalist country—note issue, carrying out the government's financial policy, re-financing other banks, supervising (or directly administering) foreign payments, and in addition servicing the State budget. It also prescribes the rules governing bank deposits, the extension of credit, interest rates and bank accounting and statistics. In most Socialist countries it is responsible to the Ministry of Finance, but in Bulgaria and the German D.R. it answers directly to the Council of Ministers.

In addition to the State Bank, in each country there is usually an investment (or industry), an agricultural, a savings and a foreign trade bank. Some of them also have a bank of commerce, a bank of liquidations, a maritime bank and a number of co-operative banks. The latter are owned collectively, their function being to cater for the needs of handicrafts, small farms and shops. They are best developed in the German D.R. and Yugoslavia.

The structure of the banking system in each European Socialist country is represented in Fig. 11. Where there are no specialized banks, the banking services in question are provided by the State Bank (the extreme case is represented by Albania, which has only one bank with specialized departments). All European Socialist countries, except Albania and Yugoslavia (but including Mongolia), belong to the International Bank for Economic Co-operation. It has its head office in Moscow, it started operations in 1964 and its function is to facilitate payment settlements among member countries.

The role of the banking system in a Socialist economy differs in two important respects from that in a developed capitalist country.

FIG. 11. *The Structure of the Socialist Banking Systems*

Country	Central (State) Bank	Industry (Investment) Bank	Agricultural Bank	Co-operative Bank(s)	Savings Bank	Bank of Foreign Trade	Other Bank(s)
Bulgaria	×	×	×	—	×	×	×[1]
Czechoslovakia	×	—	—	—	×	×[2]	×[3]
German D.R.	×	×	×	×	×	×	×[4]
Hungary	×	×	—	×	—	×	×[5]
Poland	×	×	×	×	×	×[6]	×[7]
Rumania	×	×	×	—	×	×	—
USSR	×	×	—	—	×	×	—
Yugoslavia	×	×	×	×	×	×[8]	×[9]

[1] The Maritime Commercial Bank.

[2] The Bank of Trade.

[3] The Bank of Commerce (also handles foreign transactions).

[4] The Berlin People's Bank, The Berlin Municipal Bank—both handling transactions between East and West Germany.

[5] Public Bank for the Exchange of Valuables.

[6] The Bank of Trade.

[7] The Polish Guardian Bank (which also handles internal exports, i.e. sales in the domestic market for foreign currencies) and the Bank of Domestic Economy (responsible for transfers of property and liquidation).

[8] In addition fifteen other banks have the right to engage in foreign financial operations.

[9] Mostly small banks serving particular regions.

Source. Adapted (and up-dated) from: Academy of Sciences of the USSR, Institute of International Socialist Economics, *Mirovaya sotsialisticheskaya sistema khoziaistva* (The World Socialist Economic System), Mysl, Moscow, 1966, Vol. I, p. 361.

On the one hand banks, not being privately owned, cannot pursue their activities independently in pursuit of their microeconomic interest. Banking operations are subordinated to the needs of the economic plan, in which the overall and major structural developments are predetermined. On the other hand, banking policy is in a sense a more powerful weapon because there is no short-term money market, no stock exchange and no 'fringe' banking institutions (hire purchase companies, personal loan establishments, development financiers, building societies, etc.). All these functions are performed by the banking system, and its regulation provides an air-tight control over the flow and distribution of finance.

C. CREDIT AND INTEREST

Under Socialism economic development is never allowed to be hampered by a lack of finance. If there are physical resources available and if the production is socially desirable, it goes without saying that the means of financing will be provided. The economic plan has a counterpart of the credit plan which is worked out by the central bank in co-operation with other banks.

As was shown in Ch. 5 D, the role of the State budgetary allocations of finance to enterprises has been declining; instead enterprises are increasingly relying on their own liquid resources and on repayable bank credits. There is no doubt that the increased ability of the enterprises to obtain credit on their own initiative is a great step forward in giving effective meaning to decentralization and a more effective utilization of resources.

The total amount of credit and the proportions allowed to different branches are, as before, centrally fixed according to the planned needs of the economy. But otherwise the microeconomic distribution is left to the judgment of the banks and enterprises concerned. Loans are extended on the condition of good management and the soundness of the purpose for which credit is sought. As under capitalism, a distinction is made between short-term (also known as 'turnover' or 'production') and long-term ('investment') credits.

Short-term credits, particularly on commodity turnover, are not as important in Socialist countries as in the West. Trade credits on commodity turnover are extended only by banks, not by the selling enterprises. They are strictly regulated because they could easily interfere with the planned utilization of resources. The same applies to credits in trade among Socialist countries—the loans are granted by banks (including the IBEC) to the designated banks in the importing countries.

Consumer credit, which is extended only by savings banks and consumer co-operative shops, is as yet of smaller importance than in the West, but its role is gradually increasing. The proportion of consumer goods sold on this basis is about one-tenth, but in Hungary it is as high as one-quarter.[6] There are usually strict conditions imposed, such as that the borrower must be in regular employment and that the amount of credit must not exceed a certain proportion of the person's annual earnings (e.g. one-third in Yugoslavia).[7]

In extending long-term credits emphasis is no longer on the sheer size of the projects but rather on their suitability and efficiency. Banks participate in planning investment ventures and evaluate their prospective profitability. Preference is given to the projects promising quick returns, those directly affecting exports and import-replacement production and those intended for the less-developed regions.

To ensure financial discipline, banks have considerable powers of control over the users of bank funds. In case credits are not applied for the approved purpose, or the project is not completed on time, or if credits are not repaid on maturity banks can apply the following sanctions against the offending enterprises:

(i) charging penalty interest for the period originally approved;
(ii) requiring the repayment of the credits before maturity;
(iii) withholding the funds for wage and salary payments, especially for material incentives;
(iv) refusing credits in the future (but enterprises can appeal to the arbitration court in such cases).

As the total amount of credit and its broad distribution are determined on a planned basis, it is obvious that *interest* cannot play such a decisive role as under capitalism. However, although interest rates are of little significance in programming investment at the central level, they are now used as an important instrument of promoting the most efficient distribution and application of credits at the operational level.

Until the early 1960s, a large proportion of the enterprises' investment needs in the European CMEA countries was met by interest-free non-repayable grants from the State budget. But this practice only encouraged enterprises to place extravagant demands for larger and larger allocations, leading to an alarmingly increasing capital–output ratio and tremendous waste (see Ch. 5 C, p. 83).

---

[6] *Acta Oeconomica*, Vol. 2, No. 1–2, 1967, p. 96.
[7] For an example of the new regulations on consumer credit, see Decree 292 of the Council of Ministers of Bulgaria, dated 17/7/1968, *Durzhaven vestnik*, 30/7/1968, pp. 1–4 (an English translation can be found in: US Dept. of Commerce, Joint Publications Research Service, *Translations on Eastern Europe: Economic and Industrial Affairs*, 23/9/1968, pp. 14–30).

However, this wasteful practice has been almost completely dis-continued since the mid-1960s by the introduction of annual capital charges. It is now recognized that interest is ideologically justified because capital is nothing else but materialized labour, and as such it should be rationally distributed, because it represents a means of economizing live labour. In fact, there is nothing new about interest under Socialism—it existed even under Stalin. But it applied only to turnover credits obtainable directly from banks; interest was also payable on personal savings deposits.

The capital charge in most of these countries is uniform for the whole economy. In Bulgaria it is 3 per cent p.a. of the value of fixed assets, in Hungary it is 5 per cent and in Poland—6 per cent. In Czechoslovakia the charge is levied on fixed capital (6 per cent p.a.) *and* on circulating assets (2 per cent p.a.). But in some countries the annual charges on fixed capital are differentiated according to industries—in the German D.R. they range from 1 to 6 per cent p.a., and in the USSR from 3 to 9 per cent. The purpose is to regulate the profitability rate of different industries, which otherwise would differ greatly owing to the imperfect price structure. The differentia-tion of the rates is treated as temporary, and it will disappear when the price structure is improved.[8]

The rates of interest on bank credits are not determined in the free market for loanable funds, but are fixed centrally to suit a variety of objectives. The rates charged are now highly differentiated, but they mostly fall within the range 1–5 per cent p.a. In addition there are heavy penalty rates which may reach (in Yugoslavia) 20 per cent p.a.[9]

To attract deposits from enterprises, institutions and individual persons, interest is payable by banks. For example, up to 7 per cent p.a. is offered in Hungary and Yugoslavia on long-term deposits. Savings banks pay about 3 per cent p.a. on personal deposits.

D. SOCIALIST INFLATION

A well-known assertion advanced in Socialist countries in the past is that 'the possibility of inflation in a Socialist economy is extremely

[8] A. Wołowczyk, ('Financing of Investments in the CMEA Countries'), *Życie gosp.*, 15/1/1967, p. 7; R. Evstigneiev and V. Kayie, ('Economic Reforms in the CMEA Countries'), *Voprosy ekonomiki*, 10/1968, p. 110.

[9] As reported at the beginning of 1969, the ranges of interest rates p.a. charged (including penalty rates) were as follows: Bulgaria: 2–8 per cent; Czechoslovakia: 1·5–12 per cent; the German D.R.: 1–12 per cent; Hungary: 2–16 per cent; Poland: 2–10 per cent; Rumania: 1–12 per cent; the USSR: 0·5–8 per cent; Yugoslavia: 5–20 per cent. W. Jaworski, ('Stocks, Credits and the Banking System'), *Finanse*, 1/1969, p. 52.

remote'.[10] This contention is based on the assumption that the Socialist State is committed to 'planned proportional development' and it has sufficient powers to ensure a balance between production and spending, so that stability of prices can be assured. In reality this mechanism has not worked up to expectations.[11]

In practice, it is impossible to measure the extent or degree of Socialist inflation. First, the official price indexes cover only retail prices, and these are still largely controlled. Even so these indexes have shown annual increases of 1–2 per cent in most CMEA countries following the economic reforms since the early 1960s.[12] A better indication of the continuing inflationary pressure is provided by the retail price index in Yugoslavia, where economic reforms had begun much earlier (1952) and have been more liberal; in the 1950s the index rose on the average by 4 per cent p.a., whilst over the period 1960–8 it rose by 12 per cent p.a.[13]

Second, Socialist money is an imperfect measure of value (however defined) and changes in its purchasing power are selectively restricted. There is no conventional market for the factors of production, and thus money cannot buy the means of production or secure labour for hire unless it is done through recognized planned channels. But even the prices of consumer goods are not indicative of their value. The existence of sellers' markets means that the official prices are under-stated. The very existence of the two-tier price system shows that Socialist money is not a uniform measure of value.

There is a number of factors distinctive of Socialism which contribute to the inflationary tendencies, and it may be observed that the economic reforms have created new sources of pressure. Those on the supply side are as follows:

(i) The overcommitment of resources and the overexpansion of industries in the name of 'all-round development' and high rates of growth, irrespective of the available raw material base.

(ii) A relatively high proportion of national income fixed for accumulation at the expense of consumption.

(iii) Unfulfilled targets caused by planning errors or unexpected

[10] *Mała encyklopedia ekonomiczna* (Concise Encyclopedia of Economics), Warsaw, PWE, 1962, p. 227.

[11] Some economists, both Western (such as R. Hutchings, B. Mieczkowski, W. G. Nutter, H. Olsienkiewicz, G. J. Staller and E. Zaleski) and Socialist (e.g. N. Cobelijic of Yugoslavia, J. Goldmann of Czechoslovakia, W. Przelaskowski of Poland and H. Rost of the German D.R.) believe that Socialist economies are developing regular economic cycles. E.g. see the references 5, 9, 11, 13 and 14 at the end of this chapter.

[12] *Życie gosp.*, 7/4/1968, p. 3.

[13] *Statistički godišnjak Jugoslavije 1968* (Statistical Yearbook of Yugoslavia for 1968), p. 270.

developments; the burden of adjustment is usually shifted to consumer goods industries to safeguard priority production.

(iv) A tendency on the part of enterprises to hoard raw materials, components and labour as a reaction to sellers' markets ('Socialist speculation').

(v) Insufficient motivation to economy and exertion, a natural consequence of the absence of private enterprise, the limited scope for individual initiative and very well-developed social security.

(vi) Increasing freedom given to enterprises to influence or fix their own prices.

(vii) A growing proportion of production exported on credits, especially to developing countries.

At the same time there are contributing causes operating on the demand side:

(i) The artificially low prices officially enforced, encouraging wasteful use (e.g. at the time of the disastrous crop failures in the early 1960s bread was so cheap that it was fed to cattle and pigs for fattening).

(ii) A higher velocity of monetary circulation consequent upon decentralization and the increasing role of the market.

(iii) The increasing role of material (as distinct from non-material) incentives which represent extra spending power.

(iv) An increasing popular pressure for consumer credit and immediate consumption (a trend described as 'consumerism').

(v) A tendency for social consumption to exceed planned levels.

(vi) Limitations placed on the import of consumer goods in favour of producer goods.

There are many Socialist economists and political leaders who believe that there is no need to be unduly concerned about inflationary pressure. The State has sufficient powers to prevent inflation reaching undesirable proportions. In fact, there is a well-established belief that a mild state of inflation, or the existence of sellers' markets, is perfectly normal and in fact evidence of the superiority of Socialism over capitalism. In a capitalist economy the growth of consumption by the masses falls short of the expansion of the production capacity, which tends to lead to recessions and stagnation, whilst in a Socialist economy the growth of demand constantly outstrips the growth of production and thus the former provides a continuous healthy driving force to the latter.[14]

[14] W. Wilczyński, *Rachunek ekonomiczny a mechanizm rynkowy* (Economic Accounting and the Market Mechanism), Warsaw, PWE, 1965, pp. 143–5.

RECOMMENDED REFERENCES AVAILABLE IN ENGLISH

*1. Ács, L., 'The Effects of the Banking System on Enterprise Management under the New Hungarian Economic Mechanism', *Acta Oeconomica*, Vol. 3, No. 1, 1968, pp. 41–52.

*2. Bajt, A., 'Yugoslav economic reforms, monetary and production mechanism', *Econ. of Planning*, Vol. 7, No. 3, 1967, pp. 201–18.

*3. Batyrev, V., 'The Economic Reform and the Increasing Role of Credit', *Problems of Economics*, Sept. 1966, pp. 50–8.

4. Bednarik, M., 'The Moscow Bank: The International Bank for Economic Cooperation', *Amer. Rev. of Soviet and Eastern Europ. For. Trade*, Jan.–Feb. 1966, pp. 3–36.

*5. Čobeljić, N., and Stojanović, R., *The Theory of Investment Cycles in a Socialist Economy*, translated from the Yugoslav, New York, IASP, 1968.

*6. Erdös, P., *Contribution to the Theory of Money*, translated from the Hungarian, New York, IASP, 1969.

*7. Garbuzov, V., 'Finances and Economic Stimuli', *Problems of Economics*, Feb. 1966, pp. 3–10.

8. Garvey, G., *Money, Banking and Credit in Eastern Europe*, New York, Fed. Res. Bank of New York, 1966.

*9. Goldmann, J., 'Short- and Long-term Variations in the Growth Rate and the Model of Functioning of a Socialist Economy', *Czechosl. Econ. Papers*, No. 5, 1965, pp. 35–46.

10. Herman, A., 'Czechoslovak Banking in the Wind of Change', *The Banker*, June 1968, pp. 506–12.

11. Hutchings, R., 'Periodic Fluctuations in Soviet Industrial Growth Rates', *Soviet Studies*, Jan. 1969, pp. 331–52.

*12. Meznerics, I., *Banking Business in a Socialist Economy with Special Regard to East–West Trade*, translated from the Hungarian, rev. ed., Leyden, Sijthoff, 1968.

13. Mieczkowski, B., 'The Unstable Soviet-Bloc Economies', *East Europe*, Oct. 1967, pp. 2–7.

14. Olsienkiewicz, H., 'Problems of General Imbalance, Inflation and Cyclic Fluctuations in the Communist Economy', *Bulletin*, Munich, Aug. 1968, pp. 13–25.

*15. Tuček, M., 'Monetary Equilibrium and Future Economic Growth', *Eastern European Economics*, Summer 1968, pp. 3–12.

* indicates contributions by writers from Socialist countries.

CHAPTER 11

Fiscal Policy and Control

A. BASES OF BUDGETARY PLANNING

The Socialist budget performs three basic functions: (i) the control and co-ordination of physical economic processes through financial discipline, (ii) the promotion of economic activities through fiscal incentives and disincentives to achieve the targets postulated in the economic plan, and (iii) the redistribution of national income in conformity with the 'law of planned proportionate (or balanced) development' of the entire economy. Although these functions are similar to those under capitalism, their extent and pervasiveness are far greater in the case of the Socialist economy.

The importance of budgetary planning under Socialism derives from the size of the budget and its focal position in relation to different facets of the economy, and from several peculiarities of the economic and social conditions. First, the scope of public finance is naturally much greater. This is a reflection of the State's direct participation in the economic and social life of the country. The budget includes not only the receipts and expenditure of the central government but also of provincial and local authorities and other 'non-productive' organizations, and the *balances* of productive enterprises. About two-thirds (about one-half in the federal countries, viz. the USSR and Yugloslavia) of the national income passes directly through the Socialist budget as receipts or expenditure, compared with about a quarter in capitalist countries (if national income is brought to the Socialist basis).

Second, the State budget is a financial expression of the economic and social tasks laid down in the overall economic plan. The budget is the key element in economic planning and growth, and it links the requirements of the plan with the production and financial plans of the enterprises. The plan and the budget are worked out simultaneously (by the State Planning Commission and the Ministry of Finance respectively) and presented to Parliament annually[1] at the same session.

[1] However, with the emphasis shifting to medium- and long-term economic planning, there have been some attempts to increase the time range of budgetary

Third, the importance of the budget is further enhanced by the fact that it is integrated with other financial plans, viz. the cash plan, credit plan, personal wage fund, and the financial plans of the enterprises. Finally, the role of the budget has been increased under the new economic system, where directives have been largely replaced by sophisticated forms of fiscal and financial instruments. On the other hand, the new emphasis attached to self-financing and bank credits as sources of enterprises' ways and means has tended to reduce the proportion of funds passing directly through the State budget[2] (also see Chs 5 D and 10 C).

In contrast to capitalist countries, under Socialism there is no need for budget deficits to promote full employment. Historically speaking, budget deficits were a rule in the post-revolutionary years, when they were met by inflationary note issues to strike at the holders of large monetary assets. In the last ten to fifteen years there has been a tendency to plan for budget surpluses, to provide for larger reserves and counteract the inherent predisposition of the Socialist economy towards inflation (see Ch. 10 D).

As has been indicated before, local budgets form an integral part of the State budget.[3] The reason is that the Socialist State cannot remain indifferent to the independent raising and spending of finance, as it might be in conflict with the State's overall financial policy, economic planning and the utilization of resources. The proportion of the State budget expenditure allocated to local budgets ranged in the early 1960s from 15 per cent in Rumania and 20 per cent in Hungary to 60 per cent in the USSR and Yugoslavia.[4] The federal system of administration and decentralization naturally enhances the role of regional, branch and local entities, and as a result of the economic reforms the proportion of funds passing through local budgets has tended to increase.

The budgetary systems of different Socialist countries are broadly similar, but differences of detail naturally exist. The differences increase with the lower levels of budgetary administration. They are greater on the receipts than on the expenditure side, reflecting planning. The first experiment was undertaken in the USSR in 1963, when a two-year budget was prepared for 1964 and 1965, and in Poland in 1964 for 1965 and 1966. W. Karpiński, *Zagadnienia systemu budżetowego państw socjalistycznych* (Problems of the Budgetary System in Socialist Countries), Warsaw, PWE, 1965, pp. 97–8.

[2] E.g. in Czechoslovakia before the economic reforms, 80 per cent of national income passed through the central budget, but the proportion has declined since to about 65 per cent. *Życie gospodarcze*, 21/4/1968, p. 7.

[3] E.g. in the USSR there are nearly 50,000 local budgets and they are all reflected in the State budget. D. A. Allakhverdyan (ed.), *Soviet Financial System*, Moscow, Progress Publishers, 1966, p. 311.

[4] W. Karpiński, op. cit., p. 22.

different degrees of socialization of the economy. In spite of some efforts under the auspices of CMEA, there are still considerable differences of classification.

B. BUDGETARY RECEIPTS

Most of the State budget receipts in Socialist countries are contributed by enterprises (including farms) and less than 10 per cent comes from the direct taxation of individuals.[5] This fact can be explained on two grounds. Firstly, there is little personal ownership of the means of production,[6] and secondly it is considered ideologically undesirable to tax workers directly. This approach contrasts with the practice in capitalist countries, where personal taxes normally account for 30 per cent or more (70 per cent, if we include indirect taxes which are explicitly shifted on to the consumers). We shall now examine the main sources of State receipts as reflected in Socialist budgets.

a. *Deductions from Enterprises' Profits*. This class of revenue is not referred to in Socialist countries as a profits tax, but regarded as a form of deduction from the 'surplus product' which belongs to the State anyway. These deductions may be made on account of the following: (i) variable capital allocated out of the State budget; (ii) fixed capital; (iii) stocks held; (iv) differential advantages (natural or man-made, but in each case not created by the enterprise's own exertion); (v) payroll tax (being introduced in some countries, as in Hungary in 1968); (vi) residual profits (remaining after the net enterprise profit is distributed in conformity with the regulations laid down, see Ch. 3 B). Enterprise profits are assuming an increasing importance as a source of State revenue. For example in the USSR, before 1950 they represented less than one-tenth of the total, but now the proportion is over one-third (see Fig. 12, p. 157).

b. *Turnover Taxes*. This form of revenue, which is peculiar to Socialist economies, represents the difference between the producers' and the retail price, excluding the wholesale and retail margins for the trading enterprises. These taxes apply mostly to consumer goods and some consumer services (such as entertainment). In contrast to the past, there is a tendency now for these taxes to be collected by trading, rather than producing, entities. There are three bases on which the size of this tax is set. In some cases, it is calculated on an

---

[5] Op. cit., p. 60.
[6] In Poland, which in addition to Yugoslavia has the largest private sector in Eastern Europe, only 4 per cent of the budgetary receipts is derived from that sector. W. Karpiński, op. cit., p. 78.

ad valorem basis (as a percentage of the retail price) and in some on a *specific* basis (a fixed amount per unit of the product). However, in most cases, the tax is arrived at *residually*, i.e. the retail price is fixed first to balance the available (or desirable) supply with the existing demand, and the tax is the difference between this price and the price paid to the producer (minus trade margins). Some producer goods are also subject to it (e.g. oil, electricity, metalware and chemical products in the USSR) and the proportion tends to be increasing. On the other hand some consumer goods, such as foodstuffs sold directly by peasants to consumers, are free from turnover taxes (the peasants' incomes are taxed instead). Whatever the basis of fixing this tax, the effective rates are highly differentiated.[7] In a sense, the size of the turnover taxes does not determine the level of retail prices—on the contrary, the magnitude of these taxes depends on the predetermined price level. Officially, turnover taxes are not regarded as taxes but as transfers of that part of the 'surplus product' which is created by society. However, some economists disagree and maintain that at least a portion of these levies constitutes an indirect tax which is shifted to the consumer.[8] For a long time, turnover taxes were by far the most important source of budget receipts. In the 1930s in the USSR and even in the early 1960s in Bulgaria, they constituted 60 per cent of the total.[9] However, although still important they represent only one-third or less (see Fig. 14, p. 178).

c. *Income Taxes.* These forms of revenue are raised from co-operative and private enterprises (including farms) and from persons. These taxes are progressive, the rates depending on the source and size of income. The discriminatory rates are so designed as to inhibit the accumulation of excessive profits by non-State enterprises and to prevent private enrichment. Thus in Poland, if the profitability of a co-operative enterprise is 5 per cent or less, 20 per cent of the net income is payable in tax, but if the profitability exceeds 35 per cent, the rate is 90 per cent.[10] On the other hand, the tax rates applicable

[7] These taxes may be differentiated according to the branch and sub-branch of industry, the type of purchasers, the type of individual commodity (quality, colour, packaging) and the type of raw materials used. E.g. in Bulgaria in 1968 over 300 tax rates were reported for leather gloves; the tax rates for macaroni ranged from 18·5 to 62·5 per cent (*Finansi i kredit*, 7/1968, pp. 40–52). However, there is a tendency towards introducing some uniformity. E.g. a uniform rate was recently introduced in Poland on the goods exported, whilst in some Socialist countries (such as Czechoslovakia, the USSR and Yugoslavia) exported goods are exempt from turnover taxes.

[8] E.g., M. V. Kolganov, *Natsionalnyi dokhod* (National Income), Moscow, Izd. Pol. Lit., 1959, p. 285.

[9] W. Karpiński, op. cit., p. 72.

[10] *Mała encyklopedia ekonomiczna* (Concise Encyclopedia of Economics), Warsaw, PWE, 1962, p. 482.

to personal wage incomes are noted for their very low degrees of progression, roughly half the rates or less prevailing in Western countries. The figures below show average tax rates on low, average and high wage levels in the European CMEA countries.

	Low	Average	High
Bulgaria	4·0	7·7	10·1
Czechoslovakia	8·8	10·9	15·0
German D.R.	—	10·7	18·5
Hungary	3·0	3·0	6·0
Poland	—	5·7	14·0
Rumania	0·8	8·7	13·2
USSR	—	6·2	9·3

Source. United Nations, ECE, *Incomes in Europe*, Geneva, 1967, Ch. 9, p. 5.

The degree of tax progression on incomes earned by free professions (writers, artists, doctors, lawyers, expert advisers) is about four to five times as great. The proportion of the income payable in tax rises to 48 per cent in Bulgaria, 50 per cent in Rumania,[11] 65 per cent in Poland, 69 per cent in the USSR, 70 per cent in Hungary, and 80 per cent in Czechoslovakia and the German D.R. The progression is even greater on incomes earned by privately operating craftsmen— up to 90 per cent.[12] Personal taxes are also imposed on peasants selling privately grown produce directly to consumers (or restaurants) and in addition on the private owners of buildings, vehicles and livestock and on the lessors of buildings, rooms and equipment. Personal taxes are considered to be temporary, a survival from capitalism for which there is no justification under communism, and the Communist Parties are committed to the abolition of these taxes in the long run.

d. *State Borrowings.* This form of receipts consists of State loans mostly raised internally, on a voluntary and compulsory basis but in each case repayable. The funds may come from the public, savings banks and enterprises. The titles issued to the creditors are either bonds or a type of lottery ticket for periods ranging from ten to twenty years. The former normally carry interest of 3–5 per cent p.a., whilst the latter are entitlements to lottery prizes drawn regularly. In

[11] Plans were recently announced to increase the degree of progression in Bulgaria and in Rumania.

[12] M. Weralski, *Zagadnienia systemu podatkowego w państwach socjalistycznych* (Problems of the Taxation System in Socialist Countries), Warsaw, PWE, 1965, p. 136.

some cases the titles may embody both elements of the reward. The bonds can be freely purchased and sold at savings banks. All Socialist countries, except Czechoslovakia and Rumania, have taken recourse to State borrowings. This source of funds was heavily relied upon in the early postwar period (especially in Hungary), but owing to the lack of popular support the floating of State loans has been greatly reduced since the mid-1950s.

The relative importance of the different forms of budgetary receipts, together with historical trends in each, is shown in the example of the Soviet budget in Fig. 12.

FIG. 12. *State Budgetary Receipts and Expenditure in the USSR in Selected Years*
(In value percentages)

Forms of receipts or expenditure	1933	1950	1960	1969 (est.)
Receipts				
Deductions from enterprise profits	7	10	24	36
Turnover taxes	59	56	41	32
Other payments by enterprises	16	19	26	23
Personal taxes	9	9	7	9
State borrowings	9	6	2	*n*
TOTAL	100	100	100	100
Expenditure				
Financing of material production	60	38	44	43
Sociocultural measures	15	28	34	38
Administration	4	3	2	1
Defence	—	20	13	13
Other purposes	21	11	7	5
TOTAL	100	100	100	100

est. = estimates.
n = negligible, less than 0·5 per cent of the total.

Sources. Based on: Central Statistical Office Attached to the Council of Ministers of the USSR, *Narodnoye khoziaistvo SSSR* (The National Economy of the USSR), Moscow, different years; *Izvestiya*, 11/12/1968, pp. 3–4.

C. BUDGETARY EXPENDITURE

The items of expenditure in a Socialist budget are arranged according to their role in the creation of national income. This contrasts with the budgetary expenditure in capitalist countries, concerned mostly with financing 'non-productive' (by Socialist standards) services (see Ch. 4 A). There is naturally a basic conflict in planning Socialist expenditure. On the one hand, there is the need to channel finance to the productive sector to maximize the rate of economic growth. On the other, the Socialist State prides itself on providing a wide range of sociocultural benefits to the masses. These two purposes absorb four-fifths of the expenditure. Fig. 12 provides an example of the main items of budgetary expenditure. We shall briefly examine these items.

a. *The Financing of Material Production.* About one-half of the expenditure is earmarked for productive purposes in the economy, the proportion ranging from 40 per cent in the USSR to 60 per cent in Rumania.[13] It provides all, or a part of, the finance for the centrally determined investments. The provision of finance for stocks and reserves of materials and of subsidies to the loss-incurring enterprises is also classified as productive expenditure. However, owing to the official drive to promote the self-financing of enterprises there is a tendency for the proportion of this item of expenditure to decline.

b. *The Sociocultural Programme.* This expenditure is associated with social consumption (Ch. 6 B). About one-third of the total expenditure is devoted to this purpose, the lowest proportion being usually recorded in the less-developed Socialist countries (Bulgaria and Rumania—about 25 per cent each) the highest in the more advanced ones (Czechoslovakia, the German D.R. and the USSR—nearly 40 per cent).[14] The specific purposes of this expenditure include social insurance, social security,[15] public health, housing, workers' holiday schemes, child welfare, youth camps, education, science and arts. The benefits are quite generous. For example, in the USSR old-age pensions are available at the age of sixty (males) and fifty-five (females). The amount of the pension received is a percentage of the wage or salary earned on retirement, and it varies from 50 per cent

[13] W. Karpiński, op. cit., p. 48.
[14] Ibid.
[15] *Social insurance* applies to employed persons, the scheme being financed by contributions paid by the employing enterprises and institutions (not by the insured) and administered generally by trade unions. *Social security* applies to those disabled by war or from birth; this scheme is financed by direct grants from the State budget and benefits are administered by special social security organs.

(in the case of the highest paid employees) to 100 per cent of the lowest paid workers. The actual amount received ranges from 30 to 120 rubles per month. The average pension is 60 per cent of the average national wage (compared with 20 per cent in the USA).[16]

FIG. 13. *Defence Expenditure in Socialist and Capitalist Countries in 1968*

Country	Defence expenditure:		
	Total in US $ million	As a percentage of GNP	Per head of population in US $
Socialist countries			
Bulgaria	228	2·9	27
Czechoslovakia	1,538	5·7	105
German D.R.	1,715	5·7	100
Hungary	370	2·9	36
Poland	1,830	4·8	57
Rumania	551	3.0	28
USSR	39,780	9·3	169
Yugoslavia	543	5·7	24
Capitalist countries			
Australia	1,293	4·8	107
Canada	1,589	2·5	77
France	6,104	5·3	121
F.R. of Germany	5,108	3·9	87
India	1,452	3·6	3
Japan	1,172	0·8	12
United Kingdom	5,438	5·3	98
United States	79,576	9·2	396

Source. Based on: *The Military Balance 1969–1970*, London, Institute for Strategic Studies, 1969, pp. 57–8. The Institute's permission to quote is gratefully acknowledged.

c. *Administration.* The expenditure on (public) administration, as distinct from the direct administration of producing enterprises, is essentially considered to be unproductive. Although it constitutes only 1–2 per cent of the total budgetary expenditure, there are determined efforts to promote its mechanization and automation wherever possible, to reduce the burden of this item.

[16] D. A. Allakhverdyan, op. cit., p. 259.

d. *Defence*. The proportion of the expenditure on defence ranges from 3 per cent in Hungary and 4 per cent in Bulgaria to 7 per cent in Czechoslovakia and 13 per cent in the USSR. These percentages are of little use for making comparisons with capitalist countries because the scope of the budget differs under each system. A more satisfactory approach is to bring the production capacities of the two types of countries to a common basis. This is done in Fig. 13, where the size of defence expenditure is given as percentages of GNP and *per capita*. It may be concluded from these figures that there is not much difference in these respects between Socialist and capitalist countries.

e. *Other Expenditure*. This heading covers miscellaneous types of expenditure, such as special emergency assistance out of reserve funds, loans or grants to other countries, the servicing and repayment of internal and external public debt, etc.

D. FINANCIAL CONTROL

Financial control, as understood in Socialist countries today, has two distinct although closely related meanings. In the broader sense it involves a flexible use of instruments of financial content (prices, interest rates, credits, depreciation allowances, taxes, deductions, subsidies) to guide the activities of enterprises and other entities towards socially desirable goals. This form of control has come to be known in the USSR as 'control by the ruble', and it is opposed to the administrative control by directives. This aspect of financial control is dealt with in Chs 3, 7 C, 9 and 10.

In the narrower sense, financial control implies a system of supervision and the enforcement of financial discipline in the sphere of public finance. It is in this sense that the question of financial control is discussed in the remaining part of this chapter. The problem of fiscal control is much greater under Socialism than under capitalism. In a Socialist economy, the scope of public finance is much greater. The budget directly influences the entire process of production and social relations, there is little private ownership and interest to protect property and, as Soviet experience has shown, anti-social elements are as rife today as they were fifty years ago.

In fact in the last decade Socialist countries have substantially tightened up control in response to two different types of development. First, contrary to the traditional Marxist dream, there appears to be a reawakening of the acquisitive instinct and an increase in economic crimes, following de-Stalinization and the greater role accorded to material incentives. Thus the increased number of cases of vandalism, embezzlement of public funds, illegal operations in gold, foreign exchange and bonds, bribery, etc., in the USSR led to the strengthening of legislation against 'social parasites' (1957–65) and 'property offenders' (1961–2), and the re-introduction of the death penalty (in 1961) for economic crimes (for the details of some notorious cases of economic crimes in the USSR see reference 7 at the end of this chapter).

Economic abuses are now the subject of systematic study in Socialist countries. For example, in Poland a specialized body has been established for the purpose—the Institute for the Study of Economic Crimes. The second development strengthening financial control is the rapid computerization of the Socialist economies as a step towards optimal planning. Computer centres are being established for the collection, processing and current control of data and of plan implementation, whereby irregularities can be speedily detected.

The exercise of financial control is guided by the following objectives:

(i) to ensure compliance with the production and financial plan in respect of quantity, structure and quality;

(ii) to prevent the accumulation of capital in socially undesirable hands—either private or socialized—and to ensure that the allocated funds are utilized;[17]

(iii) to ensure the economical use of resources and to reveal untapped reserves in the economy;

(iv) to determine the extent of deviations from the plan, their causes and remedies.

The machinery through which financial control is exercised, although in many respects similar to that in a typical capitalist country, has several distinctive Socialist features. The control processes are carried out in accordance with the Leninist principle of 'democratic centralism'. There is a hierarchical system, in which the top controlling body is responsible directly (or indirectly through the Council of Ministers, as in the USSR) to Parliament. At the same time the masses are also given encouragement and power to act as watchdogs and to choose committees and individuals to carry out formal inspections and checking.

Overall financial control is vested either in the special Ministry of Control (as in Czechoslovakia and Hungary) or in the State Control Commission (as in the German D.R., Poland and the USSR). The

---

[17] E.g. in Poland before appropriate measures were taken in 1960, many local budgets finished the financial year with a surplus of up to 90 per cent because local authorities just left the allocated funds unspent. See W. Karpiński, op. cit., p. 138.

executive function of control is mostly carried out by the Ministry of Finance, which has a specialized auditing network. The State Bank and other banks also perform important controlling functions. In addition to the external control, each government department, branch association, enterprise and institution has a distinct internal auditing system.

Paralleling the above set-up is the popular control. For example in Hungary there is the People's Central Control Commission, assisted by 232 regional People's Control Boards. The field work is carried out by 25,000 Social Comptrollers, of whom one-third is composed of workers and peasants.[18]

The process of financial control involves the examination of the correctness and regularity of accounts, the value and punctuality of payments, the size and purpose of expenditure, the costs of the targets realized, the legality of receipts and expenditure and above all the degree of compliance of the financial operations with the plan laid down. The pattern of control falls into three phases.

a. *Preliminary Control.* At this stage the draft financial plans of enterprises or the estimates of other organizations are examined and corrections are made where necessary. This scrutiny is considered valuable because it can prevent waste before it occurs.

b. *Current Financial Control.* This is mostly carried out by banks at the time of the financial transactions. The purpose of the control is to ensure that the implementation of the plan proceeds smoothly and the financial and economic processes are carried out on time.

c. *Retrospective Control.* This is carried out towards the end of the financial year, supplemented with quarterly and irregular checks. The aim is to verify the purpose and regularity of the operation involving finance by checking and analysing accounts and balances. Special attention is given at this stage to the measurement of stocks and the efficiency with which the plan has been implemented.

[18] A. Iwanka, *Kontrola finansowa w państwach socjalistycznych* (Financial Control in Socialist Countries), Warsaw, PWE, 1966, p. 112.

RECOMMENDED REFERENCES AVAILABLE IN ENGLISH

*1. Allakhverdyan, D. A. (ed.), *Soviet Financial System*, translated from the Russian, Moscow, Progress Publ., 1966.

2. Bird, R., 'The Possibility of Fiscal Harmonization in the Communist Bloc', *Public Finance/Finance Publique*, Vol. XIX, No. 3, 1964, pp. 201–24.

*3. Blass, B. and Fedorowicz, Z., 'The Role of the State Budget in the Intersectoral and Inter-divisional Distribution of National Income in the People's Republic of Poland', *Public Finance/Finance Publique*, Vol. XXIII, No. 1–2, 1968, pp. 106–23.

*4. Lidke, T., 'Rehabilitation of the Disabled in Poland', *Intern. Labour Rev.*, June 1968, pp. 571–84.

5. Musgrave, R. A., 'Tax Policy under Decentralized Socialism', *Public Finance/Finance Publique*, Vol. XXIII, No. 1–2, 1968, pp. 203–11.

6. Pryor, F. L., *Public Expenditures in Communist and Capitalist Nations*, London, Allen & Unwin, 1968.

7. Staff Study, 'Economic Crimes in the Soviet Union', *Journal of the International Commission of Jurists*, Geneva, Summer 1964, pp. 3–47.

8. United Nations, ECE, *Incomes in Postwar Europe*, Geneva, 1967, Chs 7–12.

* indicates contributions by writers from Socialist countries.

CHAPTER 12

Domestic Trade

A. THE STATUS AND ORGANIZATION OF TRADE

The importance attached to trade by the authorities in Socialist countries has never been great because it is considered that its contribution to material production is limited (see Ch. 4 A). Whilst transport, storage and packaging are accepted as a continuation of production, the processes of selling goods to wholesale and retail organizations and to final users, keeping records and handling payment settlements are regarded as non-productive. In other words, only the former add to the value of the products, whilst the latter merely involve changes in ownership.[1]

Consequently, compared with capitalist countries, the trade network and services are poorly developed. The average pay of the personnel in trade is about 15 per cent below the national average (see Fig. 9, p. 107). Trade is accorded inferior treatment in the allocation of social amenities, housing, cost-free holidays, etc.[2] The purpose is not only to save on resources, but also to attract superior labour to priority industries. The social status of trade as an occupation is low. According to a study carried out in Poland, on a scale divided into 29 occupations, trade ranked as 26; only unskilled builders' labourers, charwomen and unskilled agricultural labourers were ranked lower.[3]

Trade margins are usually less than 10 per cent of the retail price, compared with about 30 per cent common in the West. The proportion of investment channelled to trade is 2–4 per cent, whilst the proportion in Western countries ranges from 8 to 20 per cent.[4] Even

[1] B. Minc, *Ekonomia polityczna socjalizmu* (The Political Economy of Socialism), Warsaw, Polish Academy of Sciences, PWN, 1961, p. 340.
[2] A. Wakar (ed.), *Teoria handlu socjalistycznego* (Theory of Socialist Trade), Warsaw, PWN, 1966, pp. 206, 218–20.
[3] Ibid., pp. 199–200.
[4] V. Kobik *et al.*, ('Action Programme for Domestic Trade'), *Noviny Vnitrniho Obchodu* (Domestic Trade News), Prague, 26/4/1968, Supplement (an English translation can be found in: US Dept. of Commerce, Joint Publications Research Service, *Translations on Eastern Europe: Economic and Industrial Affairs*, 7/6/1968, p. 14). *Życie gospodarcze*, 18/11/1968, p. 9.

in Czechoslovakia, commercially the most developed Socialist country, the floor space per 1,000 residents is less than 200 square metres, which contrasts with the average of over 370 sq.m. in Western Europe.[5] The proportion of the working population employed in trade in Socialist countries is only about 6 per cent, compared with 10–15 per cent in the West.[6]

Retail shops are relatively few and understaffed, the morale of the personnel is low and the staff turnover and absenteeism are high. For example in Poland, over the period 1964–7, one-half of the personnel employed in State trade was changed and, what is more disquietening, retail shops had to be closed on the average for twenty-eight *working* days a year.[7] One has to visit Eastern Europe to believe how small is the range of goods and how poor the service. It is not surprising therefore that, as Socialist economists like to point out with pride, the costs of distribution under Socialism are low. Thus in the USSR retailing costs represent about 6 per cent of the value of trade turnover, whilst in the F.R. of Germany, in the UK and the USA the proportions range from 22 to 33 per cent.[8]

Socialist domestic trade is almost exclusively concerned with consumer goods. Its sphere of operation is limited to the purchases of such goods from industry, agriculture and foreign trade corporations, and sales to and through shops and to the establishments of collective feeding (restaurants, factory canteens, communal kitchens, etc.). In each country there is a separate Ministry of Internal Trade responsible for the planning and co-ordination of domestic trade.[9] It is assisted by regional trade associations, and these are usually further subdivided into specialized urban and rural distributing centres. Centrally controlled Inspection Squads, and local trade unions, consumer protection societies and housewives' associations participate in the supervision of retail shops, but in the past their work did not produce much improvement in service.

Socialist trading activities are based on the social ownership of the means of production. Supplies are obtained mostly from socialized entities, and trading enterprises themselves are State or co-operatively owned. All wholesale trade is socialized, but a small proportion of retail trade is still in private hands.[10] As with other branches of the

[5] V. Kobik, op. cit., pp. 25–6.

[6] Ibid.; United Nations, ECE, *Incomes in Postwar Europe*, Geneva, 1967, Ch. 8, p. 53; International Labour Organization, *Year Book of Labour Statistics 1967*, Geneva, pp. 41–135, 142–239.

[7] *Życie gosp.*, 15/9/1968, p. 6.

[8] B. Minc, op. cit., pp. 346–7.

[9] In Albania the Ministry of Commerce handles both domestic and foreign trade.

[10] Even in Poland, only 8 per cent of retail shops (handling 1 per cent of total retail sales by value) is privately owned. *Życie gosp.*, 23/3/1969, p. 9.

economy, trade is integrated into the general economic plan. The overall trade network, investment, finance (including consumer credit), trade margins, employment, training and wage scales are all centrally determined or regulated.

B. THE RELATION BETWEEN PRODUCTION AND DISTRIBUTION

Trade provides a link between production and consumption. But the role of this link in the Socialist economy is different from that in a market economy because in the former both production and consumption are centrally planned. In consequence, trade is not necessarily an effective transmitter of consumers' preferences to producing enterprises, and in turn it cannot be used by such enterprises to market merely the commodities which are convenient or profitable to them.

It does not mean that trading enterprises enjoy independence. On the one hand they are used by the central authorities to implement the predetermined consumption plan. On the other, should there occur discrepancies between production and consumption in the course of plan fulfilment, the trade network is used to assist in adapting *the latter to the former*.

The insulation of consumption does not have to be achieved by directives. It can be ensured by manipulating turnover taxes, whereby retail and producers' prices can move independently of each other. Thus if the demand for a particular product increases, the authorities increase retail prices but the increase is not necessarily reflected in higher prices paid to producers or higher trade margins to trading enterprises, but absorbed by the State in the form of a higher turnover tax. As the profitability of the producing enterprises is not affected, there is no responsiveness of production to consumption, and yet equilibrium in the consumer goods market is preserved. If planners decide to increase the consumption of a particular article, its retail price is reduced and its producers' price increased, whilst the turnover tax is diminished.

Whilst the insulation of consumption from production can be justified in the earlier stages of Socialist industrialization, its disadvantages have become patent enough to economists and political leaders for many years now. This system led in the past to what is known as 'fetishism of production', when producers were only interested in fulfilling quantitative targets, irrespective of the demand for such goods. The effect was piling-up stocks of unsaleable goods existing side by side with shortages of other goods, especially of higher quality.[11]

In the Socialist economy, the power to determine production cannot be unreservedly handed over to the consumer (see Ch. 6 D). But it is now widely agreed that within the broadly planned framework, the structure of production in the consumer goods sector (Department II) should correspond to consumers' preferences. To ensure this, conditions would have to be created to enable and induce the trade network to act as an effective transmitter of the consumers' needs and changing tastes, and the producing enterprises to respond accordingly. The reforms initiated in Socialist countries since the early 1960s (since the early 1950s in Yugoslavia) represent several steps in this direction.

There is a tendency for a higher share of investment to be allocated to trading enterprises, for an improvement in the conditions of work for the personnel and for greater importance to be attached to commercial training. The acceptance of profit as the criterion of enterprise success, and as a basis for material incentives to the staff personnel, together with flexible and differentiated trade margins, combine the interest of the trading enterprises, the consumers and society.

As a rule, trading enterprises now have the power to refuse to accept goods not corresponding to the specifications and quality indicated in the contract. Improved systems of penalties have been introduced whereby producing enterprises and transport agencies are fined for the non-fulfilment of contracts, delays and negligence.[12]

As a result of decentralization and an increased capacity for self-financing, producing enterprises have acquired a greater ability and inclination to produce what the consumer wants. Quantitative fulfilment (or over-fulfilment) of targets has been largely discarded in favour of output actually sold. Enterprises now have their own 'development fund' providing them with some scope for independent

[11] The amount of waste was particularly widespread in the USSR in the 1930s after the 1930 payments reform. According to that system, enterprises making deliveries of goods according to the plan were *automatically* entitled to receive payment from the State Bank, irrespective of the suitability or quality of the goods. But even in Czechoslovakia, usually regarded as the most advanced Socialist country industrially, in 1968, 15 per cent of the goods examined under the State testing scheme was obsolete, 73 per cent was of only average quality, and only 12 per cent was up to world standards (reported in *East Europe*, April 1969, p. 45).

[12] For an example of a scale of penalties, see the Soviet schedule effective since 1/1/1968: ('Decree on the Material Responsibilities of Enterprises'), *Ekonomicheskaya gazeta*, No. 47, Nov. 1967, pp. 3–4 (an English translation can be found in: US Dept. of Commerce, JPRS, *USSR International Economic Relations*, 22/12/1967, pp. 30–40).

decisions to respond, within limits, to current and anticipated market demand.

C. SELLER'S AND BUYER'S MARKETS

In contrast to capitalist countries, Socialist economies have been continuously saddled with seller's markets noted for an excess of aggregate demand over supply of consumer goods at the official prices, and the consequent privileged and dominant position of producers and distributors over consumers. There are many deep-seated reasons for this state of affairs on both the supply and demand sides.

Insufficient supply can be explained by: (i) planning for high investment at the expense of current consumption to maintain high rates of economic growth; (ii) balancing with unduly low (or no) reserves; (iii) strictly controlled imports and the priorities given to exports; (iv) irregularities in the supply of inputs ('unfulfilled targets'); (v) official reluctance to commit more resources to distribution. On the demand side we may mention such contributory causes as the lack of sufficient correlation between the production of consumer goods and the growth of the wage fund and social consumption, changing tastes and the official desire to maintain price stability. Queues, low quality and a small range of goods and indifferent or rude service in shops are still familiar features that hit even a recent visitor to Eastern Europe.

There is still rationing of housing, cars and many other consumer durables and of foreign travel (especially to capitalist countries) in the form of long waiting lists. But even many small items of domestic use are still in insufficient supply. According to a recent investigation, the proportions of unsatisfied demand for selected items in Poland in 1966 were as follows: sugar tongs: 85 per cent, bath soap holders: 83 per cent, cabbage shredders: 78 per cent, soup cups: 58 per cent, baking tins: 52 per cent, egg spoons: 50 per cent, strainers: 50 per cent, nail scissors: 40 per cent, and so on.[13]

Whilst sellers' markets were reluctantly tolerated in the past as a necessary sacrifice during the periods of post-war reconstruction and accelerated industrialization, their liabilities are now recognized not only by consumers but also by many economic writers, administrators and political leaders. Buyer's markets and high rates of economic development are not necessarily mutually exclusive. In fact the waste produced by seller's markets in some respects slows down growth. 'The analysis of the conditions and ways of developing buyer's markets in a Socialist economy', concluded a Polish economist,

[13] *Życie gosp.*, 22/1/1967, p. 1.

'inspires optimism. There are no significant barriers to the creation and operation of such a mechanism. The difficulties seen are of a subjective nature.'[14] The same economist also pointed out significantly that, 'In a Socialist economy a buyer's market would remove the basic contradiction between the quantitative maximization of the National Product and the optimum utilization of resources from the standpoint of social benefit.'[15]

There is no need to fear that buyer's markets will produce adverse social contrasts, because under Socialism income disparities are not large. Some Socialist economists, such as W. Brus (of Poland), E. Liberman (of the USSR) and Ota Šik (of Czechoslovakia) advocate the so-called 'shallow buyer's markets', with only a slight excess of supply over demand to stimulate improvements in the structure of production and the quality of commercial service.[16]

The need of buyer's markets is paralleled by an improved capacity of the more developed Socialist economies to evolve such markets for consumer goods. The high level of investment in the past has laid down foundations for a solid industrial base which is starting to yield widespread benefits now. Productivity is rising rapidly and the Socialist leadership is now more inclined to respond to the public pressure for better living. There has been a trend towards increasing the proportion of national income for current consumption, and the discrepancy between the rates of growth of the means of production and the means of consumption has tended to decline (see Ch. 6 A, p. 91).

The production of many consumer durables has been substantially increased in recent years and is likely to rise faster in the future. The growing stocks of some consumer goods indicate that shortages are not as widespread as they used to be.[17] Buyer's markets are developing, especially in the private sector which is being rejuvenated, and where the State sector is open to competition from small private producers, as in fruit and vegetable growing and preparation, catering, fashion and children's footwear, various handicrafts, clothing, haberdashery, sports goods, and cosmetics. The authorities

---

[14] W. Wilczyński, *Rachunek ekonomiczny a mechanizm rynkowy* (Economic Accounting and the Market Mechanism), Warsaw, PWE, 1965, p. 200.

[15] Ibid., p. 29.

[16] E.g., W. Brus, *Ogólne problemy funkcjonowania gospodarki socjalistycznej* (General Problems of the Functioning of the Socialist Economy), Warsaw, PWN, 1961, p. 263.

[17] However, these stocks are not necessarily indicative of buyers' markets, as a large proportion of such goods have proved unsaleable—a legacy of poor correlation between the structure of supply and consumers' preferences. This problem, as arising in the more developed Socialist countries, is analysed in: T. Wojciechowski, ('Problems of Stocks Management'), *Gospodarka planowa*, 1/1968, pp. 13–17.

appear to accept changes in fashions as legitimate consumer needs because they have 'a deep sociological and psychological justification'.[18] The traditional divorce of production from distribution, which resulted in the enterprises being exclusively interested in producing large quantities and not necessarily in the suitability of the articles is now being replaced with closer links between industry, trade and consumers (Part B of this chapter).

These encouraging developments are paralleled by a growing liberalization of foreign trade in consumer goods. The former tight monopoly of imports held by the foreign trade corporations is being relaxed so that the right of imports is being extended to industrial enterprises, co-operatives and internal trading enterprises. Licences are freely granted for exchanges of consumer goods not involving foreign exchange expenditure, especially with other Socialist countries. A substantial increase of exchanges of industrial consumer goods has taken place in recent years amongst CMEA countries and a further expansion in the near future is a certainty. The authorities are also responding to the demands by local consumers and to the pressure from capitalist countries to admit more and more quality consumer goods.

Other recent developments strengthening the cause of buyer's markets may be briefly stated. Official blessing and active encouragement is given to regional co-operative councils, housewives' associations and consumer advisory committees which champion the cause of the consumer.[19] The daily and periodical press in many cases now proves to be an effective medium for publicizing shortages, abuses by enterprises and even official incompetence, as a result of which deficiencies are often rectified. Besides, the authorities are attaching increasing importance to market research and advertising, which we shall consider next.

D. MARKET RESEARCH AND ADVERTISING

The orthodox view of market research and advertising under Socialism could be reduced to disinterest and indeed contempt. These

[18] M. Pohorille (ed.), *Ekonomia polityczna socjalizmu* (The Political Economy of Socialism), Warsaw, PWE, 1968, p. 82.

[19] E.g. already in 1962 in Czechoslovakia there were over 136,000 co-operative workers organized in 41,743 committees to scrutinize the working standards affecting consumers in shops, bars, butchers' shops and bakeries, and they carried out over 114,300 investigations in that year. In Poland, there is a network of quality control centres and branch commissions with about 2,300 quality experts; in 1967 these experts were called upon to examine goods in over 24,000 cases, as a result of which prices of inferior items had to be reduced to purchasers to the value of 180 m. złotys and goods valued at 380 m. złotys were returned to the

practices were regarded as hallmarks of the higher stages of capitalism, noted for an insufficiency of effective demand and for fierce struggles amongst greedy monopolies for markets. It was generally accepted that under central planning both production and distribution are systematically planned, there is no shortage of demand and thus there is no need, or scope, for demand creation. Market research and advertising not only represent social waste of resources, but could in fact lead to unplanned changes in consumer demand and the disruption of the overall economic plan.

This attitude, although warranted in the early stages of the industrialization drive, has been largely discarded in the last decade. It is now generally agreed that both market research and advertising can perform useful functions to planners, producing and trading enterprises and to consumers. The importance being attached to marketing is indicated by the dozen or more major conferences held under the auspices of CMEA in the latter 1960s on such problems as consumption models, methods of demand analysis, the development of buyer's markets, stocks and warehousing, sales promotion and economic forecasting and prognoses. In 1965 the CMEA countries held an advertising exhibition in Warsaw and another was staged in Moscow in 1968. The authorities have created or revitalized such bodies as market research institutes, commodity study associations, standards commissions and testing (including tasting) centres.[20]

It is widely recognized that market analysis is indispensable in the higher stages of Socialist development, characterized by decentralized decision-making and a greater concern for the consumers' preferences. The planning of consumption models can be greatly improved if they are based on systematic studies of the factors affecting consumers' preferences. The greater independence of decision-making at the operational level, the profit criterion and the developing buyer's markets are placing Socialist producing and trading enterprises in a similar position with regard to sales promotion as the firms in capitalist countries.

'A rare book about the despicable methods of foreign intelligence agents. Unforgettable scenes from the life of an exotic Oriental land. Spies wear masks. Foul play.'[21] This is not a case of bourgeois trickery to cheat a poor unsuspecting reader, but an advertisement by a Soviet bookshop, quoted in the official organ of the Supreme

producing enterprises. See A. Wakar, op. cit., p. 242; P. Sztuk, ('Trade and the Quality of Goods'), *Życie gosp.*, 7/4/1968, p. 6.

[20] For examples of studies on the income elasticity of demand carried out in Czechoslovakia, the German D.R., Hungary and Poland see *Incomes in Postwar Europe*, op. cit., Ch. 10, esp. pp. 20–2.

[21] *Izvestiya*, 18/3/1965, p. 3.

Soviet in 1965 as a good example of sound sales promotion. Which way the wind was blowing was further indicated by the advice tendered by the organ of the Communist Party of the Soviet Union that, 'Advertising is a broad rewarding field of work for the poet, the writer and the artist.'[22]

Since that time great strides have been made in advertising. In addition to window dressing and merchandise displays, advertisements are now common in the press, on radio and television, in cinemas and through the medium of attractive packaging and neon signs. Advertising is considered to be rendering two important social functions. Firstly, informative advertising enables the consumer to make a more rational choice in spending his income. Secondly, the judicious use of persuasive advertising is a tool of 'consumer education' and 'consumption steering', whereby on the one hand consumers' preferences can be adapted to socially desirable planned patterns, and on the other unwanted stocks of goods can be easily disposed of.[23] It can be seen that in this respect, as a Socialist economist pointed out, 'the utilization of advertising has incomparably greater significance in a planned than in a capitalist economy'.[24]

Further evidence of the new approach to advertising is provided by the fact that foreign, including capitalist, firms are now allowed to advertise in Socialist countries in the daily press, in magazines, technical journals, trade directories and in some countries even on radio and television.[25] The condition of acceptance is that it must be 'informative and intelligent' rather than demand-creating, and it is mostly limited to producer goods. A very effective means of foreign advertising is provided by trade fairs and exhibitions which have become of inestimable value in promoting East–West trade (see Ch. 14 A).

However, it must be realized that market research and advertising under Socialism cannot be left to the anonymous market forces. They are carried out on a planned and centrally co-ordinated basis to maximize social, not private or merely microeconomic, benefit. They are used as instruments for consumption steering and for promoting market equilibrium consistent with social production goals. As to advertising, it can never become so lavish and persuasive or so deceitful and wasteful as under capitalism.

[22] *Pravda*, 4/5/1965, p. 2.

[23] A. Wakar, op. cit., p. 75.

[24] K. Białecki, ('Application of Mass Advertising in the Socialist Economy'), *Gospodarka planowa*, 5/1966, p. 46.

[25] E.g. as reported in 1968, the rates for foreign advertisers on Soviet radio were $600 and on television $2,000 per minute (*American Review of East–West Trade*, 6/1968, p. 91).

RECOMMENDED REFERENCES AVAILABLE IN ENGLISH

*1. Fenyo, I., 'The New System of Management in Hungarian Home Trade', *Acta Oeconomica*, Vol. 2, No. 1–2, 1967, pp. 93–103.

*2. Fogaras-Zala, Julia, 'The Stock Problem in Hungary', *Review of Income and Wealth*, Dec. 1968, pp. 403–10.

3. Goldman, M. I., *Soviet Marketing: Distribution in a Controlled Economy*, New York, Free Press of Glencoe, 1963; and his 'Trade and the Consumer', *Survey*, July 1967, pp. 129–42.

*4. Kodet, Z., 'Monopoly and Competition in a Socialist Economy', *Czechosl. Econ. Papers*, No. 6, 1966, pp. 31–44.

*5. Kürthy, P., 'Market Research—Marketing', *Soviet and Eastern Europ. For. Trade*, July–Aug. 1967, pp. 48–67.

*6. Szabo, L., 'Scientific Research into the Problems of Home Trade'. *Acta Oeconomica*, Vol. 3, No. 3, 1968, pp. 342–6.

*7. Varga, S., 'The Importance of Market Research in Socialism', *Øst Økonomie*, Oslo, Dec. 1962, pp. 233–43.

8. Vishniak, M., 'Since the October Revolution: A Chronicle of Unredeemed Promises', *Studies on the Soviet Union*, Vol. VI, No. 3, 1967. pp. 1–10.

* indicates contributions by writers from Socialist countries.

CHAPTER 13

Foreign Trade

A. THE ROLE AND ORGANIZATION OF FOREIGN TRADE

Up to Stalin's death (1953) the foreign trade of Socialist countries was dominated by national autarkic ambitions.[1] This attitude was conditioned by such factors as the wide fluctuations in capitalist markets to which these countries had been exposed under pre-communist regimes, the hostility of the Western countries (including the strategic embargo initiated in 1948), and the desire for industrialization to achieve a balanced economic structure in traditionally agricultural countries. The newly established Socialist States uncritically adopted the Soviet model of self-sufficiency. Under these conditions trade was essentially regarded as a necessary evil to facilitate the industrialization programme—a means of obtaining machinery and other equipment, whilst exports were looked upon as a sacrifice to pay for such imports.

Although these sentiments are still present, the ideal of autarky has been gradually forsaken officially since the mid-1950s. Even the USSR, which has the greatest potential of all countries in the world for self-sufficiency, has been increasingly turning to foreign trade. Her interest has been nourished partly by political motives, but trade is also recognized now as an important means of economizing resources through international specialization and a channel for the incorporation of the latest technological achievements in the West into her otherwise unsophisticated industrial structure.

The economic need for trade has been, of course, felt much more strongly by other Socialist countries which have a narrow raw material base and small domestic markets. There is probably no other more nationalistically minded Socialist country than Rumania, but a Rumanian expert on international trade recently concluded: '. . . foreign trade appears to us as an indispensable avenue for promoting technological progress, which in turn constitutes an organic factor for the development of international exchanges and economic

---

[1] With the exception of Yugoslavia, which by necessity (upon her expulsion from Cominform in 1948) had to turn to capitalist countries for trade and aid.

174

co-operation'.[2] The virtual cessation of the Cold War since 1963 and the recent economic reforms have greatly enhanced the role of foreign trade in Socialist countries.

The growing interest of the European Socialist countries in foreign trade is indicated by their increased share in world trade, which is higher today, 10 per cent, than it was in 1953, viz. 8 per cent (see Fig. 14, p. 178). However, viewing their trade in the world scene, the small Socialist participation is conspicuous even today. Although these countries represent nearly 20 per cent of world area, and they claim 31 per cent of the world's industrial output,[3] they contribute only one-tenth of world trade. But, contrary to what is often said in the West, this low participation is not due to Socialism. These countries' share in world trade was even lower before World War II—only about 7 per cent.

The institutional framework in foreign trade is vastly different from that in a typical capitalist economy.[4] In each Socialist country (Yugoslavia excepted[5]), there is a *State foreign trade monopoly* (to the exclusion of private traders) 'made necessary by the political nature of international exchanges and by the specific needs of the Socialist economy'.[6] The State monopoly is exercised, as a rule, through a separate ministry of foreign trade.[7]

The actual foreign trade activities are, exclusively or mostly, carried on by specialized *foreign trade corporations*. Their number varies from country to country—from 7 in Albania and 20 in Rumania to about 40 in Hungary, Poland and the USSR. Each corporation usually has the exclusive right to export and/or import a defined class of goods. It is normally a large organization, and as such it can be in a strong bargaining position in dealing with small un-

[2] I. Kun, ('Foreign Trade and Technical Progress'), *Probleme economice*, 8/1967, p. 34.

[3] *Ekonomicheskaya gazeta*, No. 12, March 1968, p. 41.

[4] But State trading was an important feature of the developed capitalist countries' trade during World War II and in the early postwar period, whilst a number of developing countries have reorganized their trade partly or wholly along Socialist lines. For details see, M. Quin, 'State Trading in Western Europe', *Law and Contemporary Problems*, Summer 1959, pp. 388–419; UNCTAD, *State Trading in Countries of the ECAFE Region*, Doc. E/CONF. 46/32, Geneva, 1964; J. Panglaykim and I. Palmer, *State Trading Corporations in Developing Countries*, Rotterdam U.P., 1968.

[5] The State monopoly has been discontinued in Yugoslavia since 1952. There are now several hundred State, co-operative and private entities freely engaging in foreign trade.

[6] A. Wakar, *Handel zagraniczny w gospodarce socjalistycznej* (Foreign Trade in the Socialist Economy), Warsaw, PWN, 1968, p. 260.

[7] In Albania the Ministry of Commerce is responsible for both foreign and domestic trade, whilst in Yugoslavia the overall co-ordination of external trade is in the hands of the Federal Secretariat for Foreign Trade.

organized capitalist traders. For example, the annual value of trade handled by average foreign trade corporations in the USSR, Czechoslovakia and Poland exceeds $550 m., $200 m. and $150 m. respectively.[8]

The economic reforms since the early 1960s (since 1952 and again since 1965 in Yugoslavia) have introduced some elements of decentralization. The corporations have been granted greater independence, and profit (where practicable, in terms of foreign exchange) has been accepted as the main criterion of their performance and the basis for bonuses for the personnel.

Of greater consequence is the fact that branch (or industrial or economic) associations, selected enterprises (especially those producing for export), and even some domestic trading enterprises have been granted the right to direct dealings in foreign markets.[9] This reorganization has gone furthest in Bulgaria, Rumania and, of course, in Yugoslavia, but it has hardly touched the Soviet foreign trade set-up.[10] In Bulgaria, only one-half of imports is now handled by the foreign trade corporations, whilst in Yugoslavia since the beginning of 1967 any enterprise has had complete freedom of export.[11]

As a result of this growing trend for combining production and trade, the former rigid central control by the ministries of foreign trade has been relaxed, and it is now shared with production ministries and branch associations. The tendency is to reserve to the ministry of foreign trade only the overall co-ordination of exports and imports in accordance with the economic plan.

In addition to the entities discussed above, in each Socialist country there is a chamber of commerce and one (or more) foreign trade arbitration commission. In contrast to capitalist countries, Socialist chambers of commerce are concerned with foreign trade only; the Soviet and Yugoslav chambers are exceptions in so far as they handle domestic trade as well. The foreign trade arbitration commission is attached to its national chamber of commerce, and its responsibility is limited to settling disputes in foreign trade only.[12]

[8] Based on, IMF and IBRD, *Direction of Trade*, June 1968, p. 178, and August 1968, pp. 19, 102.

[9] Examples: in Bulgaria: *Bulgarsko Pivo* (production, export and import of beer); in Czechoslovakia: *Škoda* (production and export of cars); in the German D.R.: *DIA Technocommerz* (domestic and foreign trade in power plants, engines and industrial fittings); in Hungary: *Medicor* (production and export of pharmaceuticals); in Poland: *Befama* (production and export of machinery).

[10] But in 1967 Export Councils were established to co-ordinate the activities of the foreign trade corporations with those of the enterprises producing for export, and the right of direct export by producing enterprises is strongly advocated.

[11] *Gospodarka planowa*, 7/1968, p. 60.

[12] In Yugoslavia the Foreign Trade Arbitration Board (established in 1946) was abolished in 1954 to be replaced by Economic Courts (remodelled in 1958).

The Socialist system differs from that prevailing in capitalist countries, where foreign trade disputes are handled by ordinary courts, or by *ad hoc* arbitration tribunals, or by the International Court of Arbitration attached to the International Chamber of Commerce in Paris.

B. REGIONAL DISTRIBUTION AND TRENDS

The regional distribution of the Socialist countries' foreign trade is presented in a historical setting in Fig. 14. As has already been observed, the share of these countries in world trade has never been large; well below what one would expect from their area and industrial output (p. 207). However, these countries cannot be accused of autarkic tendencies after the Korean War, since when the value of their trade has been rising faster (on the average 9 per cent p.a. over the period 1953–68) than that of the capitalist world (7 per cent p.a.).[13]

As far as intra-trade amongst the Socialist countries is concerned, it is possible to distinguish two stages since World War II. Up to 1954 there was a gradual diversion of trade into intra-Socialist channels, so that in 1953 over two-thirds of their foreign trade was within the group. Common ideology, geographical proximity and the difficulty of earning foreign exchange in capitalist countries have favoured mutual trade. Although this drive was already obvious in the early postwar years, it was further accelerated by the Western strategic embargo (after 1947), the formation of the Council for Mutual Economic Assistance (1949) and the Korean War (1950–3).

Since that time, although the absolute value of intra-trade has been well maintained, its proportion of total trade has tended to decline to a little over 60 per cent. On the one hand, the solidarity of the group has been weakening owing to increasing political–national differences and the relaxed Soviet grip over the satellite countries. On the other, for economic as well as for political reasons, trade with capitalist countries has become more attractive (for further details, see Ch. 14 C, D).

The group's trade with other Socialist countries[14] has never been

[13] Based on United Nations sources: *Yearbook of International Trade Statistics* and *Monthly Bulletin of Statistics*.

[14] I.e. with the Asian Socialist countries (China, the D.P.R. of Korea, Mongolia and the D.R. of Vietnam). The share of the European Socialist countries in Yugoslavia's trade fell from 50 per cent in 1947 to practically nil in the next five years, then it recovered to 37 per cent in 1965, but subsequently fell to 31 per cent in 1968. The group's share in Cuba's trade increased from less than 2 per cent in 1959 to about 60 per cent in 1968. Based on: *Direction of Trade*, and the author's estimates.

large, except during the Korean War when the proportion reached was 14 per cent. However, the Sino-Soviet dispute has adversely affected the trade between the two groups since the early 1960s so that

FIG. 14. *Regional Distribution of the European Socialist Countries' Foreign Trade,*[1] *1938–68*

Year	Total value (at current prices)		Intra foreign trade	Trade with the Asian Socialist countries[2]	Trade with Western countries[3]	Trade with developing countries[4]
	In US $m.	*As a percentage of world trade*	*As a percentage of the European Socialist countries' total foreign trade*[5]			
1938	3,010	6	13	2	74	10
1948	6,050	5	46	3	40	8
1953	12,670	8	68	14	15	3
1960	25,890	10	60	11	20	10
1961	27,930	10	64	6	19	10
1962	30,990	11	66	5	19	9
1963	33,330	11	66	4	19	10
1964	36,020	11	66	3	21	9
1965	38,740	10	64	3	21	10
1966	40,570	10	62	3	24	10
1967	43,960	10	62	3	23	10
1968	47,980	10	63	3	23	9

[1] The countries included: Albania, Bulgaria, Czechoslovakia, the German D.R., Hungary, Poland, Rumania, the USSR. Yugoslavia is excluded because her trade has followed different trends; in accordance with the UN classification, she is treated as part of developed countries. Similarly, Cuba is treated here as a developing country throughout the period.

[2] China, Mongolia, D.P.R. of Korea, D.R. of Vietnam.

[3] North America, Western Europe (including Yugoslavia), Japan, Australia, New Zealand, South Africa.

[4] Other than Socialist and Western countries, but Cuba is included.

[5] The total foreign trade figure includes trade of unknown destination, so that the four component percentage figures do not necessarily add up to 100.

Source. Based on United Nations sources: *Yearbook of International Trade Statistics* and *Monthly Bulletin of Statistics.*

the share of the European Socialist countries' trade now claimed by the Asian group has been reduced to 3 per cent.

Although before World War II the present developed capitalist countries claimed three-quarters of the Socialist group's trade, the share has been drastically reduced since the war. The proportion declined to 15 per cent during the Korean War, largely on the initiative of the Co-Com and other co-operating countries, through the administration of strategic export controls.[15] Since the Korean War the role of Western countries has been steadily increasing and they now claim one-quarter of the group's total trade. Both sides have displayed increasing interest in expanding East–West trade. Socialist countries have found that as they reach the higher stages of economic development their need of trade with the highly industrialized countries of the West does not diminish, but in fact increases. They want the sophisticated instruments, machinery and even complete plants containing advanced technology. Moreover, these countries have found it necessary to import large quantities of grains.

Trade with developing countries slumped to insignificance during the Korean War, but since then it has been expanding most remarkably. On the one hand, in the East–West competition, the uncommitted nations of the Third World appeared (to the USSR in particular) an obvious sphere of ideological and political influence. On the other, the growing industrialization in Socialist countries has been creating an increasing need for imports of raw materials and creating the capacity for the export of manufactures.

C. PRICES, EXCHANGE RATES AND TARIFFS

1. PRICES

In dealing with capitalist traders, Socialist countries trade, as a rule, at the prices prevailing in world (capitalist) markets. The actual prices paid or received may depart from current levels in the case of long-term contracts, when prices may be agreed upon in advance, irrespective of subsequent changes. On the whole, there is evidence to suggest that Socialist countries often receive lower than world prices on their exports to capitalist nations (owing to various forms of dis-

---

[15] Co-Com countries are the fifteen capitalist nations (Belgium, Canada, Denmark, France, the F.R. of Germany, Greece, Italy, Japan, Luxemburg, the Netherlands, Norway, Portugal, Turkey, the UK and the USA) observing the embargo on strategic exports to Socialist countries, and which have representatives on the Co-ordinating Committee (based in Paris), which compiles lists of embargoed items. The Co-ordinating Committee (Co-Com) is a working committee of the Consultative Group (established in 1949) which consists of the ambassadors of the member countries.

crimination encountered and to poor marketing techniques), whilst on very large purchases (typical of the foreign trade corporations) they may pay lower than world prices.

As was shown in Ch. 9, Socialist countries have not so far worked out a practical system for rational price determination. The criteria for pricing differ in each country, and they may change from time to time. Consequently, even in trade amongst themselves these countries have found it necessary to use capitalist prices. In practice, the CMEA countries adopt the average prices prevailing during a selected period, and make various adjustments for transport costs and other conditions peculiar to the region.[16] For example, the prices used over the period 1966–70 were based on the average world market prices which prevailed during 1960–4, and for the 1971–5 plan period a new basis is envisaged.

Traditionally, there has been an almost complete insulation of domestic from foreign prices. This policy has been conditioned by practical considerations to prevent disruptive fluctuations originating from foreign, particularly capitalist, countries. Thus foreign trade corporations have normally paid domestic wholesale prices to the enterprises producing for export, irrespective of the prices received in foreign markets. At the same time, imported goods have been sold in the domestic market at the prices of the nearest domestically produced substitutes, irrespective of the prices paid in foreign markets.

Although this insulation in essence still prevails in most Socialist countries, there has been a growing tendency to link domestic with foreign prices, especially in the sphere of internationally traded goods. This has been almost completely achieved in Yugoslavia and to a considerable extent in Czechoslovakia and Hungary. In the remaining countries, the enterprises producing for export now receive prices from the foreign trade corporations in accordance with those actually obtained in foreign markets. Bonuses to the personnel engaged in foreign trade are no longer based on accounting 'profits' arising out of the domestic pricing anomalies, but on net foreign exchange earned or saved.

---

[16] These calculations and adjustments are carried out by the CMEA Permanent Commission for Foreign Trade (established in 1956). Capitalist prices are 'cleansed' of fluctuations and monopolistic elements. To the price so established, one-half of the transport costs between the principal world market and the Socialist country in question is added (the other half is meant to be borne by the Socialist exporter). The mark-up on behalf of other costs ranges from 5 per cent (on raw materials) to 60 per cent or more (on complete plants) of the starting price. See F. Bartha, ('Trends in the Development of Socialist Foreign Trade Prices'), *Külkereskedelem*, 9/1967, pp. 271–4.

2. EXCHANGE RATES

In market economies, exchange rates normally relate domestic to foreign prices, and they roughly indicate the purchasing power of the national currency in terms of foreign currencies. Exchange rates directly determine the profitability of foreign trade, and they largely influence the size and direction of trade. Although the currencies of the European Socialist countries (except Albania) are defined in gold for the purposes of official exchange rates, this fact is of little practical consequence. These rates are not indicative of the purchasing power of the Socialist currencies and none, with the partial exception of the Yugoslav dinar, is convertible. The size of Socialist foreign trade is determined directly on a planned basis in which (with the exception of Yugoslavia) the exchange rates are of little relevance. The official rates applicable to visible trade exaggerate the value of the Socialist currency in terms of convertible capitalist currencies.

All Socialist countries, with the exception of the USSR and Yugoslavia, administer multiple exchange rates, i.e. in addition to the basic rate applicable to visible trade there is also a tourist rate which is more favourable to the holders of foreign currencies. This fact reflects the higher level of retail prices of goods and services (the cost of living) compared with producers' prices. Thus in Bulgaria, the basic rate is US $1.00 = 1·17 lev, but the tourist rate is 2.00 lev. Moreover, the tourist rate may be multiple, too—a larger sum of convertible currency is exchanged at a more favourable rate to the foreigner. For example in Rumania, the ordinary tourist rate is $1.00 = 12.00 leu, but if $50 or more is exchanged the rate becomes 18.00 leu.

The disadvantages of the absence of equilibrium exchange rates have been long recognized in Socialist countries. So far only Yugoslavia has adopted equilibrium exchange rates (since 1965), and regularly publishes her international reserves (being the only Socialist member of the International Monetary Fund). In other Socialist countries, strict direct controls are still considered to be the only practical way of ensuring a balance of payments equilibrium. Hungary and Czechoslovakia have recently taken steps to gradually evolve 'realistic' exchange rates. But this requires a good deal of structural readjustment in the economy.[17]

---

[17] E.g., it was estimated in Czechoslovakia in 1967 that if such a uniform rate were introduced, 25 per cent of industry would prove uneconomic and some 800,000 people would have to be shifted to other branches of the economy. Even after the far-reaching price reform of 1967, the Czechoslovak price level still deviated 15–20 per cent from world prices. *Hospodářské Noviny*, 11/10/1968, p. 1.

3. TARIFFS

In a centrally planned economy tariffs do not perform such an important function as in a market economy. Under Socialism there are more direct and effective methods of protecting domestic industries and collecting State revenue. Administration of tariffs involves a waste of manpower and other resources and is, in a sense, pointless, considering that payments are made by one State instrumentality to another. Besides, the flow of trade can be shaped directly on a planned basis. Up to the late 1950s (early 1950s in Yugoslavia) tariffs were, in fact, practically non-existent.

However, the Socialist attitude to tariffs has changed since that time. First, the economic integration in Western Europe (EEC and EFTA), followed by similar schemes in other parts of the capitalist world, has led in effect to tariff discrimination against non-member countries. Consequently, Socialist countries decided to revive or introduce two-column tariffs in order to be able to reciprocate tariff concessions.

Secondly, as a result of the economic reforms greater reliance is placed on motivational rather than directive means, and tariffs are more consistent with decentralized management. Czechoslovakia (a foundation member), Poland (since 1967) and Yugoslavia (since 1966) are members of the General Agreement on Tariffs and Trade, and so they have benefited from the recent tariff reductions under the Kennedy Round negotiations.

4. FOREIGN TRADE EFFICIENCY CALCULATIONS

Owing to the distorted price structures, disequilibrium exchange rates and the insulation of the domestic from foreign markets, Socialist countries (with the exception of Yugoslavia and partly of Hungary) have no automatic mechanism for ensuring the most gainful flow of foreign trade. To overcome this disability, since the early 1950s these countries have been pursuing systematic studies of foreign trade efficiency under Socialist conditions.

A number of formulae has been devised whereby it is possible to compare the foreign trade effectiveness of different exports, imports and relevant investments. This analysis, which has reached a high degree of sophistication, was applied for the first time on a systematic basis to work out the foreign trade plans for 1966–70 and integrate them with the overall plan. In the practical conduct of foreign trade, the calculations of effectiveness are applied to most exports, whilst imports are largely predetermined to fulfil developmental targets.

An example of a simplified formula to calculate the foreign exchange effectiveness of exports (actually used in Poland) is given below:

$$feE_x = Mr \cdot nfeX - sC > 0;$$

feE_x = foreign exchange effectiveness of export
Mr = marginal foreign exchange profitability rate for the currency area;
$nfeX$ = net foreign exchange value of the exportable article;
sC = social cost of production for export (average factory price + trade margin + turnover tax).

Source: Adapted from: *Życie gospodarcze*, 17/9/1967, p. 5.

The 'marginal foreign exchange profitability rate' is determined periodically by the ministry of foreign trade (in co-operation with the ministry of finance). It is based on the least profitable batch of products which still has to be exported to ensure a balance of payments equilibrium (or its planned disequilibrium). In the 'net foreign exchange value of the exportable article' the marketing cost incurred in foreign currency is deducted.

If the formula is applied to a particular product, it shows what is known as 'computational profit'. The condition of export is that this profit is a positive value, but under certain conditions this requirement may be waived.[18]

D. PAYMENTS

Socialist countries have always suffered from shortages of foreign exchange. The contributing causes on the demand side include the growing need for imports of equipment and industrial equipment created by the planned rapid industrialization, the non-fulfilment of targets (which have to be made good by imports), the low quality of domestic production and unsatisfied consumer demand. At the same time, on the supply side, the development is not usually geared to build up export capacity, the prevailing seller's markets at home reduce the inclination to export, and besides Socialist exports are confronted with various forms of discrimination in capitalist markets.

Although Socialist countries keep the size of their international reserves secret,[19] there are reasons to believe that, with the possible

[18] The reader interested in further details is referred to J. Wilczynski, *The Economics and Politics of East–West Trade*, London, Macmillan, 1969, Ch. 14 B.

[19] With the exception of Yugoslavia which, being a member of the International Monetary Fund, regularly publishes her reserves in the IMF monthly, *International Financial Statistics*. Her reserves oscillate around $150 m., sufficient to pay for about 8 per cent of her annual imports. See *Int. Fin. Stat.*, June 1969, p. 353.

exception of the USSR, they are very small.[20] This being the case, Socialist imports, particularly from capitalist countries, are subject to fluctuations conditioned not by the instability of demand for imports but by fluctuating export earnings and the low reserves held. Faced with continuous pressure on their balance of payments, Socialist countries administer the strictest form of exchange control. Trade with capitalist nations is carried on exclusively in Western currencies, mostly in sterling and US dollars. Within the CMEA region, the Soviet ruble is used for statistical purposes and partly as a means of settlement.

Largely as a consequence of the inconvertibility of their currencies and of the foreign exchange problems, Socialist countries are noted for their preference for *bilateralism*. They endeavour to balance their imports and exports with each trading partner annually. To facilitate the integration of foreign trade into the overall economic plan, they prefer to sign *bilateral trade agreements* with the governments (or chambers of commerce, in the absence of diplomatic relations). The agreements may cover periods from two to six years, and are subsequently supplemented with more specific annual *trade protocols*.

Such agreements usually indicate the total value of trade, the broad classes of goods to be exchanged, the method of payment and other conditions, such as tariffs, transport, the exchange of trade missions, the settlement of disputes, etc. In relations with other Socialist countries (especially those within the CMEA group), these agreements are quite detailed and they carry firm commitments as to deliveries and purchases of specified items by specified dates. The agreements with capitalist countries are now less specific, mostly indicating intentions to exchange broad classes of goods ('umbrella agreements'). Only signed contracts are legally binding.

Trade amongst all Socialist countries is on a bilateral agreement basis, but not necessarily with all capitalist countries. In 1968 there were 390 bilateral trade agreements in force between the nine European Socialist countries and about 100 capitalist nations. Of this total, 140 agreements were with developed, and 250 with developing, countries.[21]

In their trade amongst themselves, Socialist countries have as a

[20] The USSR is the second largest world producer of gold (after South Africa) and her international liquidity reserves are estimated to be about $2,500 m., sufficient to pay for about 30 per cent of her annual imports (the reserves held by Western countries on the average represent about 40 per cent of their annual imports). The reserves of the remaining seven European Socialist countries (Yugoslavia excluded) are estimated at about $700 m.–$800 m., i.e. 5–10 per cent (or less on occasions) of their annual import bill. See J. Wilczynski, op. cit., pp. 196–7.

[21] Based on: J. Wilczynski, op. cit., pp. 108–9.

rule been planning for *bilateral balancing*, i.e. the equality of exports and imports, if we disregard the small amount of grants and credits (and reparations before 1955). The disadvantages of trading on such a basis have been long recognized, and as a move towards the multilateralization of their trade the CMEA countries established the International Bank for Economic Co-operation in 1963. Each member country has a clearing account with the Bank and is supposed to balance its trade annually with the group as a whole, not bilaterally. In other words, a trade surplus with one member country can be used, under certain conditions, to offset a deficit with another, and this is carried out by means of the 'transferable ruble'.

However, these operations are possible only if they are planned in advance or the partners concerned agree. The point is that credit balances with some countries are less useful than with others. Consequently, the ruble so far is not only inconvertible (into gold or hard currencies) but not even automatically transferable. Although the recent economic reforms are expected to gradually create conditions for rational and linked price structures and realistic exchange rates, the road to multilateralism will be long and arduous.[22]

In trade with capitalist countries, bilateral balancing has been less common. In fact some currency areas, especially the Sterling Area and the European Payments Union, have been treated by Socialist countries as convenient reservoirs for multilateral balancing settlements. Thus the group as a whole, excluding Yugoslavia,[23] regularly earns substantial trade surpluses in the United Kingdom and in other parts of Western Europe (including Yugoslavia) and uses them to offset its deficits with Australia and New Zealand. The group incurs substantial deficits with the United States and Canada, but normally finishes with credit balances in Africa, Asia and Latin America (see Fig. 15, for details).

[22] For further details see, J. Wilczynski, 'Multilateralization of East–West Trade', *Economia internazionale*, May 1968, esp. pp. 308–16.

[23] Yugoslavia's trade patterns do not necessarily conform to those of other European Socialist countries. Her exports to, imports from, surpluses (+) or deficits (−) with, in that order, the same major areas of the world as shown in Fig. 15 were (annual averages over the period 1966–8 in US $ million): European Socialist countries: 450, 480, −30; Asian Socialist countries: 1, 6, −5; Developing Asia: 100, 80, +20; UK: 50, 90, −40; Other Western Europe: 45, 40, +5; Africa: 25, 30, −5; Japan: 3, 33, −30; Latin America: 10, 45, −35; EFTA (excluding the UK): 95, 125, −30; Australia and New Zealand: practically nil, 20, −20; EEC: 350, 580, −230; North America: 85, 140, −55. Based on, IMF and IBRD, *Direction of Trade*, April 1968, p. 179, and April 1969, p. 80.

FIG. 15. *Trade Surpluses and Deficits of the European Socialist Countries*[1]
with Major Areas of the World

(Annual averages over the period 1966–8 in US $ m.)

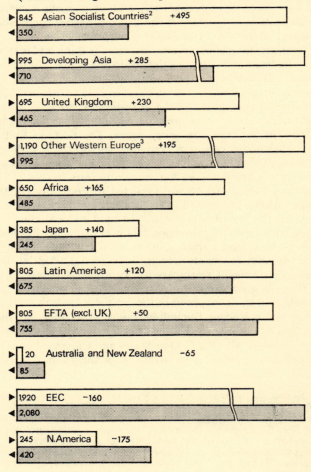

▶ □ Exports (valued f.o.b.) from the European Socialist
countries to.

◀ ▨ Imports (valced f.o.b.) into the European Socialist
countries from.

[1] Albania, Bulgaria, Czechoslovakia, the German D.R., Hungary, Poland, Rumania and the USSR. Yugoslavia ia treated as part of 'Other Western Europe', and Cuba is included in 'Latin America'.

[2] China, the D.P.R. of Korea, Mongolia, the D.R. of Vietnam.

[3] Other than EEC, EFTA (incl. UK). Yugoslavia is included here.

Source. Based on: United Nations *Monthly Bulletin of Statistics*, June 1969, pp. xii–xv.

RECOMMENDED REFERENCES AVAILABLE IN ENGLISH

1. Adler-Karslsson, G., 'Problems of East–West Trade—A General Survey', *Econ. of Planning*, Vol. 7, No. 2, 1967, pp. 119–82; and his *Western Economic Warfare 1947–67*, Stockholm, Almqvist & Wicksell, 1968.

*2. Bash, Y., 'Mathematical Programming and Optimisation of Foreign Trade', *Foreign Trade*, Moscow, 4/1969, pp. 42–4.

*3. Bránik, J., 'Internal and World Prices in the New System of Management', *Eastern Europ. Econ.*, Spring 1967, pp. 39–48.

*4. Brass, H., and Schulmeister, D., 'Input–Output Analysis as an Instrument for Co-ordinating Production and Foreign Trade', *Amer. Rev. of Soviet and Eastern Europ. For. Trade*, May–June 1966, pp. 25–49.

5. Brown, A. A., and Neuberger, E., *International Trade and Central Planning—An Analysis of Economic Interactions*, Univ. of California Press, 1968.

*6. Faude, E., and Maier, W., 'The New Economic System of Planning and Managing the Economy and Foreign Trade Profitability', *Amer. Rev. of Soviet and Eastern Europ. For. Trade*, March–April 1966, pp. 27–68.

*7. Kohlmey, G., 'Economic Growth and Foreign Trade', *Amer. Rev. of Soviet and Eastern Europ. For. Trade*, May–June 1966, pp. 3–24.

*8. Lazaroiu, D., 'Ways of Increasing the Efficiency of Exports', *Soviet and Eastern European For. Trade*, Spring 1968, pp. 18–34.

*9. Nyerges, J., 'Effective Tariff Policy in the New Economic Policy', *Soviet and Eastern Europ. For. Trade*, July–Aug. 1967, pp. 41–7.

*10. Petrov, M., 'Foreign Exchange Planning under the Conditions of the New System of Planning and Management of the National Economy', *Eastern European Economics*, Summer 1968, pp. 44–54.

*11. Pleva, J., 'Monopoly and Central Management (A Consideration of the State Monopoly in Foreign Trade)', *Soviet and Eastern Europ. For. Trade*, Summer 1968, pp. 72–82.

*12. Rachmuth, I., 'Trade Problems Between Countries with Different Socio-Economic Systems', *Soviet and Eastern Europ. For. Trade*, Spring 1968, pp. 3–17.

13. Sawyer, Carole A., *Communist Trade with Developing Countries: 1955–65*, New York and London, Praeger, 1966.

*14. Selucký, R., 'The Impact of the Economic Reforms on the Foreign Economic Relations of the Socialist Countries', *Soviet and Eastern Europ. For. Trade*, Fall 1968, pp. 72–86.

15. Uren, P. E. (ed.), *East–West Trade*. A Symposium, Canadian Institute of International Affairs, Toronto, 1966.

*16. Vajda, I., *The Role of Foreign Trade in a Socialist Economy*, translated from the Hungarian, Budapest, Corvina Press, 1965.

17. Wilczynski, J., *The Economics and Politics of East–West Trade*. A Study of Trade between Developed Market Economies and Centrally Planned Economies, London, New York, Macmillan, 1969.

18. Wiles, P. J. D., *Communist International Economics*, Oxford, Basil Blackwell, 1967.

19. Wyczalkowski, M. R., 'Communist Economics and Currency Convertibility', *IMF Staff Papers*, July 1966, pp. 155–95.

*20. Zajíc, B., and Tokan, L., 'Production Enterprises and Foreign Trade', *Amer. Rev. of Soviet and Eastern Europ. For. Trade*, July–Aug. 1966, pp. 52–65.

indicates contributions by writers from Socialist countries.

CHAPTER 14

International Economic Co-operation

A. PARTICIPATION IN THE WORK OF INTERNATIONAL ORGANIZATIONS

During the 'frigid' phase of the Cold War, especially up to the mid-1950s, the attitude of Socialist countries to most international organizations was highly critical, considering that practically all such organizations were (and still are) dominated by capitalist nations.[1] Many Socialist countries either refrained from joining such organizations or often boycotted and obstructed the work of those to which they belonged. International meetings were frequently used as forums for communist propaganda and bitter diatribes, for which capitalist countries could be partly or equally blamed.

Since the mid-1950s, the attitude of the European Socialist countries[2] has been changing in favour of close (even though sometimes reluctant) co-operation. Many of them have decided since to join such organizations relevant to economic co-operation as the Baltic and International Maritime Conference (Czechoslovakia, Hungary, Rumania, USSR), the Food and Agriculture Organization (Poland, Rumania), the General Agreement on Tariffs and Trade (Poland, Yugoslavia), the International Labour Office (Rumania), the International Cotton Advisory Council (USSR, Yugoslavia), the

---

[1] Of about 130 countries in the world capable of joining international organizations, only fourteen are generally classed as Socialist (i.e. China, Cuba, the D.P.R. of Korea, Mongolia, and the D.R. of Vietnam, in addition to the nine European Socialist countries). Of the total number of over 2,130 international organizations listed in the *Yearbook of International Organizations*, less than 2 per cent have headquarters or subsidiary offices in Socialist countries, and of the total number of 2,230 international meetings involving these organizations in 1966, only 8 per cent were held in Socialist countries (and the proportion in 1956 was less than 3 per cent). Based on: *International Associations*, Brussels, 2/1967, pp. 166–9, and 2/1968, pp. 92–7.

[2] This contrasts with the attitude of the Asian Socialist countries, of whom hardly any belong to international organizations, partly by their own choice and partly owing to the opposition of many capitalist countries.

FIG. 16. *European Socialist Countries' Membership of Selected International Organizations*

Organization	Headquarters (and year of foundation)	Total world membership*	Albania	Bulgaria	Czechoslovakia	German D.R.	Hungary	Poland	Rumania	USSR	Yugoslavia
A. United Nations Organization											
1. United Nations	New York (1945)	115	×	×	×	—	×	×	×	×	×
2. Economic Commission for Asia and the Far East	Bangkok (1947)	28	—	—	—	—	—	—	—	×	—
3. Economic Commission for Europe	Geneva (1947)	29	×	×	×	—	—	×	×	×	×
4. Food and Agriculture Organization	Rome (1945)	113	—	—	—	—	—	×	×	—	×
5. International Bank for Reconstruction and Development	New York (1945)	103	—	—	—	—	—	—	—	—	×
6. International Labour Organization	Geneva (1919)	113	×	×	×	—	×	×	×	×	×
7. International Monetary Fund	Washington (1945)	103	—	—	—	—	—	—	—	—	×
B. Other inter-governmental organizations											
8. Bank for International Settlements	Basle (1930)	26	×	×	×	—	×	×	×	—	×
9. General Agreement on Tariffs and Trade	Geneva (1948)	81	—	—	—	—	—	×	—	—	×
10. International Exhibition	Paris (193?)	32	—	×	×	—	×	×	×	×	—

	Location (year)	Members	1	2	3	4	5	6	7	8	9
11. International Lead and Zinc Study Group	New York (1959)	25	×	×	—	×	—	—	×	—	—
12. International Sugar Council	London (1953)	45	—	×	—	×	×	—	×	—	—
13. International Union for the Protection of Industrial Property	Geneva (1883)	74	×	×	×	×	×	×	×	×	×
C. Non-governmental organizations											
14. Baltic and International Maritime Conference	Copenhagen (1905)	62	×	×	×	×	×	—	×	—	×
15. International Cargo Handling Co-ordination Association	London (1952)	70	×	—	—	×	×	—	×	—	—
16. International Organization for Standardization	Geneva (1946)	53	×	×	×	×	×	×	×	×	×
17. International Union of Official Travel Organizations	Geneva (1925)	93	×	×	×	×	×	—	×	×	—
18. Permanent International Association of Navigation Congresses	Brussels (1900)	69	×	×	×	×	×	×	×	×	—
19. Union of International Fairs	Paris (1925)	30	×	—	—	×	—	×	×	×	—
20. World Power Conference	London (1924)	61	×	×	×	×	×	—	×	×	—
			5	11	16	3	13	17	12	13	17

* A country's membership is treated as one even though in some cases other component entities of the country (such as Byelorussian SSR and Ukrainian SSR, in addition to the USSR) may also be formal members. The total number of countries in the world capable of joining international organizations was about 130 in 1970.

Sources. Based on: Union of International Associations, *Yearbook of International Organizations 1968–1969*, Brussels 1969; *International Associations* (monthly issues); *Europa Year Book 1969*, London, 1969.

International Exhibition Bureau (Bulgaria, Czechoslovakia, Hungary, Poland, USSR), the International Fur Trade Federation (Czechoslovakia, USSR), the International Organization for Standardization (Albania, Bulgaria), the International Union for the Protection of Industrial Property (German D.R., USSR), the International Wheat Council (USSR), the Union of International Fairs (Czechoslovakia, Hungary) and the World Power Conference (Bulgaria, Czechoslovakia, Rumania, USSR). Besides, Albania, Bulgaria, Hungary and Rumania have been admitted to the United Nations.[3] The European Socialist countries' membership of the twenty international organizations most relevant to economic co-operation is shown in Fig. 16.

Of all international organizations, the European Commission for Europe has proved to be the most fruitful platform for identifying and solving the economic problems arising between capitalist and Socialist countries. The Commission consists of seven 'Divisions', of which three have been most active and successful in dealing with East–West economic issues: the 'Commission Affairs and Trade Development', 'Research and Planning', and 'Transport'. The fields of co-operation have included both theoretical and practical problems. Experts from Eastern and Western Europe have worked in common sessions on such questions of mutual interest as the nature of economic growth, the criteria for investment policies, regional and intra-regional planning, macroeconomic models, technological progress as a factor in economic growth and long-term problems of international trade.

That the problems arising in relations between different economic systems are not insurmountable is demonstrated by the following common solutions of direct practical value to both sides:

   (i) The standardization of commercial documents.

  (ii) The normalization of the general conditions of sale of certain products (mostly engineering items).

 (iii) Effective reciprocity of the Most-Favoured-Nation treatment.

 (iv) Rules for preventing market disruption and discriminatory surcharges on imports and exports.

  (v) Agreed forms and conditions of insurance and re-insurance contracts in foreign trade.

 (vi) The settlement of trade balances on a multi-angular basis involving Eastern and some Western European trade partners and some developing countries as well.

(vii) Mutually acceptable procedures for the settlement of foreign trade disputes and the enforcement of arbitral awards.

[3] Based on: Union of International Associations, *Yearbook of International Organizations 1954–55* and *1968–69*, Brussels.

B. CO-OPERATION WITH CAPITALIST COUNTRIES

In a general sense, the Socialist multilateral participation in the work of international organizations is an example of co-operation with capitalist countries because, as has already been stated (see footnote 1, p. 189), most such bodies are dominated by capitalist nations. In this section we shall consider other forms of co-operation, especially those on a more or less mutual basis involving two countries or partners.

The broad basis for co-operation with capitalist countries has been provided by the declaration of 'peaceful co-existence' which was first[4] formulated at the 1956, and further reaffirmed and elaborated upon at the 1961 Congress of the Communist Party of the Soviet Union. The principle of peaceful co-existence—in addition to the postulates of non-interference in internal affairs, respect for national sovereignty and territorial integrity and the conditional renunciation of war—calls for the 'promotion of economic and cultural co-operation on the basis of equality and mutual benefit'.[5]

Evidence of a conciliatory attitude is afforded by the following examples. Since the mid-1950s, Socialist countries' trade has been rising at a faster rate with the capitalist world than with each other (see pp. 203, 217). They have established an excellent record as traders in respect of their adherence to the terms of contracts and payments—in fact better than many a capitalist country. Since the early 1960s these countries (except Albania) have increasingly inclined to import more consumer goods from developed as well as from developing nations, and have relaxed restrictions on foreign travel. International trade fairs and exhibitions have become most valuable meeting grounds for Socialist and capitalist officials, traders and engineers. The most important cities for these occasions are Belgrade, Brno, Budapest, Leipzig, Leningrad, Moscow, Plovdiv, Poznan and Zagreb in Eastern Europe, and Cairo, Frankfurt, Hong Kong, London, Milan, Montreal, Munich, Osaka, Paris, Stockholm, Sydney, Tripolis and Vienna in the capitalist world.

Most Socialist governments have also signed bilateral agreements with many capitalist countries on industrial, technical, scientific and

[4] The phrase was first used in its present meaning in the Sino-Indian declaration of 1954, which embodied 'Five Principles of Peaceful Co-existence'. Neither China, nor the D.P.R. of Korea, nor the D.R. of Vietnam, has accepted the policy of peaceful co-existence in relation to the leading capitalist powers, and indeed China did not regard herself bound by it at the time of the Sino-Indian border dispute of 1962–3.

[5] *The Road to Communism*, Documents of the 22nd Congress of the CPSU MOSCOW, FLPH, 1961, p. 506.

even cultural co-operation. For example, the USSR has signed such agreements with Algeria, Belgium, Canada, Denmark, Finland, France, India, Iran, Italy, Japan, Malaysia, the Netherlands, Pakistan, Sweden, the United Arab Republic, the United Kingdom, the USA and other countries. Practically all European Socialist countries maintain permanent trade missions in the more important trading centres in the capitalist world. A number of joint chambers of commerce has also been established, such as Anglo-Czechoslovak, Anglo-Hungarian, Anglo-Rumanian, Anglo-Soviet, Finnish-Soviet, Franco-Soviet, and Italo-Soviet.

The most direct channel of economic co-operation is represented by joint East–West ventures. These undertakings existed before 1964, too, but they were limited to joint trading companies. Since that time, there has been a remarkable development of co-operation in the sphere of production as well. The most dynamic Socialist countries in this respect are Yugoslavia, Hungary, Bulgaria, Czechoslovakia and Poland, whilst the F.R. of Germany, Austria, Italy, France, Sweden, Belgium and the United Kingdom are the most active co-operators on the capitalist side. Co-operation takes the following forms: the exchange of designs, licences and other technological data, sub-contracting, joint production, joint marketing and co-operation in third markets.

In most cases, the co-operating enterprises retain their separate identity, but there are now numerous fully integrated joint companies such as *Anglodal* (Anglo-Polish), *Bu-Mac* (Australian-Bulgarian), *Dalexport* (Franco-Polish), *Dalimpex* (Canadian-Polish), *Falconda Venezolana* (Venezuelan-Polish), *Konela* (Finnish-Soviet), *Sigma-Italiana* (Italo-Czechoslovak), *Snam-Ina* (Italo-Yugoslav).

In addition to co-operation with the highly industrialized capitalist nations, Socialist countries have also embarked on a drive to strengthen their links with the developing world. This drive, which had its beginnings in the International Economic Conference in Moscow in 1952, has followed three lines—the extension of economic aid, the negotiation of trade agreements and the consequent expansion of trade. Socialist economic aid began in 1954, i.e. six years after the US programme had been launched. Up to 1969 the European Socialist countries had committed themselves to about US $10,000 m. of aid (of which the Soviet share amounted to three-quarters). This compares with the Western aid commitments to developing nations exceeding $100,000 m. (two-thirds contributed by the USA).[6] Socialist aid is mostly in the form of low-interest tied loans repayable over long periods in local products, and as such it lays

[6] Based on J. Wilczynski, *The Economics and Politics of East–West Trade*, London, Macmillan, 1969, p. 254.

foundations for the continued growth of mutual trade. Between 1954 and 1969, the number of bilateral trade agreements between the nine European Socialist countries and about eighty developing nations increased from 125 to 260, mostly on Socialist initiative.[7] Trade agreements may not only initiate or expand trade, but they also have substantial value in a broader sense—the promotion of Socialist goodwill and economic thinking and practices. As a result, the developing countries' share in Eastern Europe's (including the USSR's) foreign trade increased from 3 per cent in 1953 to 10 per cent in 1968 (see Fig. 14, p. 178).

C. CO-OPERATION AMONG SOCIALIST COUNTRIES

Systematic economic (as distinct from political) co-operation among the European Socialist countries dates from the formation of the Council for Mutual Economic Assistance (CMEA or Comecon) in 1949.[8] Up to the mid-1950s co-operation was limited to the mutual co-ordination of trade. Since that time there has been a systematic drive towards economic integration through the co-ordination of investment plans, specialization, joint undertakings and financial, scientific and technical co-operation.

How varied the scope of co-operation is under the auspices of CMEA is conveyed by the Permanent (or 'Standing') Commissions, of which there are now twenty-one. Their headquarters and dates of establishment are stated in parentheses:

1. Agriculture (Sofia, 1956).
2. Building and Construction (East Berlin, 1958).
3. Chemicals (East Berlin, 1956).
4. Coal (Warsaw, 1956).
5. Co-ordination of Scientific and Technical Research (Moscow, 1962).
6. Currency and Finance (Moscow, 1962).
7. Economic Questions (Moscow, 1958).
8. Electric Power (Moscow, 1956).
9. Engineering (Prague, 1956).
10. Ferrous Metals (Moscow, 1956).
11. Food Processing Industries (Sofia, 1958, 1963[9]).

[7] Ibid., pp. 108–9.

[8] It included all the European Socialist countries, except Yugoslavia, whilst other Socialist countries were granted an observer status. Albania has ceased participating in CMEA's activities since 1961, whilst Mongolia was admitted in 1962. Yugoslavia was admitted as an associate member in 1964.

[9] The Light and Food Processing Industries Commission was established in 1958, but it was divided into two separate Commissions in 1963.

12. Foreign Trade (Moscow, 1956).
13. Geological Surveys (Ulan Bator, 1963).
14. Light Industries (Prague, 1958, 1963[9]).
15. Non-Ferrous Metallurgy (Budapest, 1956).
16. Oil and Gas (Bucharest, 1956).
17. Radio and Electronics (Budapest, 1963).
18. Standardization (East Berlin, 1962).
19. Statistics (Moscow, 1962).
20. Transport (Warsaw, 1958).
21. Utilization of Nuclear Energy for Peaceful Purposes (Moscow, 1960).

Each Commission usually includes a number of agencies, sub-committees, working parties, etc. We shall now examine some examples of achievements in the most important spheres.

a. *Economic Planning*. This is the most fundamental form of co-operation, and one, of course, that distinguishes CMEA from other groupings. In the first decade of CMEA's existence, planning was virtually limited to that of mutual trade. But since 1958 consistent dovetailing of production plans has been pursued. Since the early 1960s efforts have been directed toward co-ordinating perspective plans (for fifteen to twenty years). In 1963 a special Bureau for Planned Integration Problems was established with its head office in Moscow. Attention is focused on the co-ordination of investment plans.

b. *Specialization*. Since the mid-1950s, the CMEA countries have practically discarded autarkic policies in favour of specialization, which in manufacturing alone now covers over twenty groups of industries, such as food processing, agricultural machinery, sugar refining equipment, mining machinery, metal rolling, ball-bearings, machine tools, textile machinery, transport equipment and electronics. By 1967, the number of recommendations concerning specialization in mechanical engineering embraced 2,300 kinds of machinery and instruments.[10] There have also been attempts to promote specialization in agriculture. Thus Bulgaria, Hungary and Rumania are concentrating on the production of fruit, vegetables and wines to supply the growing needs of the other member countries.

c. *Joint Undertakings*. These are ventures in which the capital, know-how and even manpower of several member countries are pooled

[10] D. Fikus, *Rada Wzajemnej Pomocy Gospodarczej* (The Council for Mutual Economic Assistance), Warsaw, PWE, 1967, p. 74.

together. Such enterprises are mostly concerned with the extraction, treatment or transport of key industrial raw materials, such as bauxite, cellulose, coal, copper, iron ore lead, phosphates, potash, sulphur and zinc.[11] The most publicized examples of such undertakings are: the Kingisep Potash Works (in the USSR) jointly developed by Bulgaria, Czechoslovakia, the German D.R., Hungary, Poland and the USSR; the 'Friendship' pipeline, linking the Urals with Poland, the German D.R., Czechoslovakia and Hungary; the electric power transmission grid 'Peace', linking all CMEA countries; 'Intermetal', an iron and steel community being developed by Czechoslovakia, Hungary and Poland. A scheme has been put forward to establish 'Interelektronika', to co-ordinate and speed up the computerization of the member countries.

d. *Technological Co-operation.* The exchange of blueprints, descriptions of technical processes and results of scientific research have been practised ever since the foundation of CMEA (and even before). Over the twenty years of existence of CMEA (1949–68) the USSR alone supplied 21,000 sets of documentation to other member countries and received 10,000 sets from them.[12] No charges are made for such data, but by world market prices the value of the know-how passed on by the member countries to each other in 1966 was estimated at US $13,000 m.[13]

e. *Standardization.* The member countries have embarked upon a consistent policy of standardization designed to produce types, models and parts that conform to agreed standards of quality and specification. To place this form of co-operation on a systematic basis, the Institute of Standardization was established in Moscow in 1962 (in addition to the Commission on Standardization in East Berlin). There is now a unified trade nomenclature and a common industrial classification. Steps have also been taken towards further systematization of national statistical reporting, including a common basis for certain index numbers.

f. *Transport and Communications.* The road and railway networks of the member countries have been linked and traffic has been rationalized. In 1964 the Common Freight Railcar Pool, administered from Prague, went into operation. There is a scheme to link all the European CMEA countries by 1980 with a system of canals joining the

[11] *Voprosy ekonomiki*, 1/1969, pp. 47–57.
[12] *Trud*, 14/1/1969, p. 3.
[13] *Życie gospodarcze*, 15/9/1968, p. 10.

Danube, Elbe, Oder, and Vistula.[14] In the sphere of communications, there is a unified, semi-automatic telephone system connecting the capitals and major industrial centres of all member countries, a telecommunications cable linking East Berlin, Prague, Warsaw and Moscow, and the television network 'Intervision' covering all the European CMEA countries.

g. *Intra-CMEA Foreign Trade.* Of all the economic groupings, the CMEA region has attained the highest degree of mutual trade concentration, viz. 61 per cent in 1968, compared with 45 per cent in the European Economic Community and 24 per cent in the case of the European Free Trade Area.[15] The proportions for the respective groups of countries in 1948 were 45 per cent, 35 per cent and 17 per cent (and in 1938: 9 per cent, 30 per cent and 18 per cent).[16] The share of the CMEA countries is highest in the foreign trade of Bulgaria (72 per cent) and the German D.R. (69 per cent), and lowest in that of the USSR (57 per cent) and Rumania (47 per cent).[17] It is often pointed out with pride in Socialist literature that intra-CMEA specialization and trade are not 'vertical', between producers of raw materials and manufactures, typical of capitalist trade, but 'horizontal', i.e. involving all stages of production without the division of the countries into 'developed' and 'undeveloped'.[18] The extent of economic co-operation is indicated by the fact that 98 per cent of coal, 95 per cent of machinery and equipment, 90 per cent of oil and products, 80 per cent of iron ore, and large proportions of the non-ferrous metals, mineral fertilizers, timber and cotton required by these countries are obtained from within the grouping.[19]

h. *Finance and Payments.* Some of the richer CMEA countries (the USSR, Czechoslovakia, the German D.R.) have been extending economic aid to other member countries at low interest rates (1–3 per cent p.a.). Under the system administered by the International Bank for Economic Co-operation, in certain circumstances trade surpluses with the member countries can be used to pay for trade deficits with others. The Bank also extends credits, at low interest

[14] D. Fikus, op. cit., p. 48.

[15] Based on: United Nations *Monthly Bulletin of Statistics*, June 1969, p. xii.

[16] Based on: United Nations *Yearbook of International Trade Statistics 1962*, pp. 20–9.

[17] *Życie gosp.*, 3/11/1968, p. 11.

[18] Z. Kamecki, J. Sołdaczuk and W. Sierpiński, *Międzynarodowe stosunki ekonomiczne* (International Economic Relations), Warsaw, PWE, 1964, p. 79.

[19] O. Tarnovskii, ('Regional Value and the CMEA Market'), *Vop. ekon.*, 10/1967, p. 91.

rates,[20] and it performs a very useful integrating function. It is assumed that in the long run the grouping will develop sound exchange rates, a truly multilateral system of payments and perhaps a common currency.[21]

Although to a lesser extent than amongst themselves, the European CMEA countries also co-operate with other Socialist countries. Mongolia is a full member of CMEA, and nine-tenths of her trade is with the grouping. Yugoslavia has been admitted to several Permanent Commissions, a number of joint ventures have been formed and there is increasing commercial and financial co-operation; the CMEA group now claims one-third of Yugoslavia's trade. Various forms of economic aid are extended to Cuba, the D.P.R. of Korea and the D.R. of Vietnam, and the relatively large amount of trade with these countries is largely conditioned by political motives. Although in the 1950s there was a lively industrial, commercial and scientific co-operation with Albania and China, relations have drastically deteriorated since the early 1960s owing to the Sino-Soviet dispute.

D. PROBLEMS OF INTRA-SOCIALIST CO-OPERATION

The main stumbling blocks to continued progress in economic co-operation amongst Socialist countries derive from national differences, the lack of a supra-national authority, the absence of a rational basis for prices, a non-fulfilment of commitments and the growing preference for trade with the capitalist world. We shall now discuss the significance of these problems.

a. *National Differences.* The divergent forces within the Socialist family of nations are well known: the ideological blacklisting of Yugoslavia, the Sino-Soviet rift, Rumanian opposition to CMEA integration, Czechoslovak popular dismay at the military intervention by the Warsaw Pact countries (without Rumania). The monolithic unity of the Socialist bloc is a fact of the past, instead each country is now intent on following its 'own path to socialism'.[22] There are still considerable differences in economic development and

[20] The new rates (introduced in 1968) are: on seasonal and trade expansion credits: 1·5–2·5 per cent p.a., on clearing credits: 2·0–3·0 per cent p.a. The rates are slightly higher than they were before. *Vunshna turgoviya*, 1/1969, p. 5.

[21] B. W. Reutt, ('Socialist Integration—The Forms of Organic Links'), *Życie gosp.*, 21/7/1968, p. 10.

[22] This possibility was formally conceded at the 1956 Congress of the Communist Party of the Soviet Union.

the standard of living, even within the CMEA region. Thus if the real national income per head of Poland is taken as 100, that of Rumania is only 82 and of Bulgaria 83, whilst that of Czechoslovakia is 144 and of the German D.R. is 165.[23]

b. *The Question of Supra-National Authority.* In each Socialist country (with the possible exception of the USSR) there is a strong body of opinion interested more in national sovereignty and self-development than in the cohesion of the CMEA grouping or the strength of the 'Socialist camp'. CMEA has proved powerless to prevent its obstinate member countries from developing similar economic structures. Khrushchev's dream of vesting the CMEA Executive Council (established in 1962) with supra-national powers failed in 1963, due to the stubborn opposition of Rumania, supported by other smaller countries. This set-up contrasts with that in the EEC where the Common Market Commission and the Iron and Steel Community have such powers. With directive planning and management being abandoned on a national scale in favour of decentralization, there is little chance for directive planning and control eventuating at the CMEA level in the future.

c. *The Pricing Conundrum.* So far Socialist countries have not evolved a practical system of their own to guide their specialization and trade in accordance with comparative advantage. When this writer visited Moscow recently, a Russian cynic asked him the following riddle: 'Why is the Communist Party in favour of eternal peaceful co-existence?' The answer obligingly provided was: 'Because if there were no capitalist market, we would have no clue as to the prices for carrying on our foreign trade.' A huge output of literature has been produced on the rationalization of prices, and yet so far no solution that is acceptable to all countries—in fact the disagreement appears to be widening. Socialist countries are still using capitalist prices in their own trade, which amounts to an admission of the failure of Socialism and produces demoralizing effects. Yet it is widely realized that capitalist prices are not a reliable guide to intra-CMEA specialization and trade, because they do not reflect the conditions of production and exchange under Socialism. A Polish economist summed up:

'Using world market prices, it is impossible to evaluate the effectiveness of the foreign trade of Socialist countries, because such prices do not indicate the comparative advantage these countries may have

[23] K. Łaski, ('Problems of Economic Growth of Socialist Countries'), *Nowe drogi*, 1/1968, p. 89.

in relation to each other as members of a regional grouping. . . . These prices do not facilitate further economic integration of the member countries . . . they only promote adjustment to capitalist markets.'[24]

Consequently, many Socialist economists, such as S. Ausch and F. Bartha of Hungary, V. Diachenko and Yu. Olsevich of the USSR, Z. Knyziak and J. Soldaczuk of Poland, G. Kohlmey of the German D.R. and G. Zhelev of Bulgaria, advocate that the CMEA group adopt a price basis of its own, divorced from world capitalist markets.[25] But some, such as S. Polaczek of Poland, K. Popov of the USSR and Ota Šik of Czechoslovakia, strongly oppose such proposals,[26] whilst others (such as O. Tarnovskii of the USSR) are in favour of a compromise solution.[27]

d. *Suspicion of Exploitation.* The actual prices used in intra-CMEA trade embody 'corrections' to the average world market prices (see Ch. 13 C, p. 180). Thus mark-ups of 50 per cent are common, and some items carry much more. In effect, in the case of most items Socialist countries charge each other higher prices than in their trade with capitalist countries.[28] This inevitably leads to suspicions of exploitation, which are particularly strong against the Soviet Union, as she is in a position to exercise superior bargaining power economically and politically.[29] These misgivings cannot, of course, be

[24] Z. Knyziak, ('The Role of the System of Foreign Trade and Internal Prices in Socialist Integration'), *Życie gosp.*, 2/6/1968, p. 11.

[25] E.g. see, V. Diachenko, ('Main Directions for Improving Prices in Intra-CMEA Foreign Trade'), *Vop. ekon.*, 12/1967, pp. 64–74; J. Sołdaczuk, ('The System of Prices in Intra-Socialist Foreign Trade and Problems of the Socialist International Division of Labour'), *Ekonomista*, 1/1966, pp. 73–89: G. Kohlmey, ('Foreign Trade Prices and Growth Effects in the Economic Co-operation among the CMEA Countries'), *Staat und Recht*, East Berlin, Oct. 1968, pp. 1642–54. Also see references 1 and 20 at the end of this chapter.

[26] E.g., S. Polaczek, ('Problems of the Price System in Intra-Socialist Foreign Trade'), *Gospodarka planowa*, 8–9/1967, pp. 45–51; K. Popov, ('Objective Principles of Constructing a Price System for Trade among Socialist Countries'), *Vop. ekon.*, 8/1968, pp. 67–72.

[27] E.g., O. Tarnovskii, ('Regional Value and the CMEA Market'), *Vop. ekon.*, 10/1968, pp. 81–92.

[28] E.g. in 1964, expressed in rubles, the prices of drilling machines were from 16 to 107 per cent (according to size) and of turning machines from 54 to 128 per cent higher in intra-CMEA trade than in world capitalist markets. See Z. Knyziak, op. cit.

[29] It was disclosed by a Soviet writer that to obtain one passenger car, the USSR would have to export 3,400 tons of oil at world market prices, but at CMEA prices she needs to forgo only 1,300 tons of oil. The respective costs of obtaining one vertical milling machine are 520 tons of iron in capitalist markets, but only 140 tons in the CMEA market. The point is that the USSR is the chief

publicly articulated in Eastern Europe, but this question has received considerable attention from a number of Western economists, as reflected particularly in the Mendershausen–Holzman controversy (see references 9 and 14 at the end of this chapter). The problem of proving or disproving exploitation in trade between Socialist economies is complex.[30] But it may be observed that some Soviet economists deny the fact of exploitation by the USSR,[31] whilst others go further in claiming that it is the USSR who is being exploited commercially by other CMEA countries.[32] If these countries adopt a structure of prices completely divorced from world market prices, there will be more grounds for the suspicion of exploitation.

e. *Non-fulfilment of Commitments.* A failure to honour undertaken deliveries, faulty specifications, poor quality and delays have been common complaints ever since World War II. In the context of planned economic development, breaches of this nature produce disruptive effects. Such irregularities are often caused by unexpected events that cannot be avoided. But in some cases they are deliberate —particularly in the case of 'hard' items for which hard currencies can be earned in capitalist markets. Czechoslovak machinery for the chemical industry, East German precision instruments, Polish coal and Soviet iron ore and non-ferrous metals have on occasions been diverted to Western countries, in spite of acute shortages within the CMEA region. The temptation to do this is becoming greater under the new economic system because, as a Polish economist pointed out, '. . . decentralization and material incentives . . . weaken enterprises' discipline in honouring contractual obligations which turn out to be unprofitable'.[33]

f. *The Declining Role of Intra-CMEA Trade.* Owing to the problems

supplier of oil and iron to other CMEA countries, whilst she mostly imports manufactures from them in exchange. V. Zhukov and Y. Olsevich, ('International Costs and Co-operation among the CMEA Countries'), *Vop. ekon.*, 3/1967, p. 78.

[30] For a discussion of this problem see J. Wilczynski, op. cit., pp. 336–42.

[31] E.g., F. Abramov, ('Pseudo-scientific Investigations by Bourgeois Economists'), *Vneshnaya torgovlya*, 10/1963, pp. 13–17; S. Zavolzhky and L. Lukin, ('Bourgeois Criticism of Socialist Economic Co-operation'), *International Affairs*, Moscow, 1/1967, pp. 8–13.

[32] E.g., O. Bogomolov, ('Current Problems of Economic Co-operation among Socialist Countries'), *Mirovaya ekonomika i mezhdunarodnye otnosheniya*, 5/1966, pp. 15–27; his arguments are further developed in his *Teoriya i metodologiya mezhdunarodnogo sotsialisticheskogo razdeleniya truda* (The Theory and Methodology of the International Socialist Division of Labour), Moscow, Mysl, 1967.

[33] S. Polaczek, ('Fundamental Factors Relevant to the Integration of Socialist Countries'), *Gospodarka planowa*, 7/1968, p. 20.

considered above, the continued inconvertibility of the ruble and their inability to free themselves from bilateralism, the CMEA countries have displayed an increasing preference for expanding trade with capitalist countries. Since the Korean War, the share of intra-CMEA trade has declined from 68 per cent to about 63 per cent, whilst the share with capitalist countries has increased from 18 per cent to 33 per cent (see Fig. 14, p. 178). Most CMEA countries have regarded the expansion of their trade with the capitalist world as a means to some degree of economic emancipation from Soviet domination. Some of them, notably Czechoslovakia, have tended to look upon the specialization and trade with other CMEA countries as being imposed and in fact having a 'primitivizing effect' on their economies.[34]

[34] See e.g., *Hospodářské Noviny*, 16/8/1968, Special Supplement.

RECOMMENDED REFERENCES AVAILABLE IN ENGLISH

*1. Ausch, S., and Bartha, F., 'Theoretical Problems Relating to Prices in Trade Between the Comecon Countries', *Soviet and Eastern Europ. For. Trade*, Summer 1968, pp. 35–71.

2. Benoit, E., 'The Joint-Venture Route to East–West Investment', *Amer. Rev. of East–West Trade*, June 1968, pp. 39–45.

*3. Bogomolov, O., 'Problems in Production Specialization Among CMEA Countries', *Soviet and Eastern Europ. For. Trade*, Spring 1968, pp. 68–89.

*4. D'iachenko, V., 'Main Trends in Improving Prices in Trade Among Comecon Members', *Problems of Economics*, June 1968, pp. 40–9.

*5. Chossudovsky, E. M., 'The Role of the United Nations Economic Commission for Europe in the Co-existence Process—Some Notes on a Possible Case Study', *Co-existence*, July 1967, pp. 151–77.

6. Gamarnikow, M., 'Is Comecon Obsolete?', *East Europe*, April 1968, pp. 12–18.

7. Goldman, M. I., *Soviet Foreign Aid*, London and New York, Collier–Macmillan, and Praeger, 1967.

*8. Hetényi, I., 'Problems of Long-Term Planning and the International Coordination of National Plans under CMEA', *Acta Oeconomica*, Vol. 3, No. 3, 1968, pp. 283–96.

9. Holzman, F. D., 'Soviet Foreign Trade Pricing and the Question of Discrimination', *Rev. of Econ. and Stat.*, May 1962, pp. 134–47, and 'More on Soviet Bloc Trade Discrimination', *Soviet Studies*, July 1965, pp. 44–65.

10. Kaser, M., *Comecon. Integration Problems of the Planned Economies*, London, Oxford U.P., 1967.

*11. Kiss, T., *Economic Cooperation Among Socialist Countries*, translated from the Hungarian, New York, IASP, 1968.

12. Köhler, H., *Economic Integration in the Soviet Bloc* (with an East German Case Study), New York and London, Praeger, 1965.

*13. Ladygin, B. and Shiriaev, 'Problems of Improving Economic Co-operation Between Countries Belonging to the Council of Mutual Economic Assistance (CMEA)', *Amer. Rev. of Soviet and Eastern Europ. For. Trade*, Sept.–Oct. 1966, pp. 3–18.

14. Mendershausen, H., 'Terms of Trade between the Soviet Union and Smaller Communist Countries', and 'The Terms of Soviet-Satellite Trade: A Broadened Analysis', *Rev. of Econ. and Stat.*, May 1959, pp. 106–18, and May 1960, pp. 152–63.

15. Rubinstein, A. Z., *The Soviets in International Organizations: Changing Policies towards Developing Countries, 1953–1963*, Princeton U.P. and Oxford U.P., 1964.

16. Siotis, J., 'ECE in the Emerging European System', *International Conciliation*, 1/1967 (whole number).

*17. Sulieva, L., 'Currency and Financial Cooperation Among Comecon Members', *Problems of Economics*, Oct. 1967, pp. 45–50.

18. Szawlowski, R., 'The International Economic Organizations of the Communist Countries', *Canadian Slavonic Papers*, Vol. X, No. 3, 1968, pp. 254–78, and Vol. XI, No. 1, 1969, pp. 108–19.

19. Tansky, L., *US and USSR Aid to Developing Countries. A Comparative Study of India, Turkey and the UAR*, New York and London, Praeger, 1967.

*20. Zhelev, G., 'On Using a Proper Base of Price Formation on the International Socialist Market', *Amer. Rev. of Soviet and Eastern Europ For. Trade*, July–Aug. 1966, pp. 3–22.

* indicates contributions by writers from Socialist countries.

CHAPTER 15

Socialism *v.* Capitalism

In the preceding chapters we have discussed the institutional set-up and the laws, policies and practices determining the operation of the Socialist economy. It is appropriate in the last chapter to make an overall economic appraisal of Socialism. This can be done more meaningfully if made against the backdrop of its rival—capitalism. We shall first project Socialist and capitalist economies onto the world scene, and then we shall bring out the economic strengths and weaknesses of Socialism. We shall conclude by examining the extent to which the two economic systems are 'converging'.

A. SOCIALIST AND CAPITALIST COUNTRIES IN THE WORLD SCENE

To make international comparisons involving objective quantities, such as area and population, is simple. But where value judgments have to be made, as in the case of national income, industrial output and foreign trade, many problems arise, even if the countries concerned belong to the same economic system. However, where different social systems are involved, these problems are magnified because the basis, methods and consistency of valuation differ fundamentally and moreover Socialist countries do not publish systematic returns. In most studies published in the Socialist bloc and in the capitalist world, achievements made under the economic system of the writer are usually exaggerated, whilst those of the other system are belittled or ignored. Thus whilst in some Socialist studies, the Socialist bloc is credited with 40 per cent of the world's industrial output,[1] in some Western sources the proportion conceded is only 30 per cent.[2]

Although no precise calculations are possible (or advisable), rough comparisons are feasible and interesting. This is done in Fig. 17, where comparative data for area, population, national income, industrial output and national income per head are given for Socialist and capitalist countries. The figures are based on Socialist and

[1] *Peace, Freedom and Socialism*, 1/1966, p. 30.
[2] E.g., Institute of Public Affairs, Melbourne, *IPA Facts*, April–May 1968, p. 8.

FIG. 17. *Comparative Economic Data on Socialist and Capitalist Countries, 1968*

World division	Area	Population	National income[6]	Industrial output	Foreign trade	National income per head[6] (In US $)
		(As a percentage of world total)				
Socialist countries[1]	26	35	26	34	12	400
European Socialist countries[2]	18	10	20	30	11	1,150
USSR	16	7	15	20	4	1,150
Other Socialist countries[3]	8	25	6	4	1	150
Developed capitalist countries[4]	26	21	61	59	69	1,750
EEC	2	6	15	14	26	1,600
United Kingdom	n	2	4	4	7	1,800
United States	6	6	33	34	14	3,300
Developing capitalist countries[5]	48	44	13	7	19	200
World	100	100	100	100	100	600

[1] Albania, Bulgaria, China, Cuba, Czechoslovakia, the German D.R., Hungary, D.P.R. of Korea, Mongolia, Poland, Rumania, the USSR, D.R. of Vietnam, Yugoslavia.

[2] Including all the USSR.

[3] China, Cuba, D.P.R. of Korea, Mongolia, D.R. of Vietnam.

[4] Western Europe, North America, Japan, Australia, New Zealand, South Africa.

[5] Other than Socialist and developed capitalist countries.

[6] The Western concept of national income is used.

n = negligible, less than 0·5 per cent.

Sources. Based on: United Nations, Socialist and Western sources. The figures relating to national income and industrial output are author's own estimates.

Western sources; those involving values are the author's estimates, representing a 'reasonable' compromise between Socialist and Western claims.

Of particular interest to us are the European Socialist countries. Their large share in the world's industrial output, over one-quarter, is noteworthy—it is higher than that of the European Common Market and nearly as large as that of the USA. The national income per head in Eastern Europe and the USSR (US $1,150) although about twice as high as the world average ($600) is only two-thirds of the Western figure ($1,750). The relatively small participation in world trade by both European (11 per cent) and especially non-European Socialist countries (1 per cent) is striking.

It may also be added that the European Socialist countries claim the following shares in the production of:

	%
Mineral fertilizers	28
Pig iron	28
Steel	28
Coal	27
Cement	26
Sugar	25
Electric power	20
Oil	17
Chemical fibres	16

Source. Voprosy ekonomiki, 1/1969, p. 48.

B. ADVANTAGES OF THE SOCIALIST ECONOMIC SYSTEM

As compared with capitalist-oriented economies, Socialism can be considered superior in the following respects:

a. *The Mainspring of Economic Activity*. Production processes are not determined by a whimsical market mechanism powered by the private profit motive, but basically by the economic plan which is an expression of society as a whole. Appeal is made to higher social instincts and profit is treated merely as a means rather than an end. The market is harnessed within the framework of planning and so it becomes a useful instrument, a servant instead of a master.

b. *The Level of Employment*. The social ownership of the means of production and central economic planning enable the maintenance of continuous full employment. A Socialist economy does not have to suffer from over-production and cyclical fluctuations as it has an in-built capacity for making appropriate planned adjustments to the wage and social consumption funds. Where unemployment and fluctuations have occurred (in Yugoslavia) it can be shown that they were caused by excessive trust in the market mechanism.

c. *Rates of Growth.* By virtue of its control over the means of production and macroeconomic proportions, a Socialist economy has a more effective system for developmental take-off and sustained rapid growth. Over the period 1950–68 the average annual rate of growth of the national income of the European Socialist countries was 8 per cent, compared with 5 per cent attained by the capitalist world, and the respective growth rates in industrial output were 11 per cent and 5 per cent (see Fig. 6, p. 72). These countries' share in the world's industrial output increased from less than 10 per cent in 1938 to about 29 per cent in 1968, and by 1980 it is expected to reach about 37 per cent.[3] In the leading Western nations, basic industrialization took some twenty-five to fifty years to achieve, but in the European Socialist countries this process was completed in twelve to twenty years. In view of the semi-feudal conditions inherited, the absence of colonies, the widespread wartime devastation, Western boycotts and the strategic embargo, and practically no aid from the capitalist world, their achievements can be described by objective observers as spectacular.

d. *The Dignity of Labour.* Under the social ownership of the means of production, workers are co-owners of their employing establishments. There is no fundamental cleavage between the employer and the employee—no feeling of exploitation, no fear of unemployment, no disruptive strikes. Instead there is a prevailing atmosphere of co-operation and pride in the work performed. Workers, however humble, participate in the management and control of the entities employing them.

e. *The Distribution of National Income.* As there is virtually no private ownership of the means of production, wages and salaries (to the exclusion of rent, interest and private profit) are the only source of earned income. Furthermore, even though earnings from labour differ, personal income is supplemented by generous benefits out of the social consumption fund. Although the standard of living in

[3] R. Chwieduk *et al.*, *Ekonomia polityczna* (Political Economy), Warsaw, PWN, 1966, Vol. 2, p. 493; J. Kleer, J. Zawadzki and J. Górski, *Socjalizm—Kapitalizm* (Socialism v. Capitalism), Warsaw, KiW, 1967, p. 104.

Socialist countries is lower than in the West, there are no striking cases of abject poverty—in contrast to even the most affluent developed capitalist countries. There is no place for the exploitation of labour and of consumers by unscrupulous employers for private gain. Educational and advancement opportunities are more related to one's abilities and effort than to family influence or the possession of wealth.

f. *Social Cost–Benefit.* Under Socialism, 'The primacy of social over private preferences is ensured by the entire political and ideological superstructure'.[4] The Socialist State is in a good position to study social cost and benefit, which the market mechanism can never fully reflect. Capitalist economic concepts have traditionally been conditioned overwhelmingly by microeconomics, which is partly responsible for the anti-social individualism still prevalent in many Western countries and (as John Galbraith has shown) for the neglect of social amenities.

g. *Prevention of Certain Forms of Waste.* As has been vividly demonstrated by Vance Packard and Arnold Toynbee, free-enterprise capitalism is noted for its wasteful use of resources, as exemplified by artificial product obsolescence, unnecessary product differentiation, the unwarranted fragmentation and duplication of equipment and services, the excessive number of people employed in sales promotion, misleading advertising, conspicuous consumption and reckless military expenditure sometimes caused by vested private interests or used as a measure to fight unemployment. To this we must add recessions, uncertainty and monopolistic practices leading to the restriction of output, the division of markets, boycotts, etc. Such forms of waste are virtually absent, or can be easily prevented, under Socialism.

h. *Dynamism.* An objective observer, who is familiar with the two social systems which have been confronting each other for more than fifty years, has little doubt that Socialism has demonstrated a greater vitality. It has created a new socioeconomic order. It has pioneered in the sphere of social justice and accelerated economic growth, and it has committed itself to catching up with, and outstripping, the most advanced capitalist countries. Socialist leaders are convinced of the ascendancy of Socialism, particularly in the economic sphere. It is to their credit that they have been able to rise above their own prejudices, and incorporate the desirable elements from the rival system to perfect the operation of their own economies.

[4] M. Pohorille (ed.), *Ekonomia polityczna socjalizmu* (The Political Economy of Socialism), Warsaw, PWE, 1968, p. 67.

There is little doubt that in a relatively short span of time, Socialism has radically transformed the countries of Eastern Europe from backward, agricultural countries (with the partial exception of Czechoslovakia and the German D.R.), noted for a high degree of illiteracy, low productivity, recurring crises, unemployment, and dominated by semi-feudal conditions, a conservative church and foreign capital into progressive, diversified economies capable of continued rapid growth. For these reasons, many underdeveloped countries, such as Algeria, Burma, Guinea, India, Mali, Syria, Tanzania and the United Arab Republic, have at least partly adopted the Socialist road to economic development.

C. ECONOMIC WEAKNESSES OF SOCIALISM

The economic appraisal of Socialism would be incomplete without examining its disadvantages. Briefly stated they are as follows. First, there is undue *ideological and political dominance of the economic scene*. The ideological loyalty to Marxist ideas, such as the labour theory of value, often overrides economic common sense. On these grounds, land and capital are not considered scarce, and rent and interest are not fully accepted as costs, which often leads to an extravagant and wasteful use of these resources. Far-reaching economic decisions are made by Party leaders, invariably distinguished Communists but not necessarily competent economists. There is no lack of opponents of liberalization who regard economic reforms as a dangerous form of revisionism which should be sabotaged.

Second, the system is still bedevilled with *bureaucracy and inflexibility*. Central economic planning, even with a considerable degree of decentralization, requires a large number of highly skilled planners, administrators, controllers and a large supporting staff, who even by Socialist standards are 'unproductive'. The hierarchical nature of planning and administration makes the system unwieldy, not easily adaptable to the changes demanded by modern developments.

Third, not enough significance is attached to the problems arising at the *microeconomic level*, and there is *poor correspondence of decision-making between macro and micro levels*. Although the Socialist economy is in a favourable position to tackle macrosocial issues, it has neglected the problems of the management and utilization of resources at the operational level, further accentuated by a traditional contempt for marginal analysis. The dual system of decision-making, which cannot be avoided in the absence of free enterprise, contains a danger of incongruity and divergence. Experience shows that it is not easy in practice to reconcile targets set at the central level, even though they may be optimal, with the interest of the enterprises and their personnel so that the latter do not act contrary to social interest.

Fourth, the system is *liable to errors being committed on a large scale*. Central planners are political appointees owing their success to the social set-up in force. Their decisions are likely to be biased in favour of the Party and the perpetuation of communism, which may be in obvious conflict with economic rationality and the best interest of the public. But even in the absence of doctrinaire and political bias, the likelihood of errors of judgment is very real. Some of the planners' decisions must necessarily be arbitrary, as in the sphere of social cost–benefit, because so far no satisfactory quantitative, or other sound, evaluation of such considerations has been devised (see references 4, 8, 11 and 16 at the end of this chapter). Their decisions may be erroneous when made, or otherwise they may be made erroneous by subsequent developments. The point is that so much depends on the top planners' judgment, and when errors occur at the macro level they assume large proportions. Moreover, under the complex and unwieldy institutional set-up errors may not be easily detected and rectified to prevent a whole chain reaction of bottle-necks and waste with magnifying effects. On the other hand, a capitalist economy has an effective in-built error-correction system under which private firms are directly threatened with losses, and unless they avoid errors or apply swift correctives they have no chance of survival.

Fifth, so far *no rational and workable pricing system* has been devised. Prices do not fully reflect factor costs, as rent and interest are not necessarily fully accounted for in them, and furthermore different criteria for price-setting are used for different categories of products. As a result, prices do not, and cannot, perform a rational allocative function. The irrationality of prices in this sense in fact makes the whole system of economic decision-making largely arbitrary—as Tinbergen put it, 'optimization of what?' This, combined with virtual insulation from world market prices and specialization largely based on bilateral trade, militates against the optimum utilization of resources and the optimum distribution of the goods and services produced.

Sixth, there is *insufficient effective competition*. This applies to both enterprises and persons. On the one hand there is practically no private enterprise or the chance of accumulating private property. Instead, there is bureaucratic control, a predominance of large enterprises and a prevalence of seller's markets. On the other, there is hardly any fear of unemployment, social security is very well developed and in general the adventurous and capable have limited scope and incentive, whilst the indifferent and inefficient are sheltered by the system.

Next, there is *a neglect of current consumption*. The consumer has little influence on the size and structure of production, even in the consumer goods sector. So far, Socialist countries have assigned low priority to housing, public utilities, agriculture, product differentiation and 'luxuries'. All this, together with the prevailing seller's markets, reduces the consumer to an inferior position and acts against his welfare more than is perhaps necessary.

Finally, contrary to the dreams of Marx and other idealist writers who had not experienced Socialism in practice, the system tends to produce what has come to be known as *alienation*. This can be described as estrangement from higher authorities and a lack of respect for social property. It may appear in relations between enterprises and higher level officials, between workers and the enterprise, and between the ordinary man in the street and the ubiquitous and monolithic State.

The overall effect of the weaknesses discussed above is reflected in limited personal freedom and low efficiency. The productivity of labour, although rising, continues to be disproportionately low by Western standards.[5] The absence of rational pricing and effective competition mean that under Socialism, to a far greater extent than under capitalism, resources are not employed and products are not distributed in accordance with the *equi-marginal principle* to ensure maximum economic welfare (see references 1 and 8 at the end of this chapter). Although Socialist achievements have been spectacular, they have been attained at tremendous cost in terms of resources and of sacrifices borne by the public.

D. ARE THE TWO SYSTEMS CONVERGING?

In 1961, Jan Tinbergen put forward his 'convergence hypothesis' (see reference 15 at the end of this chapter). Since that time, his idea has received a good deal of attention both from Western thinkers (such as R. Aron, J. K. Galbraith, R. Schlesinger, K. E. Svendson, P. J. Wiles and G. v. Wrangel) and Socialist writers (e.g. E. Bregel, A. P. Butenko, S. Dalin, G. Kallai, K.-H. Domdey, G. Rose and I. Vajda).

According to this theory, Socialist and capitalist economies are departing more and more from centralized economic planning and

---

[5] E.g., a Soviet economist recently frankly admitted that productivity in Soviet agriculture is only about 25 per cent of that in the USA. See K. Popov, ('Objective Bases for the Construction of a Price System in Trade among Socialist Countries'), *Voprosy ekonomiki*, 8/1968, p. 71.

from *laissez-faire* private enterprise respectively, and instead are evolving patterns of thinking, institutions, methods and practices which are increasingly similar. Some idealists in fact believe that economic development based on essentially similar technological progress makes the coalescence of advanced Socialism and capitalism not only possible but also highly desirable, and indeed historically inevitable. We shall now briefly examine the convergence thesis by first bringing out the evidence in its support and then the arguments in its refutation.

a. *Micro- Macro Tendencies.* In the last decade the European Socialist countries have been giving more attention to the previously neglected sphere of microeconomics, both in theoretical writings and in matters of practical policy. On the other hand, in capitalist countries the Keynesian revolution, the interest in the problems of social welfare, the economics of growth and inflation have led to an increasing emphasis being placed on macro studies.

b. *Economic Planning.* Recent developments in the advanced Socialist countries have been marked with departures from detailed centralized planning in favour of broad 'orientational' planning and planning 'from below'. Planning in quantitative terms is giving way to that in value terms and, in contrast to the previous attitude, mathematical methods and computers are now ideologically accepted and applied in planning. At the same time, most capitalist countries have adopted some form of economic planning—'indicative', 'frame', 'goal', 'structural' or 'regional'—to promote high levels of employment, stability, social welfare and development.

c. *Economic Administration.* Decentralization has been one of the important features of the economic reforms in Eastern Europe and the USSR. Central authorities have been relieved of some details of administration, allowing a greater scope and independence to the lower administrative levels. On the other hand, capitalist economies have been experiencing centralization and increasing State intervention. Cartels, amalgamations and takeovers tend to produce larger economic units and a concentration of economic power. State marketing bodies, public authority business undertakings, control of big business (through anti-monopoly and industrial legislation), the administration of social security and the policies of protection, show that 'invisible hand' and unrestricted competition are no longer trusted.

d. *Management.* In the European Socialist countries, the idea that workers can successfully manage enterprises was dropped long ago. The position of local management has been recently strengthened, and a 'director' of a Socialist enterprise in several respects now resembles a 'manager' in capitalist countries. In the latter countries at the same time, management is increasingly divorced from ownership. As a result of the proceeding industrial integration, the management of the parent company and of its subsidiaries is becoming similar to that of an industrial (or branch) association in a Socialist country. Many large concerns allow trade unions to participate in some details of management.

e. *Money and Banking*. The directive and administrative methods of economic management are being replaced in the European Socialist countries with financial incentives and disincentives. Banks now actively participate in selecting and financing economically sound investment projects and commercial ventures. Liberalization has tended to release inflationary pressure, which is giving new significance to monetary policy. On the other hand, in capitalist countries the role of monetary policy is no longer as great as it was in the past and it is being increasingly supplemented with fiscal, wage and income policies, and even direct controls. Banks have largely lost their former dominant position in the economy.

f. *Profit*. This is now accepted in the European Socialist countries (Albania excepted) as the main criterion of enterprise performance, and part of the profit is shared by the workers and management. At the same time, in capitalist countries profit is no longer such a decisive factor in determining economic activity. To many firms the goodwill of the public is more important than the short-run maximization of profits, and State participation in business is not usually prompted by the profit motive. There are also profit-sharing schemes, and in some cases the State regulates the size of profits.

g. *Property Ownership*. In some Socialist countries there has been some de-collectivization of farming land. A large proportion of livestock is now privately owned, and individual plots are playing an increasing role in food production. Private enterprise has also been revitalized in handicrafts, retail trade, catering and fishing. In capitalist countries there is a tendency for increasing State ownership (the nationalization of key industries) and for some diffusion of property in favour of the working classes (heavy death duties and a tendency for workers to own homes, bonds, savings certificates and shares).

h. *The Distribution of National Income*. The dream of the equalization of incomes has been discarded in Socialist countries long ago. The wide disparity existing between the earnings of leading authors, actors and scientists on the one hand, and unskilled workers and collective farmers on the other, are well known. The increased role recently assigned to material incentives is further militating against the communist egalitarian principle. On the other hand, inequalities of income in capitalist countries are being reduced by progressive taxation and the expansion of social services, and in many of them there are legal or *de facto* minimum wage schemes protecting the lower-grade workers.

i. *Social Structure*. There are several indications of the existence of social classes in Socialist countries. Even in the USSR three social classes are officially recognized (workers, peasants and intelligentsia), not to mention the Communist Party elite. The increasing role of the technocrats and managers is further accentuating the distinctions. But in the capitalist world, the former class distinctions are being gradually reduced by the broadening of educational opportunities, rising affluence and increasing social mobility. The power of the employers has been moderated by a continuous high level of employment, powerful trade unions, the labour vote and State intervention.

j. *Prices*. Instead of the former rigid price fixing, there is a continued tendency in the advanced Socialist countries to extend the role of free market prices, and in the remaining prices to reflect a part of interest and rent as genuine costs. Some rationalization of subsidies and turnover taxes has been carried out and more is likely to follow. As far as the capitalist world is concerned, the ideal of prices being formed in free markets and closely reflecting factor costs can now be found only in textbooks, not in reality. Prices are increasingly distorted by indirect taxes, subsidies, government price stabilization schemes (especially in agriculture) and monopolistic practices.

k. *The Role of the Consumer*. Following the recent economic reforms in Eastern Europe and the USSR a greater role is assigned to consumer preferences. This trend is certain to continue with the rising standard of living and a gradual development of buyer's markets. On the other hand, the consumer in capitalist countries is no longer as sovereign as the traditional assertion, 'the consumer is king' would imply. Collusion amongst producers, persuasive advertising, State intervention and consumer habits reduce the consumer's ability to dictate patterns of production.

1. *Mutual Trade*. Contrary to the trend up to the early 1950s, trade between Socialist and capitalist countries has been increasing since that time most remarkably. Between 1953 and 1969 this trade was increasing at the average annual rate of 13·9. This rate was much higher than that attained either in intra-Socialist foreign trade: 6·0, or in trade amongst capitalist countries: 8·1.[6] Solutions have been found to many problems inherent in trade between different social systems, and the former political interference has been substantially reduced on both sides.

The converging trend has been further facilitated by the tacit acceptance of the policy of peaceful co-existence, a virtual discontinuation of the Cold War and the divergent trends on each side weakening the unity and chauvinism of the respective power blocs confronting each other.

If the foregoing instances of developments on each side have convinced the reader of the trend towards the convergence of Socialism and capitalism, his enthusiasm will be tempered by the following observations. It must be pointed out that the emerging similarity of forms does not necessarily lead to substantive identity, as is illustrated, for example, by profit. Most of the modifications taking place on each side are not conscious imitations but rather selective adaptations to a variety of economic and technical changes, independent of the other system. In this process, it is easy to confuse means with the end. 'The reforms being carried out in Socialist countries', it was stated in a recent Polish study, 'have nothing in common with the convergence of Socialism and capitalism. They are merely used to perfect our system of planning and management whereby the objectives of the Socialist society can be attained in a more effective way.'[7]

Whilst the economic reforms in the European Socialist countries have been quickly hailed by many eager Western commentators as a desirable move towards capitalism, the Socialist leadership essentially views the departures from *laissez-faire* free enterprise in the capitalist world not as evidence of a welcome converging trend towards Socialism but as a process further aggravating 'inherent contradictions' bound to lead to the breakdown of capitalism. As to the content of peaceful co-existence, Socialist leaders basically look upon it as 'peaceful competition' on the economic front and they have no doubt of the eventual victory of Socialism over capitalism.

In fact most Socialist writers on the subject, whilst not denying the need for greater economic co-operation, most definitely refute the

[6] Based on United Nations sources: *Yearbook of International Trade Statistics* and *Monthly Bulletin of Statistics*.
[7] J. Kleer *et al.*, op. cit., p. 126.

possibility of *ideological reconciliation*. Shortly before the military intervention in Czechoslovakia in 1968, it was significantly pointed out in *Pravda*: 'In our day, the ideological struggle is the sharpest front of the class struggle. In the field of ideology, there is and there can be no peaceful co-existence, just as there can be no class peace between the proletariat and the bourgeoisie.'[8]

[8] *Pravda*, 20/8/1968, p. 1.

RECOMMENDED REFERENCES AVAILABLE IN ENGLISH

1. Bergson, A., *Essays in Normative Economics*, Harvard U.P., 1966, Part III.

2. Campbell, R. W., *Soviet Economic Power*, 2nd ed., London, Macmillan, 1967.

3. Dobb, M., *Welfare Economics and the Economics of Socialism*, Cambridge U.P., 1969.

*4. Drewnowski, J., 'Valuation Systems Implied in Planning Decisions. Shall We Reveal Them?', *Co-existence*, Jan. 1969, pp. 39–41.

5. Feinstein, C. H. (ed.), *Socialism, Capitalism and Economic Growth*, Essays Presented to Maurice Dobb, Cambridge U.P., 1967.

6. Grossman, G., *Economic Systems*, Englewood, Prentice-Hall, 1967.

7. Halm, G. N., *Economic Systems—A Comparative Analysis*, 3rd ed., New York, Holt, Rinehart & Winston, 1968.

8. Köhler, H., *Welfare and Planning. An Analysis of Capitalism versus Socialism.* New York, John Wiley & Sons, 1966.

*9. Kotkovskii, I., 'Contemporary Conditions of Economic Competition Between the USSR and the USA', *Problems of Economics*, Dec. 1967, pp. 24–36.

10. Mazour, A. G., *Soviet Economic Development Operation Outstrip: 1921–1965.* Princeton and London, Van Nostrand, 1967.

11. Morgan, T., 'The Theory of Error in Centrally Directed Economic Systems', *Quart. Jour. of Econ.*, Aug. 1964, pp. 395–419.

12. Prybyla, J. S. (ed.), *Comparative Economic Systems*, New York, Appleton-Century-Crofts, 1969.

13. Shaffer, H. G. (ed.), *The Soviet System in Theory and Practice*, New York, Appleton-Century-Crofts, 1965.

*14. Smolianskii, V., 'Soviet Planning and the "Synthesis" Theorists', *Problems of Economics*, Dec. 1965, pp. 43–8.

15. Tinbergen, J., 'Do Communist and Free Economies Show a Converging Pattern?', *Soviet Studies*, April 1961, pp. 333–41; and 'Concrete Concepts of Co-existence', *Co-existence*, Jan. 1964, pp. 15–20.

16. Tinbergen, J., 'Optimization of What?', *Co-existence*, Jan. 1968, pp. 1–5.

*17. Trukhanovsky, V., 'Proletarian Internationalism and Peaceful Coexistence—Foundation of the Leninist Foreign Policy', *Intern. Affairs*, Moscow, 11/1968, pp. 54–62.

*18. Tsyrlin, L., 'Development of Industrial Production in the USSR and the USA (Summing Up the Last Fifty Years)', *Problems of Economics*, May 1968, pp. 37–45.

19. West, E. G., 'The Political Economy of Alienation: Karl Marx and Adam Smith', *Oxford Econ. Papers*, March 1969, pp. 1–23.

20. Zauberman, A., 'The Rapprochement between East and West in Mathematical Economic Thought', *Manch. School of Econ. and Soc. Studies*, March 1969, pp. 1–21.

* indicates contributions by writers from Socialist countries.

A GUIDE TO PERIODICALS RELEVANT TO SOCIALIST ECONOMICS

A. MAIN PERIODICALS PUBLISHED IN EASTERN EUROPEAN LANGUAGES

For actual article references, as well as books, see the footnotes to the relevant chapters.

1. *Acta Oeconomica* (Economic Papers), Hungarian Academy of Sciences, Budapest; quarterly (some articles are in English, other articles include summaries in English).
2. *Aussenhandel* (Foreign Trade), East Berlin; monthly (the table of contents also in English).
3. *Dengi i kredit* (Money and Credit), the State Bank of the USSR, Moscow; monthly.
4. *Deutsche Finanzwirtschaft* (German Financial Studies), East Berlin; fortnightly.
5. *Ekonomicheskaya gazeta* (Economic Gazette), Central Committee of the Communist Party of the Soviet Union, Moscow; weekly.
6. *Ekonomicheskie nauki* (Economic Studies), Ministry of Tertiary and Vocational Secondary Education of the USSR, Moscow; monthly.
7. *Ekonomicko-Matematicky Obzor* (Review of Econometrics), the Institute of Econometrics, Czechoslovak Academy of Sciences, Prague; quarterly (some articles also in English).
8. *Ekonomika i matematicheskie metody* (Economics and Mathematical Methods), Central Institute for Economic and Mathematical Studies, Moscow; bi-monthly.
9. *Ekonomist* (The Economist), Yugoslav Association of Economists, Belgrade; quarterly.
10. *Ekonomista* (The Economist), Polish Economic Society, Polish Academy of Sciences, Warsaw; bi-monthly (with summaries in English).
11. *Ekonomska politika* (Economic Policy), Belgrade; weekly.
12. *Ekonomski pregled* (Economic Review), Zagreb; monthly.
13. *Figyelo* (Economic Observer), Budapest; weekly.
14. *Finance a Uvěr* (Finance and Credit), Prague; monthly.
15. *Finanse* (Finance), State Economic Publications Centre, Warsaw; monthly.
16. *Finansije* (Finance), State Secretariat for Finance of Yugoslavia, Belgrade; monthly.
17. *Finansi i kredit* (Finance and Credit), the Ministry of Finance and the State Bank of Bulgaria, Sofia; monthly.
18. *Finansy SSSR* (Soviet Finance), the Ministry of Finance of the USSR, Moscow; monthly.
19. *Finanţe şi credit* (Finance and Credit), Bucharest; monthly (with summaries in English).
20. *Gospodarka planowa* (Planned Economy), State Economic Publications Centre, Warsaw; monthly (with summaries in English).

21. *Handel zagraniczny* (Foreign Trade), Polish Chamber of Foreign Trade, Warsaw; monthly (with summaries in English).
22. *Hospodářské Noviny* (Economic News), Central Committee of the Communist Party of Czechoslovakia, Prague; weekly.
23. *Ikonomicheska misul* (Economic Thought), Institute of Economics, Bulgarian Academy of Sciences, Sofia; 10 issues a year.
24. *Ikonomicheski zhivot* (Economic Life), Central Committee of the Bulgarian Communist Party, Sofia; weekly.
25. *Kommunist* (The Communist), Central Committee of the Communist Party of the Soviet Union; Moscow; 18 issues a year.
26. *Közgazdasági Szemle* (Economic Review), Institute of Economics, Hungarian Academy of Sciences, Budapest; monthly (with summaries in English).
27. *Külkereskedelem* (Foreign Trade), Hungarian Chamber of Foreign Trade, Budapest; monthly.
28. *Medjunarodni problemy* (International Problems), Institute for International Politics and Economics of Yugoslavia, Belgrade; quarterly (with summaries in English).
29. *Mirovaya ekonomika i mezhdunarodnye otnosheniya* (World Economy and International Relations), Institute of World Economics and International Relations, Academy of Sciences of the USSR, Moscow; monthly (with summaries in English).
30. *Nowe drogi* (New Paths), Central Political Committee of the Polish United Workers' Party, Warsaw; monthly.
31. *Plánované Hospodářství* (Planned Economy), the State Planning Commission of Czechoslovakia, Prague; 10 issues a year (the table of contents also in English).
32. *Planovo stopanstvo i statistika* (Planned Economy and Statistics), the State Planning Commission and the Central Statistical Office of Bulgaria, Sofia; monthly.
33. *Planovoe khoziaistvo* (Planned Economy), the State Planning Commission of the USSR, Moscow; bi-monthly.
34. *Politicka Ekonomie* (Political Economy), Institute of Economics, Czechoslovak Academy of Sciences, Prague; monthly (with English summaries of some articles).
35. *Probleme economice* (Problems of Economics), Institute of Economic Research, Rumanian Society of Economic Sciences, Bucharest; monthly (with summaries in English).
36. *Sovietskaya torgovlya* (Soviet Domestic Trade), the Ministry of Internal Trade of the USSR, Moscow; monthly.
37. *Vestnik statistiki* (Herald of Statistics), Central Statistical Board of the USSR, Moscow; monthly.
38. *Viata economica* (Economic Life), Rumanian Society for Economic Studies, Bucharest; weekly.
39. *Vneshnaya torgovlya* (Foreign Trade), Ministry of Foreign Trade of the USSR, Moscow; monthly (the table of contents also in English).
40. *Voprosy ekonomiki* (Problems of Economics), Institute of Economics, Academy of Sciences of the USSR, Moscow; monthly.

41. *Vunshna turgoviya* (Foreign Trade), Ministry of Foreign Trade of Bulgaria, Sofia; monthly.
42. *Wirtschaft, Die* (The Economy), East Berlin; fortnightly.
43. *Wirtschaftswissenschaft* (Economic Science), East Berlin; monthly (with summaries in English).
44. *Życie gospodarcze* (Economic Life), Warsaw; weekly.

All European Socialist countries publish annual statistical yearbooks which, with the exception of the German D.R. and the USSR, also include annexes with English translations of captions. They also, regularly or occasionally, publish statistical pocket-books entirely in English.

B. MAIN PERIODICALS PUBLISHED IN ENGLISH

There are now about 1,000 periodicals published in the well-known Western languages dealing specifically with the USSR and Eastern Europe (for details see *USSR and Eastern Europe. Periodicals in Western Languages*, Revised 1967, Library of Congress, Washington). Space permits the inclusion of only a selected number here. For actual articles, as well as books, in English see the references at the end of the relevant chapter.

45. *American Review of East–West Trade, The*, Symposium Press, New York; monthly.
46. *A.S.T.E. Bulletin, The*, Association for the Study of Soviet-Type Economies, University of Pennsylvania, Philadelphia; 3 issues a year.
47. *Bulgarian Foreign Trade*, Bulgarian Chamber of Commerce, Sofia; bi-monthly.
48. *Bulletin*, Institute for the Study of the USSR, Munich; monthly.
49. *Canadian Slavic Studies/Revue Canadienne d'Études Slaves*, Loyola College, Montreal; quarterly.
50. *Co-existence*, Oxford; semi-annual.
51. *Commercial Information*, the Federal Chamber of Commerce of Yugoslavia, Belgrade; monthly.
52. *Co-operation in Rumania*, Central Union of the Consumers' Co-operatives in Rumania, Bucharest; semi-annual.
53. *Czechoslovak Economic Papers*, Czechoslovak Academy of Sciences, Prague; 1–2 issues a year.
54. *Czechoslovak Foreign Trade*, Czechoslovak Chamber of Commerce, Prague; monthly.
55. *Current Digest of the Soviet Press*, Joint Committee on Slavic Studies, New York; weekly.
56. *East Europe*, Free Europe Committee, New York; monthly.
57. *Eastern European Economics*, a journal of translations from leading Eastern European journals of economics, International Arts and Sciences Press, New York; quarterly.
58. *Economic Bulletin for Europe*, Economic Commission for Europe, Geneva; about 3 issues a year.
59. *Economic Journal, The*, Royal Economic Society, Cambridge; quarterly. In addition to occasional articles on the economics of planning, it

regularly gives English titles of articles appearing in the leading economic journals and a selected number of books published in Bulgaria, Czechoslovakia, the German D.R., Hungary, Poland, Rumania, the USSR and Yugoslavia.

60. *Economic Survey of Europe*, Economic Commission for Europe, Geneva; annual.

61. *Economics of Planning*, Norwegian Institute of International Affairs, Oslo; 3 issues a year.

62. *European Economic Review*, sponsored by the European Scientific Association for Medium- and Long-Term Economic Forecasting, Brussels; published by the International Arts and Sciences Press, New York; quarterly.

63. *Foreign Trade*, Ministry of Foreign Trade of the USSR, Moscow; monthly.

64. *Hungarian Exporter*, Hungarian Chamber of Commerce, Budapest; monthly.

65. *International Affairs*, All-Union Society 'Znaniye', Moscow; monthly.

66. *Management Science and Operations Research in the USSR and Eastern Europe*, a journal of translations, International Arts and Sciences Press, New York, quarterly.

67. *Mathematical Studies in Economics and Statistics in the USSR and Eastern Europe*, a journal of translations, International Arts and Sciences Press, New York; quarterly.

68. *Peace, Freedom and Socialism*, Prague; monthly.

69. *Problems of Communism*, United States Information Agency, Washington; bi-monthly.

70. *Problems of Economics*, a journal of translations from the leading Soviet economic journals, International Arts and Sciences Press, New York; monthly.

71. *Rumanian Foreign Trade*, Rumanian Chamber of Commerce, Bucharest; quarterly.

72. *Slavic Studies*, American Association for the Advancement of Slavic Studies, Baltimore; quarterly.

73. *Socialist Thought and Practice*, Jugoslavija Publishing House, Belgrade; quarterly.

74. *Soviet and Eastern European Foreign Trade*, a journal of translations, International Arts and Sciences Press, New York; quarterly.

75. *Soviet Studies*, University of Glasgow; quarterly. It includes an *Information Supplement*, which is an up-to-date guide to current Soviet publications classified by subjects.

76. *Soviet Studies in World Economics and Politics*, a journal of translations, International Arts and Sciences Press, New York; quarterly.

77. *Studies in Comparative Communism*, University of Southern California, Los Angeles; quarterly.

78. *Studies on the Soviet Union*, Institute for the Study of the USSR, Munich; quarterly.

79. *Survey*, A Journal of Soviet and East European Studies, International Association for Cultural Freedom, London; quarterly.

80. *Translations from KOMMUNIST*, us Dept. of Commerce, Joint Publications Research Service, Washington; 18 issues a year.
81. *Translations on Eastern Europe: Economic and Industrial Affairs*, us Dept. of Commerce, Joint Publications Research Service, Washington; irregular (about 70 issues a year).
82. *USSR International Economic Relations*, a journal of translations from the leading Soviet sources, us Dept. of Commerce, Joint Publications Research Service, Washington; irregular (about 50 issues a year).
83. *Yugoslav Survey*, Jugoslavija Publishing House, Belgrade; quarterly.

Index